ANITA STEWART'S COUNTRY INN COOKBOOK

Stoddart

First published in 1987 by
Stoddart Publishing Co. Limited
34 Lesmill Road
Toronto, Canada
M3B 2T6

CANADIAN CATALOGUING IN PUBLICATION DATA

Stewart, Anita
    Country inn cookbook

Includes index.
ISBN 0-7737-5099-1

1. Cookery, Canadian.   2. Hotels, taverns, etc. — Canada.   I. Title.

TX715.S74 1987   641.5'0971   C86-094940-0

DESIGN: Brant Cowie/Artplus Ltd.

Cover photographs: Barr Photography

Text illustrations: W. Wingfelder

Map of Inns by: Derek A. Bonnett

Printed in Canada

To Mom, for a lifetime of love
And to Dad, who made her happy

SPECIAL THANKS

There are times when "special thanks" is a rather meager offering to those people who help along the making of a book.

Thank you, Wayne! And my sons Jeff, Brad, Mark and Paul! Thanks, Mom and Dad — your help testing and typing the recipes has been marvelous. I hope that I can do the same for your grandsons.

Thanks to all my tasters, especially Lynne and Art, Eleanor and John, who responded with comments like "Okay, we'll be right there!" and "When do you need us again?"

And a final thank you to all of the innkeepers—those wonderful people who went the extra mile to provide recipes and encouragement. I wish you success, health and happiness!

THE COVER

One of the most beautiful inns in all of Canada, The Elora Mill Inn graciously allowed me to ransack their dining room for the cover photograph. The picture features dishes from coast to coast. Sooke Harbour House's Salmon in Cranberry Vinegar Sauce (pp. 98-99) is in the foreground, garnished with rose petals as well as rose geranium leaves. Moving clockwise, you can see a Spinach Salad with Poppy Seed Dressing (p. 41) from The Garrison House Inn at Annapolis Royal; The Desert Rose's Carrot Cake (p. 159) from Elora; a superb Apple-Frangipane Tart (p. 166) from the Pillar and Post in Niagara-on-the-Lake; Anadama Bread (p. 150) from Nova Scotia's Westway Inn; and Charlottetown Rye Bread (p. 146) from The Dundee Arms.

Thanks to my friends Charlie and Wyonna Peppler for the use of their antiques; to Geoffry Stevens, The Elora Potter, for the lovely cake plate; and to Mary Taylor for her pewter candlestick.

Table of Contents

Introduction

Although their numbers are relatively small, Canada's innkeepers are on the leading edge of what is happening to Canadian cuisine. Almost all have their own gardens, of the land and of the sea, which produce, on their impertinent demands, the very freshest and finest ingredients. Most are in the kitchen daily, making or supervising the careful preparation of meals. Many have rejected other successful careers, in everything from journalism to science, to allow them the lifestyle which responds directly to their own creativity and sometimes frantic hard work.

As you read this book, take a little time to reflect on Canadian cuisine — the ebb and flow of it. Our rich diversity is what makes our cuisine unique among the foods of the world.

Throughout the book, you will travel, as I have, between Canada's far-flung coasts. You will notice ever-changing food styles, which move in direct response to changing economic conditions and to past and present waves of immigration. New technology plays a large part; many inns today use food processors and microwaves. New ingredients are restlessly searched for. Tastes change. Small nuances in flavor are more obvious to us than they were a few years ago, and the innkeepers, along with their chefs, are in their kitchens developing recipes which challenge us all.

You will also read about inns that are bastions of the old ways, preserving local traditions and culture with a passion. Through them, we have a sense of history and a keener appreciation of the past.

Country Inns, both large and small, are the best and most personal way to see this land. Enjoy the recipes, the generously shared house specialties, and marvel, as I did, at the diversity of foodstuffs and preparation. Experience Canada in a most intense and beautiful way!

How to Use This Book

If you are a traveler, you will find a map in the appendix. In the appendix you will also find the inns, listed by address, along with the recipes they submitted. Always call ahead for reservations when you plan to visit an inn or dine there. Some inns are open only seasonally, especially in the Maritime regions and the Far North, while others are closed between the summer's tourists and the winter's skiers. The telephone numbers were correct at the time of publication, and they will be updated with each edition.

For those who like to cook, the recipes in this book are arranged according to dish. A complete recipe index can be found on page 207. There will be some ingredients that may not be available in the area of the country where you live. For me, in landlocked Elora, Ontario, it was most difficult to obtain some of the fresh seafoods needed to test the Maritime dishes. Farmers' and fishermen's markets are an interesting and colorful source of some of the more unusual ingredients. Some of the vendors will grow vegetables to order for you, if you wish. Otherwise, enjoy reading about the regional specialties and, when you travel across Canada, you will be able to look forward to a national tasting spree!

METRIC CONVERSIONS

$\frac{1}{8}$ tsp.	= 0.5 mL	
$\frac{1}{4}$ tsp.	= 1 mL	
$\frac{1}{2}$ tsp.	= 2 mL	
$\frac{3}{4}$ tsp.	= 4 mL	
1 tsp.	= 5 mL	
$1\frac{1}{2}$ tsps.	= 7 mL	
1 Tbsp.	= 15 mL	
2 Tbsps.	= 25 mL	
$\frac{1}{4}$ cup	= 50 mL	
$\frac{1}{3}$ cup	= 75 mL	
$\frac{1}{2}$ cup	= 125 mL	
$\frac{2}{3}$ cup	= 150 mL	
$\frac{3}{4}$ cup	= 175 mL	
1 cup	= 250 mL	
1 quart	= 4 cups	= 1 litre
$\frac{1}{4}$ lb.	= 4 oz.	= 115 g
$\frac{1}{2}$ lb.	= 8 oz.	= 225 g
1 lb.	= 16 oz.	= 450 g (454 g)
2 lbs.	= 900 g	
$2\frac{1}{2}$ lbs.	= 1 kg	
3 lbs.	= 1.3 kg	
4 lbs.	= 1.8 kg	
5 lbs.	= 2.25 kg	
10 lbs.	= 4.5 kg	

TEMPERATURE CONVERSIONS

°F	=	°C
200		100
250		120
300		150
325		160
350		180
375		190
400		200
425		220
450		230
475		240

Appetizers

MANOIR ST-ANDRE
St-André, Québec

Pâté d'Anguille Froid

(Cold Smoked Eel Pâté)

🐾🐾

CÉCILE AND EMILEEN MOREL, *Innkeepers*
MANOIR ST-ANDRÉ,
St-André, Québec

For fans of smoked fish, this pâté is great on whole wheat crackers or French bread.

1 cup	smoked eel, in chunks	250 mL
¼ cup	finely diced celery	50 mL
¼ cup	finely diced leeks	50 mL
½ cup	water	125 mL
½ cup	mayonnaise (p. 41)	125 mL
	salt and freshly ground pepper, to taste	
	lettuce leaves, as needed	
	crisp, crumbled bacon, for garnish	

In a small saucepan, combine the eel, celery, leeks and water. Bring to a boil and steam until the vegetables are tender. Drain and cool. Purée by hand or in a food processor until smooth. Add the mayonnaise, salt and pepper. Serve on lettuce leaves garnished with bacon bits.

Makes 1½ cups (375 mL).

Kettle Creek House Pâté

🐾🐾

GARY AND JEAN VEDOVA, *Innkeepers*
KETTLE CREEK INN,
Port Stanley, Ontario

The Kettle Creek Inn is one of Ontario's virtually undiscovered treasures on Lake Erie. Complete with a miniature English garden, it is truly beautiful.

¼ lb.	bacon, cut in 1 in. (2.5 cm) pieces	115 g
¼ lb.	mushrooms, sliced	115 g
1	large Spanish onion, diced	1
4 cloves	garlic, chopped finely	4 cloves
1 lb.	chicken livers, chopped	450 g
4	hard-boiled eggs, chopped	4
1 cup	butter, softened	250 mL

$\frac{1}{4}$ tsp.	ground cloves	1 mL
$\frac{1}{2}$ tsp.	mace	2 mL
1 Tbsp.	Dijon mustard	15 mL
2 Tbsps.	Cognac	25 mL
	salt and freshly ground pepper,	
	to taste	

Fry the bacon in a saucepan for 3-4 minutes. Add the mushrooms and fry for 1-2 minutes. Add the onion and garlic and cook until onion is soft. Add the chicken livers and cook until livers are firm, about 15-20 minutes. Remove from heat and add hard-boiled eggs, butter, cloves, mace, mustard, Cognac, salt and pepper. Whirl in a food processor or blender until smooth. Pack in storage containers. Seal tightly and refrigerate for at least 3-4 hours before serving. This pâté benefits from being made the night before serving.

Makes about $2\frac{1}{2}$ lbs. (1 kg).

Mushroom Pâté

GARY BURROUGHS, *Innkeeper*
MARY COLTART, *Keeper of the Inn*
THE OBAN INN,
Niagara-on-the-Lake, Ontario

1	large onion, diced	1
1 lb.	mushrooms, sliced	450 g
2	eggs	2
8 oz.	cream cheese, softened	225 g
2 cloves	garlic	2 cloves
	juice of $\frac{1}{2}$ lemon	
$\frac{1}{2}$ tsp.	salt	2 mL
$\frac{1}{2}$ tsp.	freshly ground pepper	2 mL

Preheat the oven to 350°F. (180°C). Combine the onion, mushrooms and eggs in a food processor. Whirl until smooth. Add the cream cheese, garlic, lemon juice, salt and pepper. Whirl again for 20 to 30 seconds. Spoon into a small (5-cup or 1.2 L) oiled baking dish. Cover with foil and bake for 30 minutes. Uncover and continue baking for another 30 minutes or until firm. Cool and refrigerate before serving. Serve with crackers or vegetables.

Makes $3\frac{1}{2}$ cups (875 mL).

Thee Inn Pâté

🐾🐾🐾

LYNN AND HARLEY JOPLING, *Innkeepers*
LLOYD VAN LEWEN, *Chef*
THE OLD BRIDGE INN,
Young's Point, Ontario

Perched on the banks of the Trent-Severn Waterway at Lock 27, The Old Bridge Inn provides food and restful accommodation for boaters who need a less "sloshy" atmosphere. From the old bridge, now restricted to pedestrians, you can watch hundreds of perch and pickerel make their way upriver in the springtime to spawn.

$\frac{1}{2}$ lb.	side bacon, chopped	225 g
1	large onion, diced	1
$1\frac{1}{4}$ lbs.	chicken livers, trimmed of white, connective tissue	560 g
1 tsp.	celery powder (if available) *or*	5 mL
1	small bunch celery leaves, finely minced	1
1 tsp.	dried thyme	5 mL
$\frac{1}{2}$ tsp.	dried basil	2 mL
$\frac{1}{2}$ tsp.	dried rosemary	2 mL
$\frac{3}{4}$ cup	half-and-half cream (10%)	175 mL
$1\frac{1}{2}$ cups	butter, clarified by melting slowly	375 mL
2 Tbsps.	brandy	25 mL
2 Tbsps.	rosé wine	25 mL
2	bay leaves	2
	crushed, black pepper*	

In a large, heavy pot (I use cast iron), gently cook the bacon, covered, until moisture collects. Drain off some of the fat, if necessary. Add the onion and continue to cook until it is soft. Be careful not to fry it. Add the chicken livers and cook gently until they have lost their pinkness and are firm, about 10 minutes. Stir often. Remove from the heat. Combine in batches in a food processor or blender with the celery powder, thyme, basil, rosemary and cream. Whirl in 1 cup of the butter, the brandy and wine. (You will have to pour it into a large bowl and whisk all the batches together.) Pour into the top of a double boiler with the bay leaves and pepper. Cook over lightly boiling water for 45 minutes. Taste and correct the seasonings if necessary.

Meanwhile, pour half of the remaining butter into a chilled, glass mold. Refrigerate. When cooked, pour the pâté into the mold. Smooth the top surface and seal with the last of the butter. Refrigerate until firm. This pâté will keep for several weeks refrigerated.

Makes about 3 cups.

* *The amount of pepper depends on individual taste. I like 1 Tbsp. (15 mL) black pepper, but you might also try green or pink peppercorns.*

Little-Neck Clams Steamed in Beer Broth

🐝🐝

SINCLAIR AND FREDRICA PHILIP, *Innkeepers*
SOOKE HARBOUR HOUSE,
Whiffen Spit Beach, Vancouver Island, B.C.

Little-neck clams are the small, hard-shelled East Coast variety also known as Cherrystone or Quahogs (coe-hogs). On the Pacific Coast they are called Butter Clams. This is a light and easy dish that Sinclair developed.

2 lbs.	little-neck clams	900 g
1½ cups	malty, dark beer	375 mL
1 tsp.	minced fresh ginger	5 mL
2 cloves	garlic, minced finely	2 cloves
	chive flowers (optional)	

Scrub these Pacific-coast clams; remove any sand by soaking in clean sea water or 1 gallon (4 L) of tap water to which you have added ⅓ cup (75 mL) coarse salt. Leave the clams for 25-30 minutes. Repeat three times.

Place the clams in a saucepan. Add the beer, ginger and garlic. Cover with a lid and bring to a boil. Steam until clams are tender. Arrange clams on warm soup plates or dishes and pour remaining broth over top. Garnish with the chive flowers.

Makes 4 servings as an appetizer.

Oysters Provençale Blanche

(Oysters in White Provençale Sauce)

🐝🐝🐝🐝🐝🐝🐝🐝🐝🐝🐝🐝🐝🐝🐝🐝🐝🐝🐝🐝🐝🐝🐝🐝🐝🐝🐝🐝🐝🐝🐝🐝🐝🐝🐝🐝🐝

STEVEN LYNCH, *Chef*
PAUL ALMQUIST, *Chef*
HASTINGS HOUSE,
Ganges, Saltspring Island, B.C.

Another smash hit from Hastings House. The oysters may be divided among six scallop shells and baked as directed. This makes serving slightly easier.

18	oysters, shucked, beards removed (reserve shells)	18
$\frac{1}{2}$ cup	water	125 mL
1 Tbsp.	lemon juice	15 mL
1 cup	milk	250 mL
	Beurre Manie, as needed (see page 17)	
1 Tbsp.	butter	15 mL
$\frac{1}{4}$ cup	minced onion	50 mL
2 cloves	garlic, minced	2 cloves
1 oz.	white wine	30 mL
2 Tbsps.	minced fresh parsley	25 mL
	salt, to taste	
	cayenne pepper, to taste	
$\frac{1}{2}$ tsp.	Worcestershire sauce	2 mL
1	tomato, peeled, seeded and chopped	1
8 oz.	baby shrimp, cooked and shelled	225 g
	lemon and parsley, for garnish	

Preheat the oven to 450°F. (230°C). In a saucepan, combine the oysters, water and lemon juice and poach for approximately $1\frac{1}{2}$-2 minutes. Remove the oysters from the liquid. Cover the oysters and set aside.

In a saucepan, combine the milk and $\frac{1}{2}$ cup (125 mL) of the poaching liquid.

Heat this and thicken with Beurre Manie to medium thickness. It will require about 3 Tbsps. (45 mL).

In a sauté pan, melt the butter and sauté the onion and garlic until both are tender. Add to the sauce. Stir in the wine, parsley, salt, cayenne pepper, Worcestershire sauce and tomato. Set aside.

Return the oysters to the deep half of the shell, top with a few shrimp and cover with sauce. Bake on a $\frac{1}{4}$ in. (6 mm) bed of rock salt for 10 minutes. To serve, put $\frac{1}{4}$ in. (6 mm) rock salt on each plate and place the oysters, in their shells, on the salt to balance them. Garnish with lemon and parsley. *Makes 6 servings.*

Beurre Manie
To make Beurre Manie, blend thoroughly equal parts of all-purpose flour and softened (not melted) butter. Left-over Beurre Manie can be stored in the refrigerator.

Pickerel Pâté

☙☙☙

PAT AND GAYLE WATERS, *Innkeepers*
RICHARD FITOUSSI, *Chef*
THE LITTLE INN,
Bayfield, Ontario

Using local pickerel, Richard has created a mild, delicious pâté which is wonderful with fresh Grand Harbour Rolls (p. 153) and a little Dill Sauce (p. 114) on the side.

4 oz.	pork back fat	115 g
1$\frac{1}{2}$ tsps.	coarse salt	7 mL
2 Tbsps.	ice	25 mL
10 oz.	fresh pickerel fillets	300 g
$\frac{1}{2}$ tsp.	dill weed	2 mL
$\frac{1}{2}$ tsp.	dried tarragon	2 mL
1 tsp.	pink peppercorns*	5 mL
$\frac{1}{4}$ tsp.	granulated sugar	1 mL
$\frac{1}{2}$ tsp.	ascorbic acid	2 mL
1	egg	1

The day before serving, purée the pork back fat, salt and the ice in a food processor or a blender until the mixture is smooth. Scrape it into a bowl and set aside. With a sharp knife, remove the skin from the pickerel and cut it into chunks. Purée the fish with the dill weed, tarragon, pink peppercorns, sugar, ascorbic acid and the egg. When it is smooth, add the purée to the bowl containing the pork. Stir to combine thoroughly. Cover with plastic wrap and refrigerate for 24 hours.

The next day, *preheat the oven to 350°F. (180°C).* Turn the pâté into a well-oiled 2-cup (500 mL) glass dish. Set it in a larger pan of hot water and insert a meat thermometer into the pâté, making sure that the bulb does not touch the glass. Bake, uncovered, until the internal temperature is 160°F. (75°C) or about 45 minutes. Remove from the oven. Allow to cool, cover and refrigerate until serving. After chilling, this pâté slices very thinly. *Makes 6-8 servings.*

Pink peppercorns are available dried in many specialty food stores. Crushed black peppercorns are an acceptable substitute.

Smoked Salmon Cheesecake

LISA WHITELY, *Innkeeper*
MARK BUSSIERES, *Chef*
THE BENMILLER INN,
Goderich, Ontario

When my friend Lynne McClain and I first tasted this delicious appetizer, it was a blindingly bright winter's day. Outside the window beside our table, sunlight sparkled on the icy stream. Melting snowbanks dripped into the water and danced their way through the countryside down to Lake Huron. Snuggled into a hillside, surrounded by forest and beautiful Huron County farmland, The Benmiller Inn is magical.

$\frac{1}{4}$ cup	toasted bread crumbs	50 mL
2 Tbsps.	grated parmesan cheese	25 mL
$1\frac{3}{4}$ lbs.	cream cheese (room temperature)	800 g
4	eggs	4
$\frac{1}{2}$ cup	grated oka cheese	125 mL
$\frac{1}{3}$ cup	heavy cream (35%)	75 mL
3 Tbsps.	fresh lemon juice	45 mL
$\frac{1}{2}$ tsp.	white pepper	2 mL
$\frac{1}{2}$ lb.	Canadian smoked salmon, finely diced	225 g
4	green onions, finely chopped	4
$\frac{1}{4}$ cup	fresh dill weed, chopped	50 mL
	salt, if needed	
	a few sprigs of fresh dill and lemon slices, for garnish	

Preheat the oven to 325°F. (160°C). Lightly butter the sides and bottom of a 10 in. (25 cm) spring-form pan.

In a bowl, combine the bread crumbs and parmesan. Mix well and dust the pan with the mixture until evenly coated. Shake out any excess.

In a mixmaster or food processor, blend the cream cheese until smooth, carefully scraping down the sides of the bowl. There should be no lumps. Continuing to beat, add the eggs, oka cheese, cream, lemon juice and white pepper. Mix until smooth. Fold in the salmon, green onions and dill. Taste and add salt if needed. (The quantity depends on the saltiness of the smoked salmon.) Pour the mixture into the spring-form pan. Bake for 35 minutes or until the center is firm. Allow to cool and refrigerate. Serve, garnished with dill weed and lemon slices, as an appetizer or fish course.

Makes 16 small servings.

THE MILLCROFT INN,
Alton, Ontario

Marinated Salmon with Ginger and Lime

🌸🌸🌸🌸🌸🌸🌸🌸🌸🌸🌸🌸🌸🌸🌸🌸🌸🌸🌸🌸🌸🌸🌸🌸🌸🌸🌸🌸🌸🌸🌸🌸🌸🌸🌸🌸🌸🌸🌸

FREDY STAMM, *Chef*
THE MILLCROFT INN,
Alton, Ontario

Fredy Stamm is certainly one of our best Canadian chefs. His recipes rely heavily on the freshest ingredients and are often quite simple. This appetizer is quick and very tasty.

2½ lb.	side of fresh Atlantic salmon, cleaned, skinned and deboned	1 kg
⅓ cup	rock salt	75 mL
	freshly ground black pepper, to taste	
1 oz.	ginger root, peeled and chopped	28 g
2	limes, juiced	2

With a razor-sharp knife, cut the salmon on an angle into very thin slices and arrange them on a platter. Sprinkle lightly with salt. Rock salt is preferred as it has no iodine to discolor the fish. Dust with pepper from a pepper mill. Sprinkle with finely chopped ginger root. Now, with a pastry brush, coat the salmon slices with lime juice. Cover the whole platter tightly with plastic wrap and refrigerate. The salmon will now "cure" by itself. Allow it to chill for 4-6 hours, depending on the thickness of the slices. Serve on individual plates with freshly chopped onions, capers and warm, buttered toast.

Makes 8-10 servings.

Oysters in Cider Vinegar Butter

SINCLAIR AND FREDRICA PHILIP, *Innkeepers*
PIA CARROLL, *Chef*
SOOKE HARBOUR HOUSE,
Whiffen Spit Beach, Vancouver Island, B.C.

Over a rounding, enchanted bay, teeming with sea life and bobbing seals, presides a magical inn. As you explore the perfect gardens of herbs and edible flowers, prepare yourself for the dining experience of a lifetime. Sooke Harbour House envelopes all your senses — and plays with them.

Dried seaweed is available at most fishmongers. On the eastern seaboard, it is known as dulse, and generally it is chewed, as is, for a salty snack. On the west coast, it is used for cooking and several varieties are available, alaria being the one the Philips prefer.

12	unshucked oysters*	12
$\frac{1}{2}$ cup	dry apple cider	125 mL
$\frac{1}{4}$ cup	cider vinegar	50 mL
$\frac{1}{2}$ cup	fish stock	125 mL
2	small shallots, minced	2
$\frac{1}{4}$ cup	minced leeks (white portion only)	50 mL
1 Tbsp.	dried seaweed (alaria if possible *or* laminaria *or* dulse)	15 mL
$\frac{1}{4}$ cup	heavy cream (35%)	50 mL
$\frac{2}{3}$ cup	unsalted butter, cut into $\frac{1}{2}$ in. (1 cm) cubes and refrigerated chives, for garnish	150 mL

Shuck oysters over a bowl to catch the liquor. Place the meat in a small bowl and reserve the deep halves of the shells for serving.

Transfer the oyster liquor to a small saucepan. Add the cider vinegar, stock, shallots, leeks and seaweed. Bring to a boil. Poach the oysters in this liquid, 1 minute per side. Remove and keep warm.

Warm the shells by immersing them in a pan of hot water. Add the cream to the poaching liquid. Bring to a boil over medium-high heat and reduce by half, about 4 minutes, until the mixture has thickened. Reduce the heat, and immediately whisk in the butter pieces, a few at a time, until all are incorporated. Drain the heated shells. Pat dry. Arrange for serving.

Reheat the oyster meat in the sauce. Place on the half shells and pour extra sauce over. Garnish with chives. Serve immediately.

Makes 4 inspired appetizers.

* *Puff pastry shells may be substituted for the oyster shells in this recipe.*

Marinated Abalone

🐝🐝🐝🐝🐝🐝🐝🐝🐝🐝🐝🐝🐝🐝🐝🐝🐝🐝🐝🐝🐝🐝🐝🐝🐝🐝🐝🐝🐝🐝🐝🐝🐝🐝🐝🐝🐝🐝🐝

SINCLAIR AND FREDRICA PHILIP, *Innkeepers*
PIA CARROL, *Chef*
SOOKE HARBOUR HOUSE,
Whiffen Spit Beach, Vancouver Island, B.C.

1 lb.	abalone, julienned (see Abalone, p. 44)	450 g
1	green pepper, julienned	1
$\frac{3}{4}$ lb.	fresh tomatoes, peeled, seeded and cubed	340 g
$\frac{1}{2}$	red onion, thinly sliced	$\frac{1}{2}$
1	yellow zucchini, thinly sliced on the diagonal with the skin left on	1
$\frac{1}{2}$ cup	lemon juice, freshly squeezed	125 mL
$\frac{1}{2}$ cup	diced fennel bulb	125 mL
$\frac{1}{2}$ cup	olive oil	125 mL

Marinate all the ingredients in a covered bowl in your refrigerator for about two hours. Serve on crisp lettuce leaves with crusty french bread. *Makes 4 servings.*

Les Escargots à la Crème et à l'Estragon (Snails in Tarragon Cream)

🐝🐝🐝🐝🐝🐝🐝🐝🐝🐝🐝🐝🐝🐝🐝🐝🐝🐝🐝🐝🐝🐝🐝🐝🐝🐝🐝🐝🐝🐝🐝🐝🐝🐝🐝🐝🐝🐝🐝

LUC INVERNIZZI, *Innkeeper*
L'AUBERGE LE RUÇHER,
Val David, Québec

2 Tbsps.	butter	25 mL
28	snails, rinsed, well drained	28
1 cup	dry red wine	250 mL
$\frac{1}{2}$ tsp.	powdered tarragon	2 mL
$\frac{1}{2}$ tsp.	black pepper, freshly ground	2 mL
$\frac{1}{4}$ tsp.	dried thyme	1 mL
$\frac{1}{2}$ cup	Crème Fraîche (p. 112)	125 mL
4 slices	brown bread	4 slices
1 Tbsp.	brandy	15 mL
4 leaves	romaine lettuce	4 leaves

In a skillet, melt the butter over medium heat. Add the snails and sauté for several minutes. Pour in the wine and season with the tarragon, pepper and thyme. Bring to a simmer and stir in the Crème Fraîche. Toast the bread, or grill it (if you have the facilities) with a little garlic.

Just prior to serving, splash the brandy onto the snails. Ladle them onto the toast, baste with the sauce and serve on a leaf of romaine. *Makes 4 servings.*

Escargots Dundee

DON, MARY AND JUDY CLINTON, *Innkeepers*
THE DUNDEE ARMS INN,
Charlottetown, Prince Edward Island

On Prince Edward Island, there are native snails called sea whelks. They are meaty and quite different in taste from the classy escargot. Don says that Red Feather brand snails are a close equivalent.

2 Tbsps.	butter	25 mL
2 cloves	garlic, crushed	2 cloves
$\frac{1}{2}$	medium onion, sliced	$\frac{1}{2}$
2 lbs.	fresh mushrooms, sliced	900 g
1 10-oz. can	Red Feather snails, drained	1 280-mL can
	or	
1 cup	sea whelks, washed and drained	250 mL
1	medium tomato, diced in $\frac{1}{2}$ in. (1 cm) cubes salt and freshly ground pepper, to taste	1
8	toast rounds	8

In a large sauté pan, melt the butter. Add the garlic and onion and cook until they are transparent. Toss in the mushrooms and snails. Continue to sauté until the mushrooms are cooked. Add the tomato and season with salt and pepper. Cook only until the tomato is heated through. Serve on top of toast rounds.

Makes 8 servings.

Soups

SOOKE HARBOUR HOUSE,
Whiffen Spit Beach, Vancouver Island B.C.

Sea Urchin Soup

SINCLAIR AND FREDRICA PHILIP, *Innkeepers*
PIA CARROLL, *Chef*
SOOKE HARBOUR HOUSE,
Whiffen Spit Beach, Vancouver Island, B.C.

Our son Mark, the shell collector, has sea urchin shells from both the North Atlantic — small ones washed ashore on Nova Scotia's wind-swept beaches — and large ones from the Pacific. It wasn't until I met Sinclair that I realized that sea urchins could be more than decorative.

Both the Orientals and the Europeans have used roe from sea urchins for years, but it is still *nouveau* in Canada. Sushi bars use it; probably more people have tasted it than know they have.

They are an extremely perishable shellfish. Consequently, you will find them for sale at only the very best coastal fish markets. I have not seen them anywhere throughout inland Canada, but possibly Oriental fishmongers in larger centers such as Montreal or Toronto might carry them.

If you wish to enjoy the roe raw, as Sinclair does, simply rinse it in pear cider for about 15 seconds. Only the lovely orange roe of the urchin is eaten. You will need 2 to 4 sea urchins per serving. To serve, pile all the roe back into one of the cleaned shells that has had its top removed.

The only prerequisite for this recipe is that the sea urchin must be very fresh; otherwise, the roe loses its freshness and takes on a slightly bitter taste.

2 Tbsps.	unsalted butter	25 mL
2	small shallots, minced	2
$\frac{1}{2}$	medium tomato, diced	$\frac{1}{2}$
$1\frac{1}{2}$ cups	sea urchin roe (discard all but the orange roe)	375 mL
4 cups	fish velouté*	1 L
$\frac{1}{4}$ cup	dry, Rhine-style white wine	50 mL
1	egg yolk	1
2 Tbsps.	heavy cream (35%)	25 mL
2 Tbsps.	Crème Fraîche (p. 112)	25 mL
2 tsps.	sea urchin roe (second amount)	10 mL

Melt the butter in a large saucepan. Sauté the shallots and tomato over medium heat. Add the roe, velouté and wine. As you increase the heat, whisk to combine all the ingredients well. When the soup is heated through and is ready to be served, blend together the egg yolk and cream. Add and stir well. Pour soup into 4 bowls. Divide the Crème Fraîche topping among them. Top the Crème Fraîche with $\frac{1}{2}$ tsp. (2 mL) roe.

Makes 4 servings.

To make fish velouté, thicken 4 cups (1 L) fish stock with a roux made of $\frac{1}{4}$ cup (50 mL) unsalted butter and $\frac{1}{4}$ cup (50 mL) flour which have been cooked together for 3 minutes.

Newfoundland Pea Soup

CHRISTINE AND PETER BEAMISH, *Innkeepers*
THE VILLAGE INN,
Trinity, Newfoundland

To dream is wonderful, and to pursue that dream is courageous and daring.

Peter Beamish is a marine bio-acoustician, specializing in Cetology or the study of whales, dolphins and porpoises. He and his wife, Christine, have strived to acquaint their guests with Peter's friends, the Great Whales of Trinity Bay. Setting out in sailboats or rubber dinghys, they bring people into direct contact with these awesome mammals — by sight, by sound and even by touch. Through Ocean Contact and Ceta-Research, a nonprofit organization studying the whale entrapment problem that plagues local fishermen, Peter is realizing his dream and permanently enriching the lives of many, many people.

You can almost imagine the fishermen, in their rain slicks, sloshing into the kitchen after braving the foggy Grand Banks when you dip your spoon into this rich hearty soup.

1 lb.	dried peas	450 g
2 lbs.	salt beef	900 g
	cold water	
1	large onion, diced	1
8 cups	cold water (second amount)	2 L
1-2 tsps.	Newfoundland savory	5-10 mL
	or	
1-2 tsps.	rubbed sage	5-10 mL
	salt and freshly ground pepper, to taste	
2 cups	pared and diced carrots	500 mL
2 cups	pared and diced turnips	500 mL
1 cup	pared and diced potato (optional)	250 mL

In separate large saucepans, soak the peas and the beef in lots of cold water. They should be well covered. Let stand overnight. In the morning, drain the peas and wash them under cold running water. Drain the beef and dice it into $\frac{1}{2}$ in. (1 cm) cubes. Place both the peas and the beef in a large soup pot. Add the onion, the water, and the seasonings. Be careful not to add too much salt. Cover and bring to a boil. Reduce the heat and simmer for 2 hours or until the beef is very tender. Add the vegetables and continue to cook until they are tender. If you prefer a smoother, more traditional pea soup, the vegetables may be added at the same time as the onion. Correct the seasonings and serve steaming from the soup pot.

Makes 10-12 servings.

THE AMHERST SHORE COUNTRY INN,
Amherst, Nova Scotia

Fish Chowder

🐝🐝

JIM AND DONNA LACEBY, *Innkeepers*
THE AMHERST SHORE COUNTRY INN,
Amherst, Nova Scotia

Donna says that the flavor of this chowder improves if it is made a day or so before serving. It just gets better when it is reheated.

2 6-8 oz.	halibut fillets	2 165-225 g
$\frac{1}{2}$ tsp.	salt	2 mL
2 cups	water	500 mL
$\frac{1}{4}$ cup	butter	50 mL
1 cup	finely chopped onion	250 mL
1 cup	diced celery	250 mL
1 cup	potato, chopped into small cubes	250 mL
2 cups	half-and-half cream (10%)	500 mL
$\frac{1}{4}$ cup	all-purpose flour	50 mL
	salt and freshly ground pepper, to taste	
2 Tbsps.	butter (second amount)	25 mL
	bacon bits, for garnish	

In a medium-sized, covered saucepan, poach the halibut gently in the salted water. Cooking will take only a few minutes. Remove the saucepan from the heat and let the fish cool in the poaching liquid. Remove the halibut with a slotted spoon and flake it, discarding any bones or skin. You should have at least 2 cups (500 mL) of flaked fish. Strain and reserve the poaching liquid. Again, it should equal approximately 2 cups (500 mL).

Melt the $\frac{1}{4}$ cup (50 mL) butter in a heavy saucepan. Add the onion and celery, sautéing for 2-3 minutes. Add the potato cubes and sauté for 1 minute more. Add the reserved fish stock. Bring to a boil; reduce the heat and simmer until the potatoes are cooked but not mushy. Add 1 cup (250 mL) of the cream. Blend the flour into the remaining cream and whisk into the chowder. Cook until it thickens. Add the poached fish. Season with salt and pepper. Stir in the butter. Serve in heated bowls. Garnish with bacon bits.

Makes 6 servings.

Cream of Winter Kale and Apple Soup

❀❀

SINCLAIR AND FREDRICA PHILIP, *Innkeepers*
PIA CARROLL, *Chef*
SOOKE HARBOUR HOUSE,
Whiffen Spit Beach, Vancouver Island, B.C.

Sooke Harbour House is on the southern shore of Vancouver Island. When the rest of Canada is frozen stiff, Sinclair is out in his vast garden, weeding and picking winter vegetables. Kale needs a good frost to bring it to a peak.

$\frac{1}{4}$ cup	unsalted butter	50 mL
1 clove	garlic, minced	1 clove
$\frac{1}{3}$ cup	onion, finely diced	75 mL
6 cups	curly or Siberian kale, washed and dried, thick stems discarded	1.5 L
$\frac{1}{4}$ cup	flour	50 mL
6 cups	chicken stock	1.5 L
$\frac{1}{2}$	cooking apple, cored, peeled and sliced thinly (Ida Red is suitable)	$\frac{1}{2}$
	pinch of dried thyme	
1 tsp.	dried tarragon	5 mL
	freshly ground pepper, to taste	
	Crème Fraîche (p. 112) *or* unsweetened whipped cream and minced chives, for garnish	

In a large saucepan, melt the butter over low heat. Add the garlic and onion. Sauté until transparent. Add the kale, stirring thoroughly. Cover the pan for 4-5 minutes to soften the leaves. Stir in the flour to form a roux and allow to cook for a few minutes. Slowly stir in the stock, apple, thyme and tarragon. Grind in the pepper to taste. Bring the soup to a boil. Reduce the heat and simmer for 30 minutes. Correct the seasonings. Let cool. Purée in a blender, food processor or food mill until smooth. The soup can be made ahead up to this point and refrigerated.

To serve, reheat the soup over medium heat. Pour into warmed bowls. Garnish with a small dollop of Crème Fraîche or whipped cream and a sprinkling of chives.

Makes 6 servings.

Rich Cream of Spinach Soup

&&&&&&&&&&&&&&&&&&&&&&&&&&&&&&&&&&&&&&&&&&&&&&&&

P.M. "Charlie" Holgate, *Innkeeper*
Camelot Inn,
Musquodoboit Harbour, N.S.

This is one of Charlie's standbys. She leaves it nice and thick for a soup and salad lunch or thins it with extra cream for a first course. She tops it with freshly grated nutmeg at times, too.

$\frac{1}{2}$ cup	butter	125 mL
$\frac{1}{2}$ cup	flour (scant)	125 mL
2 cups	milk	500 mL
$1\frac{1}{2}$-2 cups	beef consommé	375-500 mL
$\frac{1}{4}$ cup	puréed or grated onion	50 mL
$1\frac{1}{2}$ cups	cooked and puréed spinach	375 mL
$\frac{1}{2}$ tsp.	Worcestershire sauce	2 mL
$\frac{1}{4}$-$\frac{1}{2}$ tsp.	Fines Herbes (p. 43)	1-2 mL
3 or 4 drops	Tabasco	3-4 drops
2 cups	table cream (18%)	500 mL
	salt and pepper, to taste	
	paprika and chopped parsley, for garnish	

In a heavy saucepan, melt the butter. Stir in the flour. Add the milk and the consommé. Stir with a wire whisk on low heat until thick. Add onion, spinach and seasonings, except the salt and pepper. Add cream until soup is the desired consistency. Cook 7 to 10 minutes. Add salt and pepper. Sprinkle with paprika and chopped parsley before serving. Freezes well.

Makes 6-8 servings.

Clara's Cream of Carrot Soup

&&&&&&&&&&&&&&&&&&&&&&&&&&&&&&&&&&&&&&&&&&&&&&&&

Eve and Michael Concannon, *Innkeepers*
Marquis of Dufferin Lodge,
Port Dufferin, Halifax County, N.S.

Carrots are one of the few fresh vegetables always available on the Eastern Shore. The Concannons say that this soup freezes well; simply omit the milk and add it when you are reheating it. In an emergency, you can substitute a commercial chicken soup base or a canned chicken broth for the homemade stock.

2 Tbsps.	butter or margarine	25 mL
4	medium carrots, scraped and sliced	4
1	potato, peeled and diced	1
1 stalk	celery, sliced	1 stalk
2	medium onions, diced	2
4 cups	chicken stock	1 L
1 cup	milk	250 mL
	salt and freshly ground pepper, to taste	

Melt the butter in a soup kettle and add the prepared vegetables. Gently sauté for 10-15 minutes. Cover the kettle and allow the vegetables to "sweat" to prevent browning. Add the chicken stock, cover and simmer for 1½ hours. Purée the soup a little at a time in a blender. Return to the soup kettle and add milk until a good consistency is reached. (Thickness will vary, depending on the size of potato used). Season to taste and reheat just to boiling point.

Makes about 10 servings.

Basic Chicken Stock

JEAN AND JANINE AUTHIER, *Innkeepers*
L'AUBERGE LA PINSONNIÈRE,
Cap-à-L'Aigle, Québec

Use this full-flavored stock whenever chicken stock is required in a recipe.

3	onions, chopped	3
2	minced leeks, the white part only	2
	the chopped leaves from 1 bunch of celery	
2	bay leaves	2
1 Tbsp.	whole peppercorns	15 mL
1	large boiling fowl, including the wings and the neck	1
16 cups	water	4 L

Put the onions, leeks and celery leaves into a large soup kettle. Add the bay leaves and peppercorns. Top with the boiling fowl. Pour in the water, cover and bring to a boil. Reduce the heat and simmer slowly for 2 hours, skimming regularly. After that time, about 8 cups (2 L) of stock should remain. Strain and set aside. This stock may be refrigerated or frozen if not used immediately.

Makes 8 cups (2 L).

Mañana Lodge,
Ladysmith, Vancouver Island, B.C.

Wild Rice Soup

꽃꽃

Rena and Jim Mazurenko, *Innkeepers*
George and Thelma Stickle, *Innkeepers*
Mañana Lodge,
Ladysmith, Vancouver Island, B.C.

Mañana to me means warmth — a crackling fire, the fragrance of B.C. cedar, Cowichan Indian knits and excellent food. A carafe of sherry awaits guests in their room where, years before, an aspiring artist painted Indian murals on the cedar-lined walls. Although this soup is not on the regular menu, it has been included a number of times on gourmet nights.

1	small onion, chopped	1
2 Tbsps.	butter	25 mL
$\frac{1}{2}$ lb.	mushrooms, sliced	225 g
$\frac{1}{2}$ cup	celery, sliced	125 mL
$\frac{1}{4}$ cup	all-purpose flour	50 mL
4 cups	hot chicken stock	1 L
1 cup	cooked, wild rice	250 mL
$\frac{1}{4}$ tsp.	salt	1 mL
$\frac{1}{4}$ tsp.	dry mustard	1 mL
$\frac{1}{4}$ tsp.	curry powder	1 mL
$\frac{1}{8}$ tsp.	freshly ground pepper	0.5 mL
1 cup	cream (half-and-half —10% *or* table cream — 18%)	250 mL
$\frac{1}{2}$ cup	dry sherry	125 mL
2 Tbsps.	chopped, fresh parsley	25 mL

In a large saucepan, sauté the onion in the butter until transparent. Add the mushrooms and celery. Cook, stirring, for 2 minutes. Blend in the flour, allowing the mixture to bubble. Whisk in the chicken stock and continue to stir until it thickens.

Stir in the rice, salt, mustard, curry powder and pepper. Heat until it begins to simmer. *Do not boil.* Stir in the cream and the sherry. Serve immediately, sprinkled with parsley.

Makes 6 servings.

Cornwallis Vegetable Bisque

❀❀❀❀❀❀❀❀❀❀❀❀❀❀❀❀❀❀❀❀❀❀❀❀❀❀❀❀❀❀❀❀❀❀❀❀❀❀❀

RON AND DOREEN COOK, *Innkeepers*
VICTORIA'S HISTORIC INN,
Wolfville, Nova Scotia

Wolfville used to be known as Mud Creek. It is located in the heart of the rich Annapolis Valley where vegetables grow in profusion.

2 quarts	beef stock	2 L
½ cup	diced celery	125 mL
½ cup	potato cubes	125 mL
¼ cup	diced onion	50 mL
½ cup	diced carrot	125 mL
¼ cup	diced green pepper	50 mL
1 cup	cauliflowerettes	250 mL
1 cup	broccoli pieces	250 mL
½ cup	fresh or frozen peas	125 mL
½ cup	creamed corn	125 mL
¼ cup	butter	50 mL
¼ cup	flour	50 mL
	salt and freshly ground pepper, to taste	
2 cups	milk	500 mL

Bring the stock to a boil in a large soup pot. Add the celery and cook for 3 minutes. Add the potato cubes and continue cooking for another 3 minutes. Add the onion, carrot and green pepper. Simmer, covered, for 15 minutes.

Add the cauliflower and cook 2 to 3 minutes. Remove from the heat and stir in the broccoli. This keeps the broccoli green and attractive. Stir in the peas and creamed corn.

At this point, you may refrigerate the soup until needed, as Ron does, or you can continue the preparation and serve the soup immediately. To continue: Make a thin cream sauce by melting the butter over medium heat and stirring in the flour. Season with salt and pepper.* Add the milk and cook over medium-low heat until slightly thickened. Add to the vegetable mixture. Correct seasonings and reheat thoroughly before serving.

Makes 8-10 servings.

*Ron sometimes stirs about 1 tsp. (5 mL) of curry powder into the cream sauce for a change of flavor.

Lamb's-Quarters Vichyssoise

LINDA L'AVENTURE AND CECILIA BOWDEN, *Innkeepers*
THE COMPASS ROSE,
North Head, Grand Manan, N.B.

Linda L'Aventure has become a dedicated, patriotic "Grand Mananer." She and her great Golden Lab, Finnegan, survive through the Toronto winters to flee as fast as possible to the island and The Compass Rose. Linda has become so much a part of the island that she has the local children picking wild berries for her. The island ladies grow vegetables for her from seeds that she assembles in Ontario and takes east.

She and her partner, Cecilia, often work sixteen-hour days. One really wonders why, but then you stroll out onto the porch which overlooks the North Head Harbour and the answer is very clear.

3 cups	sliced, peeled potatoes	750 mL
3 cups	finely chopped leeks (the white part only)	750 mL
6 cups	chicken stock (p. 29) a handful of chopped lamb's-quarters	1.5 L
$\frac{1}{2}$-1 cup	heavy cream (35%) salt and white pepper, to taste	125-250 mL
2-3 Tbsps.	minced chives, for garnish	25-45 mL

In a large covered saucepan, combine the potatoes, leeks and chicken stock. Stir in the lamb's-quarters and simmer together until the vegetables are well cooked. Remove from the heat and purée in batches, either in a food processor, blender or food mill. Stir in the cream and season with salt and white pepper to taste. Cover and refrigerate for several hours or overnight. Serve in chilled soup bowls, garnished with chives.

Makes 6-8 servings.

Raspberry Bisque

DON, MARY AND JUDY CLINTON, *Innkeepers*
THE DUNDEE ARMS INN,
Charlottetown, Prince Edward Island

This unusual starter almost has the bite of yogurt. It tastes so good that our boys had a little disagreement over the ownership of the mixing bowl. The biggest brother won.

2 cups	frozen raspberries	500 mL
1 cup	dry red wine	250 mL
$\frac{1}{2}$ cup	granulated sugar (less if raspberries are sweetened)	125 mL
1-2 in. stick	cinnamon	2.5-5 cm stick
2	egg yolks	2
1 tsp.	salt	5 mL
2 cups	sour cream	500 mL
	whole raspberries, reserved for garnish	

In a saucepan, combine the raspberries, red wine, sugar, cinnamon stick, egg yolks and salt. Simmer, whisking constantly, for 10-15 minutes, or until the frozen berries are broken up thoroughly and the mixture is very hot. Cool for a few minutes and stir in the sour cream. Chill for 3-4 hours or overnight. Serve garnished with a few whole berries. *Makes 8-10 servings.*

Seafood Chowder

DORIS HALL AND GEORGE EVANS, *Innkeepers*
MACNEILL MANOR,
Chester, Nova Scotia

1 cup	water	250 mL
4 tsps.	chopped chives	20 mL
$\frac{1}{2}$ tsp.	salt	2 mL
$\frac{1}{2}$ tsp.	freshly ground pepper	2 mL
$\frac{1}{2}$ tsp.	dried tarragon	2 mL
8 oz.	fresh fish fillet, cut in small bits (haddock or halibut preferred)	225 g
8 oz.	fresh scallops	225 g
4 oz.	pre-cooked lobster or crab meat	115 g
4 Tbsps.	Beurre Manie (p. 17)	60 mL
$\frac{1}{2}$ cup	light cream (10%)	125 mL
	paprika and parsley, for garnish	

Place the saucepan with the water, chives, salt, pepper and tarragon on medium-high heat. Allow it to boil for 1 minute; then add the fish fillet and scallops. Reduce the heat and simmer for another minute; then add the lobster or crab meat, along with the Beurre Manie and cream. Stir the soup gently until steaming hot and slightly thickened. Do not allow it to boil. Garnish with a dash of paprika and a sprig of parsley. *Makes 4 servings.*

Broccoli and Cheese Soup

RESA LENT, *Innkeeper*
THE DESERT ROSE INN AND CAFÉ,
Elora, Ontario

Resa glows! Anyone who knows her will agree. She simply loves life. She came to Elora years ago, before it was fashionable to have a "shoppe" on Mill Street, to open her excellent café. She struggled through long winters without losing her sense of humor or her purpose. Her latest expansion is into a block of buildings on the Grand River where she has opened her inn. And she is still smiling!

Here's one of the all-time favorites at the café.

$\frac{1}{4}$ cup	butter or oil	50 mL
2 cups	chopped onions	500 mL
4 cloves	garlic, crushed	4 cloves
1 bunch	broccoli, chopped	1 bunch
4 cups	potato chunks	1 L
1	large carrot, chopped	1
6 cups	water or stock	1.5 L
	salt and freshly ground pepper, to taste	
1 Tbsp.	dried marjoram	15 mL
$1\frac{1}{2}$-2 cups	grated, medium cheddar cheese	375-500 mL
	grated cheese, parsley and/or garlic croutons, for garnish	

In a large soup pot, melt the butter. Gently sauté the onions and garlic until soft. Add the broccoli, potato chunks and carrot. Continue to sauté for 5 minutes. Add water or stock almost to cover. Simmer until the vegetables are soft. Let cool 10 minutes; then purée in a blender or food processor. (Resa leaves some chunks.) Return the soup to the pot and add salt and pepper to taste. Stir in the marjoram and cheddar cheese. Reheat to melt the cheese. Thin with more water or stock, if desired. Serve garnished with extra cheese, parsley and a few croutons.

Makes 6-8 steaming, fragrant servings.

Good Lobster Chowder

EVE AND MICHAEL CONCANNON, *Innkeepers*
MARQUIS OF DUFFERIN LODGE,
Port Dufferin, Halifax County, N.S.

This is not merely good. It's great. It improves with keeping and is excellent a day or two later. Keep it refrigerated and add the cream when you're ready to serve it.

6	medium potatoes, peeled and diced	6
1	small onion, minced	1
20-24 oz.	lobster meat	560-670 g
$\frac{1}{2}$ cup	butter	125 mL
2 13.5-oz. cans	evaporated milk	2 385-mL cans
4 cups	half-and-half cream (10%) salt, freshly ground pepper and grated nutmeg, to taste	1 L

Combine the potatoes and onion in a large soup kettle. Add just enough cold water to cover the vegetables. Cover the kettle and bring to a boil. Reduce heat and simmer until the potatoes are soft, but not mushy; about 10 minutes.

Meanwhile, cut the lobster into bite-sized pieces. Melt the butter in a skillet and gently sauté the lobster. Do not allow the lobster to brown, but make sure all the pieces are coated with butter. Lower the heat and add the evaporated milk. Slowly heat until the milk begins to thicken. Stir this lobster mixture into the soup kettle. Add the half-and-half cream, lightly seasoning to taste with salt, pepper and nutmeg. Reheat to serving temperature without boiling. *Makes 10-12 servings.*

Orchard Onion Soup

PAT HOGAN, *Executive Chef*
THE PILLAR AND POST,
Niagara-on-the-Lake, Ont.

Pat buys his cider locally at one of the many orchards that have made the Niagara area so famous.

2 lbs.	cooking onions	900 g
3 Tbsps.	butter	45 mL
3 Tbsps.	all-purpose flour	45 mL
$2\frac{1}{2}$ cups	sweet apple cider	625 mL
4 cups	chicken stock (p. 29)	1 L
$\frac{1}{4}$ cup	table cream (18%) salt and freshly ground pepper, to taste	50 mL
8	large croutons*	8
2 lbs.	Gruyère cheese, grated	900 g

Peel and slice the onions. Melt the butter in a large, heavy saucepan. Add the onions and sauté until transparent and soft. Stir in the flour and continue to cook until bubbly. Whisk in half the cider to dissolve the flour. Add the chicken stock and simmer for 20 minutes. Add the cream and season to taste with salt and pepper.

Heat the remaining cider in a saucepan. Divide among 8 oven-proof serving bowls. Top with the soup, croutons and Gruyère cheese. Glaze under the broiler until golden brown. *Makes 8 servings.*

*To make large croutons, cut stale French bread into 1 in. (2.5 cm) slices. Dry them out in a single layer in a 200°F. (100°C) oven for approximately 45 minutes.

Boscawen Inn,
Lunenburg, Nova Scotia

Cold Cucumber Soup

🐝🐝🐝🐝🐝🐝🐝🐝🐝🐝🐝🐝🐝🐝🐝🐝🐝🐝🐝🐝🐝🐝🐝🐝🐝🐝🐝🐝🐝🐝🐝🐝🐝🐝🐝🐝🐝🐝🐝

Leslie Langille, *Innkeeper*
Boscawen Inn,
Lunenburg, Nova Scotia

Peach yogurt is the surprise ingredient in this refreshing summer-time soup.

1	large English cucumber, peeled and sliced	1
2 cups	plain yogurt	500 mL
2 cups	peach yogurt	500 mL
2 cups	chicken stock, chilled (p. 29)	500 mL
2 Tbsps.	minced green onions	25 mL
3 Tbsps.	minced fresh mint	45 mL
	or	
1 Tbsp.	dried mint	15 mL
	salt and freshly ground pepper, to taste	
	fresh mint leaves, for garnish	

Method No. 1

Grate the cucumber finely and whisk together with the remaining ingredients in a large bowl. Cover with plastic wrap and refrigerate 3-4 hours before serving.

Method No. 2

Whirl all the ingredients together in a blender or food processor in batches until puréed. Stir together in a large bowl. Cover with plastic wrap and refrigerate until ready to serve, at least 3-4 hours.

This soup may be made 24 hours in advance and refrigerated. Garnish with fresh mint leaves.

Makes 10-12 servings.

May's Cauliflower Soup

꙳꙳

MAY DENREYER, *Innkeeper*
THE HORSESHOE INN,
Cataract, Ontario

Dating from 1870, the inn is a quiet, country retreat near the Bruce Trail; a welcome resting spot for tired hikers.

2 Tbsps.	butter or oil	25 mL
2 stalks	celery, diced	2 stalks
2 cloves	garlic, minced	2 cloves
1	medium onion, chopped	1
6-8 cups	chicken stock (p. 29) or water with soup base added	1.5-2 L
1 head	cauliflower, chopped coarsely salt and freshly ground pepper, to taste	1 head
$\frac{1}{4}$ tsp.	granulated sugar	1 mL
$\frac{1}{4}$ tsp.	dried thyme	1 mL
$\frac{1}{4}$ tsp.	dry mustard	1 mL
2 cups	cooked potatoes (optional)	500 mL
1 cup	dry milk powder	250 mL

In a large soup kettle, heat the butter or oil. Add the celery, garlic and onion. Sauté gently until tender, about 5 minutes. Pour in the stock (or water to which bouillon cubes or powder has been added). Drop in the cauliflower and stir in all the seasonings. Simmer until tender. Remove from the heat. Add the potatoes and purée in batches in a blender or food processor. Return to the heat and stir in the milk powder. Reheat and serve. *Makes 6-8 servings.*

Lentil Soup

꙳꙳

RUTH AND HAL PEETS, *Innkeepers*
UNION HOTEL,
Normandale, Ontario

Perfect on a damp November day when its warmth will reassure you that all is still right with the world.

$\frac{1}{2}$ lb.	lean, ground beef	225 g
1 cup	minced onion (1 large)	250 mL
2 cloves	garlic, minced	2 cloves
8 cups	vegetable or chicken stock (p. 29)	2 L
1 cup	brown lentils	250 mL
$\frac{1}{2}$ cup	pot barley	125 mL

1 cup	chopped carrots	250 mL
1 cup	chopped celery	250 mL
1 28-oz. tin	tomatoes, chopped	1 796-mL tin
	salt and freshly ground pepper, to taste	
1 tsp.	dried thyme	5 mL
1½ tsps.	dried sweet basil	7 mL
	juice of ½ lemon	
	fresh parsley, thyme or basil, for garnish	

In a frying pan, sauté the beef, onion and garlic until brown. Drain well. Heat the stock in a large soup kettle. Add the lentils, barley and the beef mixture. Simmer, covered, half an hour or until the lentils are cooked. Add the carrots, celery, tomatoes and seasonings. Simmer gently together for 1½ hours. Add more stock if the soup is too thick. Just before serving, add the lemon juice. Garnish with fresh parsley, sprigs of fresh thyme or basil. *Makes 6-8 servings.*

Wild Shaggy Mane Mushroom Soup

MARY AND JERRY BOND, *Innkeepers*
BLACK CAT GUEST RANCH,
Hinton, Alberta

Free for the picking, Shaggy Mane mushrooms have a super flavor and, best of all, they do not in the least resemble any of the poisonous varieties. Mary writes, "We freeze Shaggy Mane mushrooms. We pick and clean them. Scrape any sand off and wash quickly, if necessary. Drain thoroughly. Cut the mushrooms lengthwise and check for any small bugs. Pack them in small sandwich bags and freeze. When you take them out of the freezer, cut them up as soon as possible and add to what you are cooking — usually soup, spaghetti sauce or gravy for a pork roast."

½ lb.	Shaggy Mane mushrooms, cleaned and chopped	225 g
3 Tbsps.	butter	45 mL
3 Tbsps.	minced onion	45 mL
3 Tbsps.	flour	45 mL
1½ cups	milk	375 mL
½ tsp.	salt	2 mL
	paprika, to taste	
	cayenne pepper, to taste	

If the mushrooms are frozen, chop them while they are still partially solid.

In a medium-sized saucepan, melt the butter over low heat. Sauté the onion gently. Increase the heat and add the mushrooms. Cook for 1-2 minutes. Stir in the flour. Add the milk, stirring constantly. Cook until slightly thickened. Add the seasonings to taste. *Makes 4 servings.*

Salads and Dressings

High Brass Hunting Lodge,
Winnipegosis, Manitoba

Creamy Dill Dressing

೫೫೫

MARIE MUSHRUSH, *Innkeeper*
HIGH BRASS HUNTING LODGE,
Winnipegosis, Manitoba

This type of dressing is always better after a few hours in the refrigerator.

1	egg	1
1 tsp.	salt	5 mL
$\frac{1}{8}$ tsp.	freshly ground pepper	0.5 mL
1 Tbsp.	lemon juice	15 mL
1 tsp.	grated onion	5 mL
$\frac{1}{4}$ tsp.	granulated sugar	1 mL
$\frac{1}{4}$ tsp.	dried dill weed	1 mL
$1\frac{1}{2}$ cups	sour cream	375 mL

Beat the egg until slightly thickened and blend in the remaining ingredients. Fold this mixture into the sour cream. Refrigerate until serving. *Makes $1\frac{3}{4}$ cups (425 mL).*

Small Touches   Honey Yogurt Dressing

೫೫೫

Combine plain yogurt with your preferred honey until the taste is to your liking. This recipe may also be made with maple syrup, preferably syrup of the first run. Chopped, fresh herbs may also be used. (Fredy Stamm, Chef, The Millcroft Inn, Alton, Ontario)

Whitman Inn Creamy Tarragon Dressing

೫೫೫

BRUCE AND NANCY GURNHAM, *Innkeepers*
THE WHITMAN INN,
Caledonia, Queen's County, Nova Scotia

Nancy developed this recipe especially for *The Country Inn Cookbook.*

$\frac{1}{2}$ cup	vinegar	125 mL
1-2 Tbsps.	dried tarragon	15-25 mL
4 Tbsps.	honey	60 mL
2 tsps.	prepared, Dijon-style mustard	10 mL
2 Tbsps.	grated horseradish	25 mL
4 Tbsps.	sour cream	60 mL
1 cup	vegetable oil	250 mL

Blend all the ingredients except the oil in a food processor or blender until the mixture is smooth. With the machine running, add the oil in a steady stream. Blend well. *Makes about 2 cups (500 mL).*

Poppy Seed Dressing

ANNA AND PATRICK REDGRAVE, *Innkeepers*
THE GARRISON HOUSE INN,
Annapolis Royal, Nova Scotia

Anna and Patrick use this dressing on their spinach salad.

1	egg	1
$\frac{1}{4}$ cup	granulated sugar	50 mL
1 Tbsp.	Dijon-style mustard	15 mL
$\frac{2}{3}$ cup	red wine vinegar	150 mL
$\frac{1}{2}$ tsp.	salt	2 mL
3 Tbsps.	finely chopped onion	45 mL
2 cups	salad oil (preferably corn oil)	500 mL
3-4 Tbsps.	poppy seeds	45-60 mL

Combine the egg, sugar, mustard, vinegar, salt and onion in the bowl of a food processor, fitted with a steel blade. Process for 1 minute. Add oil in a slow, steady stream. Stir in the poppy seeds and refrigerate until ready to use.

Makes 1 quart (1 L).

Blender or Food Processor Mayonnaise

This is my own recipe which I have used for years. It is the basis of a number of dressings in this book.

2	eggs	2
4 Tbsps.	vinegar *or* lemon juice	60 mL
$1\frac{1}{2}$ tsps.	salt	7 mL
1 tsp.	dry mustard	5 mL
$\frac{1}{2}$ tsp.	pepper (white, if available)	2 mL
$1\frac{1}{2}$ cups	salad oil	375 mL

Have all the ingredients at room temperature. Put the eggs, 2 Tbsps. (30 mL) of the vinegar, salt, dry mustard and pepper into the container of your blender or food processor. Cover and whirl together on low speed.

Slowly drizzle the oil into the mixture, increasing the speed if necessary. When about half the oil is incorporated, add the remaining vinegar. Continue adding the oil in a thin stream until it is completely blended. Store in a covered glass jar in the refrigerator.

Makes 2 cups (500 mL).

Caesar Salad Dressing

🌸🌸🌸

LINDA L'AVENTURE AND CECILIA BOWDEN, *Innkeepers*
THE COMPASS ROSE,
North Head, Grand Manan, N.B.

This pungent variation on Caesar Salad Dressing makes almost a quart. If you wish to halve the recipe, you will still need one whole egg, but you can omit the egg yolk and halve the remaining ingredients.

1	egg	1
1	egg yolk	1
$\frac{1}{4}$ cup	lemon juice	50 mL
2 tsps.	Worcestershire sauce	10 mL
2 Tbsps.	Dijon mustard	25 mL
1 tsp.	salt	5 mL
	freshly ground pepper, to taste	
$\frac{1}{3}$ cup	wine vinegar	75 mL
3-4	flat anchovies, drained	3-4
3 large cloves	garlic	3 large cloves
2 cups	olive oil	500 mL

In a food processor or blender, process all the ingredients in order, except the olive oil, or whisk them together in a bowl, mashing in the anchovies and garlic at the end. Drizzle in the olive oil in a small stream, blending or whisking thoroughly. Refrigerate if not using immediately.

Makes 3$\frac{1}{2}$ cups (825 mL).

Swiss Salad Dressing

🌸🌸🌸

ANNE WANSTALL AND AILEEN ADAMS, *Innkeepers*
BAYBERRY HOUSE,
Granville Ferry, Nova Scotia

Use this fragrant dressing over a variety of lettuces or vegetables. Anne states firmly that basil is "the clincher."

$\frac{1}{2}$ cup	cider vinegar	125 mL
1$\frac{1}{4}$ cups	corn oil	300 mL
$\frac{3}{4}$ tsp.	Dijon mustard	4 mL
$\frac{1}{2}$ tsp.	granulated sugar	2 mL
1 tsp.	salt (optional)	5 mL
	freshly ground pepper, to taste	
1 Tbsp.	minced chives	15 mL

2 tsps.	dried dill weed	10 mL
	or	
1 Tbsp.	fresh, chopped dill	15 mL
1 Tbsp.	finely chopped, fresh basil	15 mL
	or	
2 tsps.	dried basil	10 mL
1 Tbsp.	chopped lemon balm (if available)	15 mL

In a jar, shake together the vinegar, oil, Dijon mustard, sugar, salt and a healthy grinding of pepper. Make sure that the salt and sugar are dissolved. Add the fresh herbs. Shake thoroughly. Refrigerate until needed.

Makes 1¾ cups (425 mL).

Camelot Inn Dressing Piquant

P.M. "CHARLIE" HOLGATE, *Innkeeper*
CAMELOT INN,
Musquodoboit Harbour, Nova Scotia

Charlie stopped using any other dressing years ago. Everyone chose this!

1 cup	salad oil	250 mL
⅓ cup	wine vinegar	75 mL
¼ cup	dry white wine	50 mL
1½ tsps.	Worcestershire sauce	7 mL
3-4 drops	Tabasco	3-4 drops
1 Tbsp.	brown sugar	15 mL
½ tsp.	salt	2 mL
1 tsp.	paprika	5 mL
¼ tsp.	coarsely ground pepper	1 mL
1 clove	garlic	1 clove
¼ tsp.	Herbes de Provence or Fines Herbes (see below)	1 mL

Combine all the ingredients in a jar and shake or stir until well blended. Chill several hours or overnight before using. If you are not a garlic lover, discard the garlic after 24 hours. However, Charlie crushes it and tosses in the whole clove. It can also be chopped very fine.

Makes 1½ cups (375 mL).

Herbes de Provence (Fines Herbes)

Sometimes these are available, pre-mixed, in the spice section of a supermarket or health food store. Otherwise, you can make your own by combining parsley, chives and chervil to taste. Dried tarragon is sometimes added.

Abalone

Dr. Sinclair Philip of Sooke Harbour House writes: "Our northwest abalone is a salt-water marine snail — a beautiful mollusc with a one-piece shell. Its shell is coiled like those of other snails but appears ear-shaped because its last whorl is open and flattened. Because of their appearance, abalone are called sea ears in many languages."

The Pinto Abalone

"Abalone are fairly common along most of our Pacific coast. Pity our east coast friends who have none! The most common northwest abalone is the Pinto. Local Pinto abalone are found under our kelp forests and inhabit shallow, subtidal depths with rocky bottoms, usually on surf-exposed coastlines."

Buying Abalone

"An important note of caution, for those of you who do not intend to harvest abalone yourselves: abalone blood does not contain a constituent that causes coagulation, so, if cut, they usually bleed to death. If you are buying fresh or frozen abalone in the market, avoid the ones with cuts or gouges in their flesh. They will be of inferior quality.

"Unlike some other shellfish, abalone can be harvested year round and its flesh remains consistently of high quality, although it seems at its very best in April, May and June. Males are as flavorful as females, but the males are tougher.

"Canned and dried abalone is definitely an inferior product and less desirable. "Buy abalone fresh, if possible, but first touch the dark fringe around the outside of the muscle. This will retract if the abalone is fresh and in good shape. When shucked, the "foot" or meat should be beige and slightly sweet smelling. Abalone frozen in the shell, if well frozen, can be of excellent quality and hard to distinguish from fresh."

Cleaning and Storing

"To clean abalone, remove the edible foot by sliding a knife (or abalone spoon) between the muscle base and shell in a circular motion, following the perimeter of the shell. If you are not in a hurry, let the abalone relax in the refrigerator for a few hours before cleaning. The muscle should then be more pliable and pop out of the shell easily.

"We recommend discarding *all* of the viscera. "Around the beige-colored foot is an inky, black collar which is edible. We recommend keeping the trimming of this area to a minimum and simply scrubbing off this dark pigment with a scullery brush if you do not like its appearance. At one of the narrow ends of the oval-shaped foot, you will find the mouth (*radula*) — a small vein-like structure imbedded in the muscle. Remove it with a sharp knife, being careful not to discard more flesh than necessary. Abalone is expensive to buy!

"At this point, unless you are going to use it raw for sushi or marination, let the abalone sit in the refrigerator, overnight if you can, to improve its flavor. Although it is not always necessary, you may want to cut them into steaks and pound them under a cloth with a cleaver to break down their connective fibers. Do not pound them to a pulp. Half a dozen whacks with a cleaver should suffice. The smaller the abalone, the more tender, but please obey local harvesting regulations for size limits.

"Fortunately, abalone keeps very well and is still of good quality for cooking after 3 days if stored at just above the freezing point, and can keep a bit longer than that.

"Freezing may dull the flavor of abalone slightly, but it can be nearly as good as fresh. It will keep best in a freezer bag as an uncut, unpounded whole piece. Frozen abalone usually needs little or no pounding when thawed out. Commercially frozen abalone is generally glazed with a protective coating which prevents oxidation and locks in its flavor.

Cold Abalone Salad with Oriental Flavor

SINCLAIR AND FREDRICA PHILIP, *Innkeepers*
PIA CARROLL, *Chef*
SOOKE HARBOUR HOUSE,
Whiffen Spit Beach, Vancouver Island, B.C.

2 Tbsps.	Chinese oyster sauce*	25 mL
1 tsp.	soy sauce	5 mL
$\frac{1}{8}$ tsp.	hot Chinese chili sauce*	0.5 mL
1 tsp.	minced pickled ginger*	5 mL
1 tsp.	honey	5 mL
1 Tbsp.	rice vinegar*	15 mL
1 Tbsp.	minced garlic	15 mL
1 cup	fish stock or clam juice	250 mL
1 lb.	abalone, cut into julienne strips $\frac{1}{8}$ in. (3 mm) thick	450 g
1 lb.	spinach fettucine, cooked	450 g
1 bunch	small green onions, sliced on the bias	1 bunch
	nasturtiums or other edible flowers, for garnish	

In a small saucepan, simmer together the oyster sauce, soy sauce, chili sauce, pickled ginger, honey, vinegar and garlic for 5 minutes. Remove from the heat and let cool.

In a separate saucepan, bring the fish stock to a boil. Add the strips of abalone, reduce heat and poach for 2-3 minutes or until tender. Drain and allow to cool.

In a large mixing bowl, combine the sauce mixture, abalone, cooked fettucine and the green onions. Toss well. Cover with plastic wrap. Refrigerate for at least one hour to blend the flavors. This salad may be served chilled or at room temperature. Garnish with nasturtiums.

Makes 4 servings.

* *These ingredients may be purchased at almost any Oriental grocery.*

45

Orange, Radish and Scallion Salad with Cream Cheese Dressing

LESLIE LANGILLE, *Innkeeper*
BOSCAWEN INN,
Lunenburg, Nova Scotia

This colorful salad is best displayed in a deep, glass bowl or on individual plates. It is a veritable rainbow.

Dressing

2 cups	sour cream	500 mL
1 cup	cream cheese, softened	250 mL
2	scallions, chopped*	2
$\frac{1}{4}$ tsp.	salt	1 mL
$\frac{1}{4}$ tsp.	white pepper	1 mL
$\frac{1}{4}$ tsp.	dry mustard	1 mL
2 Tbsps.	half-and-half cream (10%)	25 mL

Salad

10-14	seedless oranges, peeled and sliced into rounds	10-14
2 cups	finely sliced radishes	500 mL
1 cup	finely chopped scallions	250 mL

In a blender or food processor, whirl the dressing ingredients in order, adding a little more cream if necessary. Refrigerate until serving.

Just before serving, layer the oranges, radishes and scallions. Pour the dressing over, allowing your guests to toss it themselves. *Makes 8-10 servings.*

Scallions are also known as spring onions or green onions, depending on the area of Canada you are visiting.

Salade de Saison

(Salad of the Season)

JEAN AND JANINE AUTHIER, *Innkeepers*
L'AUBERGE LA PINSONNIÈRE,
Cap-à-L'Aigle, Québec

This salad is a picture — in fact, it has been photographed more than once — but it is the "mustardy" dressing that really makes it! Note that the recipe does not call for salt or pepper; instead, it relies on the pungent flavors in the dressing. We keep a small bottle of the vinaigrette in the refrigerator most of the time. It improves with age.

Meaux Mustard Vinaigrette

1 cup	olive oil	250 mL
1 Tbsp.	Meaux mustard (old-fashioned mustard with seeds)	15 mL
$\frac{1}{8}$ tsp.	Dijon mustard	0.5 mL
4 Tbsps.	red wine vinegar	60 mL
1 large clove	garlic, peeled and minced	1 large clove

Salad

1	head of romaine lettuce	1
1	head of iceberg lettuce	1
1	head of Boston lettuce	1
1	head of curly endive	1
1	green pepper, chopped	1
1	red pepper, chopped	1
4-5 sprigs	fresh parsley, minced	4-5 sprigs
8	radishes	8
8	tomatoes	8
2	zucchini	2
1	medium onion	1
1 cup	alfalfa sprouts	250 mL
	garlic croutons (either your own recipe or purchased)	
	a few fresh mint leaves, 8 slices of fresh orange with the peel, some sprigs of fennel (if available), for garnish	

Prepare the vinaigrette as follows: In a small bowl, mix all the ingredients thoroughly. Set aside.

To prepare the salad, have all the various lettuces washed, dried and chilled to crisp them. Tear them into small pieces. Toss the lettuces together in a large salad bowl with the green and red pepper, along with the minced parsley. Slice the radishes, tomatoes, zucchini and onion very thinly. Break the onion apart into rounds. Set aside.

On 8 large salad plates, divide the tossed lettuces and spread with alfalfa sprouts, garlic croutons, radishes and onions. Around the side of each plate, arrange the tomato and zucchini slices. Place a small sprig of mint on each slice of zucchini. Place an orange round on the center of each salad. Cut halfway through the diameter of each orange slice, pulling each side toward the other to form a cone shape. Decorate with sprigs of fennel. Pour the Meaux Mustard Vinaigrette into a sauceboat and serve it with the salad.

Makes 8 servings.

CAMELOT INN,
Musquodoboit Harbour, Nova Scotia

Crab Salad Supreme

🌸🌸

P.M. "CHARLIE" HOLGATE, *Innkeeper*
CAMELOT INN,
Musquodoboit Harbour, Nova Scotia

1 loaf	sandwich bread	1 loaf
6	hard-cooked eggs, diced finely	6
1	medium onion, chopped finely *or* 3 green onions, chopped finely	1
2 4-oz. cans	shrimp, drained	2 113-g cans
1 5-oz. can	crabmeat, drained	1 142-g can
1 cup	diced celery	250 mL
2 cups	mayonnaise (p. 41) leaf lettuce, washed and chilled paprika, chopped parsley and a radish, for garnish	500 mL

First day: Remove crusts from the bread, butter each slice and cube each slice into 16 pieces. Mix with the onions and eggs and refrigerate 3 hours or overnight.

Next day: Mix the drained shrimp, crabmeat, celery and mayonnaise with the bread mixture and store in the refrigerator 3 hours or more.

For serving, line a bowl with lettuce, add the crab salad, sprinkle with paprika and chopped parsley. Put a radish rose in the center.

Makes 10-12 servings.

Salade Niçoise

ANNA AND PATRICK REDGRAVE, *Innkeepers*
THE GARRISON HOUSE INN,
Annapolis Royal, Nova Scotia

A classic salad featuring fresh Annapolis Valley vegetables!

8	new potatoes, scrubbed	8
2 lbs.	green beans	900 g
8	ripe tomatoes, washed and quartered	8
1	small purple onion, peeled and sliced thinly	1
$\frac{1}{2}$ cup	Niçoise or Calamenta olives	125 mL
$\frac{1}{4}$ cup	chopped parsley	50 mL
	salt and pepper, to taste	
6	hard-cooked eggs, shelled and quartered	6
12 oz.	white tuna, well drained	340 g
2 oz.	anchovy fillets (optional)	56 g
	Vinaigrette Dressing	

Vinaigrette Dressing

1 Tbsp.	Dijon-style mustard	15 mL
4 Tbsps.	red wine vinegar	60 mL
1 tsp.	granulated sugar	5 mL
$\frac{1}{2}$ tsp.	salt	2 mL
$\frac{1}{2}$ tsp.	pepper	2 mL
	minced parsley and chives, to taste	
$\frac{1}{2}$ cup	olive oil	125 mL

Cook the potatoes until tender but not mushy. When cool, quarter them and transfer to a large bowl. Cook the green beans until just done and plunge them into ice water to keep their bright color. Drain thoroughly. Add the beans, tomatoes, onion, olives, parsley, salt and pepper to the potato mixture. For dressing, in separate bowl whisk together the mustard, vinegar, sugar, salt, pepper, and herbs. Slowly drizzle in olive oil, still whisking, until mixture thickens. Adjust seasonings to taste. Pour $\frac{1}{2}$ cup (125 mL) dressing over vegetables and toss gently but well. Transfer mixture to a serving platter or divide onto plates. Arrange the hard-cooked eggs around the edges. Flake the tuna over the salad and arrange the anchovy fillets in a lattice pattern. Drizzle with additional vinaigrette and serve at room temperature.

Makes 6 servings.

Palm and Artichoke Salad Remoulade

Steven Lynch, *Chef*
Paul Almquist, *Chef*
Hastings House,
Ganges, Saltspring Island, B.C.

1 14-oz. can	hearts of palm, drained	1 398-mL can
1 6-oz. jar	marinated artichoke hearts	1 170-mL jar
1½ cups	thinly sliced radishes	375 mL
2	scallions, finely chopped	2
8 leaves	lettuce	8 leaves
	radish flower or minced parlsey (optional)	

Remoulade Sauce

¾ cup	mayonnaise (p. 41)	175 mL
1 tsp.	lemon juice	5 mL
1	hard-cooked egg, minced	1
5	anchovy fillets	5
2 tsps.	parsley, minced	10 mL
1 tsp.	Dijon mustard	5 mL
½ tsp.	tarragon	2 mL
	pinch of cayenne pepper	
1 small clove	garlic, minced	1 small clove

Cut palm hearts into ½ in. (1 cm) slices. Drain artichoke hearts, reserving marinade; cut artichokes into quarters. Combine palm hearts, artichokes and onion with the reserved marinade and refrigerate. Do not add the radishes at this point as they will stain the hearts of palm.

Combine all the ingredients for the Remoulade Sauce and refrigerate the mixture for at least 2 hours. (I use my food processor for this step.)

Before serving, combine the radishes with the palm and artichoke mixture. Serve on a lettuce leaf topped with a dollop of Remoulade Sauce and garnished, if desired, with a radish flower or minced parsley. *Makes 8 salads.*

Almond and Broccoli Salad

Robert A. Corbett, *Innkeeper*
Steamers Stop Inn,
Gagetown, New Brunswick

Scattered inns open their verandahed arms down the length of the St. John River. Sip iced tea on the porch, while you watch the sailboats heading out onto the Fundy tides.

Many sailors enjoy a week of complete rest, cruising the river from one end to the other and back. They anchor for the night at various old inns such as the Steamers Stop.

1 lb.	broccoli, cut into bite-sized pieces	450 g
1	red onion, chopped fine	1
1	peeled, chopped tomato, seeds removed	1
$\frac{1}{2}$ cup	slivered almonds, toasted*	125 mL
1	small cauliflower, cut into bite-sized pieces (optional)**	1

Combine the above ingredients and cover with the following dressing, made in a blender.

Dressing

$\frac{1}{2}$ cup	granulated sugar	125 mL
$\frac{1}{4}$ cup	corn oil	50 mL
$\frac{1}{4}$ cup	white vinegar	50 mL
1 Tbsp.	prepared mustard	15 mL
1 Tbsp.	chopped onion	15 mL

Whirl the ingredients together in a blender, or simply whisk them together. Pour over the vegetables. Refrigerate, covered, 3-4 hours — the longer the better. Stir 2 or 3 times before serving. *Makes 6-8 servings.*

To toast almond slivers: Spread in shallow pan and place in oven pre-heated to 300°F. (150°C). Stir occasionally until light tan in color.
**Cauliflower helps make this a very attractive salad in green, white and red.*

Sliced Cucumbers with Whipped Cream Dressing

DONNA AND JIM LACEBY, *Innkeepers*
THE AMHERST SHORE COUNTRY INN,
Amherst, Nova Scotia

The Lacebys have a garden that covers several acres around the inn. They pick the very finest vegetables for salads like this one.

36-48	fresh, young spinach leaves	36-48
72-90	medium-thin slices of cucumber, unpeeled	72-90
$1\frac{1}{2}$ tsps.	salt	7 mL
1 cup	heavy cream (35%)	250 mL
2 Tbsps.	mayonnaise (p. 41)	25 mL
1 tsp.	lemon juice	5 mL
$\frac{1}{4}$ cup	minced chives	50 mL

Wash the spinach leaves. Drain and refrigerate. Sprinkle the cucumber slices with salt; cover and refrigerate.

Whip the cream until stiff. Fold in the mayonnaise and lemon juice. Refrigerate until serving time in a covered container.

To assemble the salads: Arrange 6-8 spinach leaves attractively on the salad plates. Drain the cucumbers. Leaving an inch (2.5 cm) or so of border, arrange the cucumber slices atop the spinach leaves. Divide the dressing equally. Sprinkle with chives.

Makes 6 very special salads.

Squid Salad and Wild Miner's Lettuce

❦❦❦

SINCLAIR AND FREDRICA PHILIP, *Innkeepers*
SOOKE HARBOUR HOUSE,
Whiffen Spit Beach, Vancouver Island, B.C.

Another of Sinclair's creations!

1 lb.	squid (whole and approx. 6 in. or 15 cm long)*	450 g
	juice of 1 lemon	
	juice of 1 lime	
1	small carrot, julienned	1
$\frac{1}{2}$ cup	olive oil, cold pressed preferred	125 mL
$\frac{1}{4}$ cup	fresh herb fennel (or substitute fresh dill)	50 mL
4 cups	miner's lettuce, washed and dried (or substitute lamb's-quarters)	1 L
	borage flowers and calendula petals (optional), for garnish	

To prepare the squid, bring a pot of water to a boil. Add the squid and cover. Lower heat to moderately high and cook for 2-3 minutes, until tender. (Be careful not to overcook.) Drain the squid into a colander and run under cold water. Fill a bowl with cold water and add squid. When squid is cold, clean as follows: Remove the heads by pulling them away from the body; then place them to one side. With a knife, cut open the body lengthwise and discard contents, including the clear cartilage. Combine bodies and heads, rinse under cold water and pat dry. Slice the squid into julienned strips and place in a bowl with the other ingredients and let marinate a few hours.

To serve, arrange squid in the middle of serving plates. Surround with the miner's lettuce and decorate with borage flowers and the petals from calendulas (Scotch marigolds).

Makes 4 decorative servings.

If you are using pre-cleaned squid, simply cook it as instructed, drain, rinse under cold water. Pat it dry and then julienne the meat.

Beef and Pork

LA PINSONNIÈRE
Cap-à-l'Aigle, Québec

Grenadins de Porc aux Bleuets
(Pork Medallions with Blueberries)

🌼🌼🌼

JEAN AND JANINE AUTHIER, *Innkeepers*
L'AUBERGE LA PINSONNIÈRE,
Cap-à-L'Aigle, Québec

The dining room at La Pinsonnière is easily one of the best in eastern Canada. The recipe that follows is an example of *nouvelle cuisine du Québec* for which the *auberge* is famous.

3½-lb.	pork fillets, without fat	3 250-g
6 slices	bacon	6 slices
1 Tbsp.	butter	15 mL
2	French shallots, minced	2
¼ cup	brandy	50 mL
1 cup	heavy cream (35%)	250 mL
½ cup	fresh or frozen blueberries	125 mL
1 cup	demi-glace (beef stock is suitable)	250 mL
¼ cup	butter (second amount) salt and freshly ground pepper, to taste	50 mL

Cut the fillets into 1¼ in. (3 cm) thick medallions. Wrap with half a slice of bacon and secure with a toothpick. Heat the butter in a heavy skillet. Sauté the medallions until they are a golden brown, turning as often as needed. When cooked, keep warm on an oven-proof plate at 250°F. (120°C).

In the same pan, sauté the shallots until tender. Flambé with the brandy. Stir in the cream, blueberries and demi-glace. Continue to cook, uncovered, and reduce until thickened. Over low heat, whisk in the butter. Season to taste with salt and pepper.

Set the medallions on a warm serving platter. Cover with the blueberry sauce and serve with small vegetables, such as carrots and zucchini.

Makes 4 servings.

Tourtière
(Québec-style Meat Pie)

🙞🙞

JOHN PARKER, *Innkeeper*
ROLLANDE THISDÈLE, *Chef*
PARKER'S LODGE,
Lac Paquin, Val David, Quebec

John was almost apologetic that all he and Rollande had to offer were old Québec recipes. To me, having grown up in central Ontario's farm land, they were as interesting as any in the book, for they reflect a way of life that is disappearing all too quickly.

Filling

½ lb.	ground pork	225 g
½ lb.	ground veal	225 g
½ lb.	ground beef	225 g
1	medium onion, chopped	1
1½ tsps.	salt	7 mL
1 tsp.	freshly ground pepper	5 mL
1 cup	water	250 mL
1 slice	white bread, cubed	1 slice

In a large saucepan, combine the meats, onion, salt, pepper and water. Bring to a boil and simmer for 20 minutes. Remove from the heat. Stir in the bread cubes to absorb the water. Taste and correct seasonings, if necessary. Set aside while making the pastry.

Pastry

1½ cups	all-purpose flour	375 mL
½ tsp.	salt	2 mL
½ cup	shortening or lard (a more traditional ingredient)	125 mL
3-4 Tbsps.	ice water	45-60 mL

Put the flour into a medium bowl and add the salt. With a pastry blender, cut in the shortening or lard until the mixture looks grainy. With a fork, stir in the ice water one tablespoon at a time until you can gather the pastry up into a ball. On a floured board, roll two-thirds of the pastry to fit the pie plate. This recipe makes enough pastry for one 9-in. (22 cm) double-crust pie.

Preheat the oven to 400°F. (200°C). Pour the meat mixture into the pie shell and spread evenly. Roll out the top crust on a floured board. Moisten the edges of the bottom crust with water. Lay the top crust over and pinch the edges together. Trim and flute the edges. Cut several slits in the top to vent the steam. Brush with a little milk. Bake until golden, about 45-55 minutes. Serve warm or cold.

Makes 6-8 servings.

Mignon de Goret aux Perles
Bleues de Charlevoix

(Pork Tenderloin in Charlevoix Blueberry Sauce)

෯෯෯෯෯෯෯෯෯෯෯෯෯෯෯෯෯෯෯෯෯෯෯෯෯෯෯෯෯෯෯෯෯෯෯෯෯

JEAN AND JANINE AUTHIER, *Innkeepers*
L'AUBERGE LA PINSONNIÈRE,
Cap-à-L'Aigle, Québec

The rocky terrain of the Charlevoix region east of Québec city grows blueberries in profusion. The inspiration of the magnificent landscape, the freshest of ingredients, and the skills of French-Canadian chefs combine to make this dish a special favorite for all who taste it.

Fillets

4	pork tenderloin fillets	4
3 Tbsps.	butter	45 mL
1	medium onion, minced	1
2 cups	white wine	500 mL
1 cup	water	250 mL
1	bouquet garni (made of thyme, a bay leaf, celery leaves and whole, black peppercorns)	1
5 cloves	garlic, peeled salt and freshly ground pepper, to taste	5 cloves

Preheat the oven to 350°F. (180°C). Trim the pork fillets of excess fat and any connective tissue. In a heavy, deep, oven-proof skillet, heat the butter until it begins to foam. When hot, sear the tenderloin on all sides until well browned. Set aside. In the same pan, brown the minced onion. Deglaze the pan with the white wine and the water. Bring to a boil, adding the bouquet garni and garlic cloves. Season with the salt and pepper to taste. Continue to boil, reducing the liquid for 3 minutes.

Add the reserved pork tenderloin. Bake, uncovered, for 15-20 minutes. While baking, make the Blueberry Sauce as follows.

Blueberry Sauce

2 Tbsps.	butter	25 mL
$\frac{1}{2}$ cup (less 2 Tbsps.)	finely minced shallots	100 mL
$3\frac{1}{2}$ oz.	brandy	100 mL
1 cup	Dubleuet*	250 mL
2 cups	blueberry purée	500 mL
2 cups	veal or chicken stock salt and freshly ground pepper, to taste	500 mL
$1\frac{1}{4}$ cups	heavy cream (35%)	300 mL

In a large, heavy saucepan, heat the butter until it begins to foam. Stir in the shallots and brown. Flambé with the brandy. Deglaze with the Dubleuet and flambé a second time. Continue to simmer and reduce for 2 minutes. Add the blueberry purée and reduce for 2 more minutes. Stir in the veal stock. Taste and add the salt and pepper. Return to a boil. Reduce for a further 3 minutes. Add the heavy cream. Stir and simmer until the sauce has begun to thicken. Correct the seasonings. Strain the sauce if desired. Keep warm.

To serve: Pour several spoonfuls of sauce onto a heated serving platter. Slice and arrange the port tenderloin on top. You might like to garnish the dish with a few blueberries. Pass the remaining sauce in a china sauceboat.

Makes 8 servings.

Dubleuet is a vermouth style of aperitif made of blueberries in the province of Québec. Cinzano could be substituted as Dubleuet has limited distribution outside of Québec.

Pork Cutlets in Sour Cream Sauce

Dorothea Dean, *Innkeeper*
Delphine Lodge,
Wilmer, British Columbia

5-6	large pork cutlets	5-6
	salt and freshly ground pepper, to taste	
$\frac{1}{2}$ tsp.	caraway seeds	2 mL
1	small onion, minced	1
1 cup	sour cream	250 mL
1 Tbsp.	dried dill weed	15 mL
1 Tbsp.	vinegar	15 mL
1	chicken bouillon cube	1
1 cup	hot water	250 mL
1-2 cups	small, white mushrooms, finely sliced	250-500 mL

Preheat the oven to 350°F. (180°C). In a heavy skillet, brown the pork cutlets lightly, being careful not to burn them. Salt and pepper them to taste. Sprinkle caraway seeds over the meat. Place in a shallow casserole. Place the onion, sour cream, dill weed and vinegar in a blender. Blend well. Dissolve the chicken bouillon cube in hot water and add to the sour cream mixture. Add sliced mushrooms. Pour over the meat. Bake, covered, for about 1-1$\frac{1}{2}$ hours at 350°F. (180°C), or until the cutlets are tender. These are wonderful served with small, whole new potatoes.

Makes 5-6 servings.

AROWHON PINES,
Algonquin Park, Ontario

Maple-Glazed Ham

🐝🐝

HELEN AND EUGENE KATES, *Innkeepers*
AROWHON PINES,
Algonquin Park, Ontario

Helen insists that you should be sure to use a fully smoked, *partially cooked* ham with the bone in and skin on. This recipe is *not* suitable for a fully cooked, water-injected ham. The right kind of ham is available by special order from a good butcher's shop. Helen notes that if the bone is protruding out of the meat at either end of the ham, it is a fully-cooked ham and *not* what you want. The ham should look plump and the bones should not protrude.

5-7 lb.	ham (fully smoked, *partially cooked*, bone in and skin on)	2.25-3.1 kg
1 cup	Dijon mustard	250 mL
1 cup	maple syrup, dark if available for a fuller flavor	250 mL
2 Tbsps.	grated horseradish	25 mL
$\frac{1}{2}$-1 tsp.	ground cloves	2-5 mL

Preheat the oven to 350°F. (180°C). Wipe the ham with a damp cloth and place it on a rack, uncovered, in a shallow pan. Insert a meat thermometer into the thickest part of the ham; it should not touch the bone. Bake until the internal temperature is approximately 155°F. (65°C) and the meat is tender. While the ham is cooking, combine the mustard, syrup, horseradish and cloves to make a glaze. Remove the ham from the oven half an hour before it is fully cooked.

Reduce the oven temperature to 325°F. (160°C). Remove the rind and excess fat from the ham. Cut diagonal gashes across the top of the ham. Cover its surface with the glaze mixture. Return ham to oven and finish baking until the internal temperature is 160°F. (70°C) and the meat is tender. Baste ham every 10 minutes.

Makes 6-8 servings.

Apple-Stuffed Pork Loin

LYNN AND HARLEY JOPLING, *Innkeepers*
LLOYD VAN LEWEN, *Chef*
THE OLD BRIDGE INN,
Young's Point, Ontario

5 lbs.	boneless pork loin, well trimmed	2.25 kg
$\frac{1}{4}$ cup	minced Spanish onion	50 mL
$\frac{1}{4}$ tsp.	dried rosemary	1 mL
$\frac{1}{4}$ tsp.	dried thyme	1 mL
10 slices	white bread, untrimmed and cubed	10 slices
2 cups	diced, fresh apples, peeled and cored	500 mL
$\frac{1}{4}$ cup	homemade applesauce	50 mL
$\frac{1}{2}$ tsp.	white pepper	2 mL
$\frac{1}{2}$ tsp.	freshly ground black pepper	2 mL
1 tsp.	fresh parsley, finely snipped	5 mL
$\frac{1}{2}$ tsp.	salt	2 mL
$\frac{1}{2}$ tsp.	freshly ground pepper (second amount)	2 mL
3 Tbsps.	applesauce (second amount, optional)	45 mL

Lay the pork loin flat and trim off any excess fat. Run your hand down the length of the loin to feel for any hard nuggets of cartilage. Cut them out. Flatten the loin by cutting three-quarters of the way through horizontally, opening it up and cutting again. With your fist or a mallet, lightly pound to flatten it further. Halve the loin vertically into 2 even pieces.

To prepare the stuffing, combine the onion, rosemary and thyme in a large bowl. Toss in the bread cubes, apples and applesauce. Season with the white and black pepper and parsley. Combine the mixture thoroughly with your hands.

To stuff the loin, lay one half of the loin flat and mound the stuffing evenly on it. Top with the second loin, centering it so that the meat entirely encases the stuffing. Tie the meat securely with butcher's string. *Begin heating the oven to 350°F. (180°C).* Set the loin on a large piece of foil, with the shiny side in. Sprinkle with salt and pepper. Spread with additional applesauce. Wrap snugly and set in a large baking pan. Bake 1 hour. Loosen foil and begin basting with pan juices. Continue roasting and basting for another $1\frac{1}{2}$ hours. The total roasting time is $2\frac{1}{2}$-3 hours. Cover the meat with a towel and allow it to stand 10 minutes before untying and slicing.

Makes 8-10 servings.

Baked Stuffed Pork Chops

🐝🐝🐝🐝🐝🐝🐝🐝🐝🐝🐝🐝🐝🐝🐝🐝🐝🐝🐝🐝🐝🐝🐝🐝🐝🐝🐝🐝🐝🐝🐝🐝🐝🐝🐝🐝🐝🐝🐝

TED AND JEAN TURNER, *Innkeepers*
GRAMMA'S HOUSE,
Port Saxon, Nova Scotia

Wonderful with Jean's Autumn Fruit Sauce (p. 113).

6	pork chops, cut 1 in. (2.5 cm) thick	6
3-4 slices	Herb Bread (p. 149)	3-4 slices
1	minced onion	1
$\frac{1}{2}$ tsp.	dried thyme	2 mL
$\frac{1}{2}$ tsp.	salt	2 mL
$\frac{1}{2}$ tsp.	freshly ground pepper	2 mL

Preheat the oven to 400°F. (200°C). Cut pockets in each pork chop. Make a dressing by finely crumbling the Herb Bread and stirring in the onion and thyme. Stuff a large mixing spoonful of the dressing into each chop. Sprinkle with salt and pepper. Bake, covered with foil, for 1 hour. Turn the pork chops over halfway through baking. *Makes 6 servings.*

Sausage and Sage Stuffing

🐝🐝🐝🐝🐝🐝🐝🐝🐝🐝🐝🐝🐝🐝🐝🐝🐝🐝🐝🐝🐝🐝🐝🐝🐝🐝🐝🐝🐝🐝🐝🐝🐝🐝🐝🐝🐝🐝🐝

RON AND DOREEN COOK, *Innkeepers*
VICTORIA'S HISTORIC INN,
Wolfville, Nova Scotia

Ron recommends this stuffing with pork roasts or in chicken. He also uses it as a filling for giant mushrooms which he calls "super colossals."

3 Tbsps.	oil	45 mL
1 cup	finely chopped celery	250 mL
1 cup	finely chopped onion	250 mL
2 cloves	garlic, crushed	2 cloves
$\frac{1}{2}$	green pepper, diced	$\frac{1}{2}$
1 lb.	bulk sausage meat	450 g
$\frac{1}{2}$ tsp.	dried thyme	2 mL
$\frac{1}{2}$ tsp.	poultry seasoning	2 mL
$\frac{1}{2}$ tsp.	dried savory	2 mL
$\frac{1}{2}$ tsp.	rubbed sage	2 mL
	salt and freshly ground pepper, to taste	

$1\frac{1}{2}$	medium potatoes, peeled, cooked, and diced	$1\frac{1}{2}$
2-3 cups	stale bread, cut into small cubes	500-750 mL
1 tsp.	dried oregano	5 mL
$\frac{1}{4}$ tsp.	cayenne pepper	1 mL
$\frac{1}{4}$ tsp.	garlic powder	1 mL

Heat the oil in a heavy saucepan. Add the celery, onion, garlic and green pepper. Sauté until soft and beginning to turn golden, about 8 minutes. Add the sausage meat and break it up evenly over the bottom of the pan. Sprinkle with the thyme, poultry seasoning, savory and sage. Continue to cook for another 30 minutes. Add salt and pepper to taste. Stir in the cooked potatoes.

Meanwhile, preheat the oven to 300°F. (150°C). Spread the bread cubes on a baking sheet. Sprinkle with oregano, cayenne and garlic powder. Bake until toasted and crispy, stirring several times, about 20-30 minutes. Toss the bread crumbs with the sausage mixture. To serve as a side dish, just continue baking at 300°F. (150°C) for another 30 minutes. *Makes 6-8 servings.*

Strip Loin Cardinal

JEAN AND PHIL CARDINAL, *Innkeepers*
THE BREADALBANE INN,
Fergus, Ontario

I love this recipe! It's fast and while your guests are having a pre-dinner glass of wine, you can enjoy their company instead of disappearing into the kitchen. I serve the Salade de Saison (p. 46), roasted potatoes and Chocolate Amaretto Cheesecake (p. 180) with the strip loin. Make sure to turn on your oven light so that as the strip loin roasts, you can watch it turn beautifully golden.

$3\frac{1}{2}$-$4\frac{1}{2}$ lbs.	piece of strip loin*	1.5-2 kg
1 tsp.	lemon pepper	5 mL
$\frac{1}{2}$ tsp.	garlic salt	2 mL
2-3 Tbsps.	melted butter	15-25 mL
3-4 Tbsps.	Keen's dry mustard	25-45 mL

Preheat the oven to 450°F. (230°C). Sprinkle the strip loin with the lemon pepper and garlic salt. Rub them in all over. Brush thoroughly with the melted butter and coat the meat with dry mustard completely. Roast in an open pan at 450°F. (230°C) for 25 minutes; then turn the oven off and allow the strip loin to finish cooking for 35 minutes (1 hour total roasting time). Remove it from the oven. Cover it with foil and allow it to rest for 10 minutes. Carve into thin, medium-rare slices and serve. *Makes 6-8 hearty servings.*

Phil says that it's important to select a piece of strip loin that has a thin layer of fat and has been aged for at least 14 days.

Deep-Dish Beef Mushroom Pie

RUTH AND HAL PEETS, *Innkeepers*
UNION HOTEL,
Normandale, Ontario

Consider the Peets for a moment. They were bored just touring around Paris; so they enrolled in La Varenne Cooking School. They are international people: Hal worked for years in the Middle East while Ruth manned the home front. Still, they are now content in a sleepy Ontario backwater. Being part of a community is very important to them; they know the meaning of "roots."

2½-3 lbs.	trimmed, lean stewing beef, cut into 1-1½ in. (2.5-4 cm) cubes	1-1.3 kg
½-¾ cup	all-purpose flour	125-175 mL
4 slices	side bacon, diced	4 slices
	or	
3-4 Tbsps.	bacon fat	45-60 mL
¾ cup	dry red wine	175 mL
3 Tbsps.	clarified butter	45 mL
2	medium onions, chopped	2
1 clove	garlic, minced	1 clove
1 lb.	fresh mushrooms, sliced	450 g
3 Tbsps.	all-purpose flour (second amount)	45 mL
1½-2 cups	beef stock	375-500 mL
1 cup	canned, undrained tomatoes, chopped	250 mL
1	bay leaf	1
½ tsp.	dried thyme	2 mL
1½ tsps.	salt	7 mL

Beurre Manie

¼ cup	butter	50 mL
¼ cup	all-purpose flour	50 mL
6-8 oz.	puff pastry (p. 165)	160-225 g
	or	
	enough flaky pastry (p. 165) to cover baking dish	

Preheat the oven to 325°F. (160°C). Pat the beef dry and dredge in flour. Shake off excess. Heat the bacon in a heavy pan until some of the fat renders out. Or simply heat the bacon fat until hot. Add the beef and brown quickly, one layer at a time. Transfer to a Dutch oven or another large, covered casserole. Pour off any excess fat. Deglaze with the wine. Pour over the meat.

In the same pan, heat the butter. Add the onions, garlic and mushrooms. Stir-fry until almost all the liquid evaporates. Stir in the flour and then add the beef stock. Cook until thickened and pour over the beef. Stir in the tomatoes and seasonings. Cover and bake for 1-1½ hours or until almost tender. Add more liquid if necessary. If there is too much liquid, thicken with a blend of butter and flour (Beurre Manie). Taste and correct seasonings. Pour into a deep baking dish. Chill until needed or continue immediately as follows.

Preheat the oven to 425°F. (220°C). On a lightly floured board, roll out the puff pastry or flaky pastry into a rectangle large enough to cover your baking dish. Bury a greased custard cup in the meat so that the pastry doesn't sink into the gravy. Dampen the edge of the dish. Cover with the pastry and crimp the edges to seal them tightly. Trim and slash the top. Brush with milk or egg wash.* Bake at 425°F. (220°C) for 20 minutes. Reduce heat to 375°F. (190°C) and bake for an additional 20 minutes. Cool slightly before cutting into squares or oblongs. This pie may be baked ahead and reheated. *Makes 8 servings.*

Make an egg wash by beating together 1 egg with enough cold water to equal ¼ cup (50 mL).

Beef Jerky

✿✿✿

DAVE AND LUCILLE GLAISTER, *Innkeepers*
MESA CREEK RANCH,
R.R. 1, Millarville, Alberta

Mesa Creek is a working, 3,000-acre cattle ranch located in the rolling foothills of the Rockies. Lucille is a beef specialist, raising prize Angus cattle, writing recipes for the *Angus Cookbook*, and promoting cattle on television. She makes Beef Jerky for her family, but she says that her guests "really go for it" too.

2	full round steaks, cut in thin ⅛ in. (3 mm) strips	2
1 Tbsp.	salt	15 mL
1 Tbsp.	garlic powder	15 mL
1 tsp.	freshly ground pepper	5 mL
1 tsp.	onion salt	5 mL
½ cup	Worcestershire sauce (Lea & Perrins is best)	125 mL
¼ cup	soy sauce	50 mL
2 tsps.	liquid smoke*	10 mL

Place the strips of steak in a large bowl. Combine all the remaining ingredients separately and pour over the meat, mixing thoroughly. Cover and marinate 12 hours or overnight.**

In the morning, cover one of your oven racks completely with aluminum foil. Lay the strips of jerky on it evenly. Turn the oven on to the lowest setting, leaving the door open 1 in. (2.5 cm). Allow the steak to dry for 10-12 hours. Pack in plastic bags and refrigerate, ready for a trail ride. *Makes 1¼ lbs. (570 g).*

Available, bottled, in most supermarkets.
**If it is more convenient, marinate the meat all day and dry all night, thus leaving the oven free for other uses.*

Barbecued Spareribs

RICHARD HILL AND RON FRIEND, *Innkeepers*
YELLOW POINT LODGE,
Ladysmith, Vancouver Island, B.C.

Yellow Point, down on the water on a point of land that pokes out into the Stuart Channel, is a lodge that has been synonymous with British Columbia hospitality for many, many years. A showplace ravaged by fire, it has risen once again because of the tenacity and dedication of scores of islanders.

The recipes from Yellow Point Lodge came after the fire and after days of difficult redevelopment of the guests' favorites. Every cookbook, every note had been destroyed. It was a monumental task. Millie and Bernice, the cooks, along with Richard and Ron, deserve our thanks!

5 lbs.	pork spareribs	2.25 kg
$\frac{1}{2}$ cup	water	125 mL
3 Tbsps.	butter	45 mL
1	large onion	1
2 Tbsps.	vinegar	25 mL
$\frac{1}{4}$ cup	lemon juice	50 mL
2 Tbsps.	brown sugar	25 mL
2 Tbsps.	prepared mustard	25 mL
1 cup	ketchup	250 mL
1 Tbsp.	Worcestershire sauce	15 mL
	pinch of salt	
	pinch of cayenne pepper	
1 cup	chopped parsley	250 mL

Preheat the oven to 350°F. (180°C). In a covered roasting pan, steam the spareribs with the water in the oven until they are tender — 1-1$\frac{1}{2}$ hours. To make the sauce, chop the onion finely and sauté it in butter in a large saucepan. When the onion is transparent, add vinegar, lemon juice, brown sugar, mustard, ketchup, Worcestershire sauce, salt, cayenne and parsley. Bring to a boil and simmer gently for $\frac{1}{2}$ hour, stirring occasionally.

When the spareribs are ready, place them on a sheet or pan and cover with the sauce. Return them to the oven and continue baking at 350°F. (180°C) for another $\frac{1}{2}$ hour. They can be served immediately or placed on a barbecue for 10 minutes.

Makes 8-10 finger-licking servings.

Calves' Sweetbreads Crozier

CROZIER AND MARY TAYLOR, *Innkeepers*
IAN GRANT, *Chef*
THE ELORA MILL INN,
Elora, Ontario

At The Elora Mill Inn, one of Canada's international inns, guests feel part of history. And the innkeepers? Well, suffice it to say that Crozier has been the model for a character in several of Richard Rohmer's novels. And oh yes, they travel to France yearly to select the Mill's own privately labeled wine. This is "Cro's" favorite dish.

1½ lbs.	sweetbreads, outer membrane removed*	675 g
4 cups	veal or chicken stock	1 L
4	bay leaves	4
1 oz.	whole, black peppercorns	28 g
1	bouquet garni**	1
½ cup	unsalted butter	125 mL
1 oz.	soft, green peppercorns	28 g
¾ cup	brandy	175 mL
1¼ cups	heavy cream (35%)	375 mL
	salt and freshly ground pepper, to taste	
2 Tbsps.	chopped, fresh parsley	25 mL

Put the first 5 ingredients into a saucepan and bring rapidly to a boil. Reduce the heat and simmer for approximately 5-10 minutes. Sweetbreads should be pink on the inside when cooked, and tender, not hard. When cooked, remove from the heat, leaving sweetbreads in the stock. Press with a weight to cover the entire surface of the meat evenly. Allow to cool. When thoroughly cooled, remove the sweetbreads from the stock and slice ½ in. (1 cm) thick at a 45° angle.

To a hot sauté pan, add the butter, green peppercorns and slices of sweetbreads. Sauté for 1 minute, turning often and keeping the pan hot. After the second minute, remove the sweetbreads and arrange on a heated platter. Keep warm. Carefully add the brandy to the hot sauté pan. Flame and reduce over medium heat to a sticky consistency. For extra flavor, Ian suggests that ½ cup (125 mL) of the veal stock could be added at this point with the brandy. Add the cream. Continue reducing until it is the consistency of a medium sauce. Taste and add salt and freshly ground pepper if needed. Pour the sauce over the sweetbreads. Sprinkle with the chopped parsley. Serve with rice or new potatoes.

Makes 4 servings.

*Sweetbreads should be a nice, light pink color and have no traces of blood.
**Tie your bouquet garni in a muslin bag. Include sprigs of thyme, celery leaves, celery stalk and some sweet basil.

Baby Beef Liver in Tomatoes and Onions

Dorothea Dean, *Innkeeper*
Delphine Lodge,
Wilmer, British Columbia

Dorothea Dean's life has been anything but run-of-the-mill and boring. Born in England, she moved to Canada to farm in Ontario's Hockley Valley. Then the pioneering urge struck, and on she moved to her beautiful Columbia River Valley. There she virtually homesteaded, renovating an old, uncared-for hotel in Wilmer. Wilmer was a real Wild West town — so wild in fact that in 1903 there was a brawl and much of the town was burned. Named after Delphine, the wife of the original builder George Stark, the inn was a relic from the 1861-64 Gold Rush.

Dorothea has been an adventurous cook for over 45 years; she recognizes when something is done in the oven by the kitchen's aroma. She is also an accomplished climber. This combination of interests made her the natural person to look after meals for the Heli-skiing camp construction on various glaciers. As she says, "Alone I cooked for 27 to 32 men daily — breakfast, coffee break, lunch, coffee break, and supper. I did want the experience of cooking for a large crew away from civilization. I have simmered down considerably since those wonderful, wild days of hard work."

But I'm not so sure that she has simmered down. She still gardens and freezes and preserves. She speaks of a new bread oven to be built in the garden. There seems no end to her tenacity, ambition and drive.

1 lb.	liver (beef or baby beef)	450 g
3-4 Tbsps.	butter	45-60 mL
	salt and freshly ground pepper, to taste	
2	medium cooking onions, sliced	2
1	beef-flavored Oxo cube	1
$\frac{3}{4}$ cup	hot water	175 mL
1 Tbsp.	cornstarch	15 mL
$\frac{1}{4}$ cup	cold water	50 mL
2 cups	chopped tomatoes	500 mL
	or	
1 16-oz. can	tomatoes	1 455-mL can

Cut the liver into small, thin strips. Melt the butter in a heavy skillet over medium heat. Add the liver. Braise quickly until lightly browned. Season with salt and pepper to taste. Cover with the onion rings. Continue to stir on medium heat to brown the onion rings. Be careful not to burn them. Add the hot water with the Oxo cube dissolved in it. Mix the cornstarch and cold water. Add to the skillet. Stir in the tomatoes. When heated through, serve with boiled rice and a tossed salad sprinkled with parmesan.

Makes 4 servings.

Chicken, Duck
and Goose

MANOIR DES ÉRABLES
Montmagny, Québec

Magret d'Oie à l'Estragon
(Goose Breast Fillets with Tarragon Sauce)

🐝🐝

LORRAINE AND RENAUD CYR, *Innkeepers*
MANOIR DES ÉRABLES,
Montmagny, Québec

The genuine warmth of Québec hospitality, a touch of true French elegance and an Olympic chef — what more could one ask for? M. Cyr participated in the 1984 Culinary Olympics in Frankfurt as a member of the province's team, and his cooking reflects his intense support of *la cuisine Québécoise*. Because the stone manor (circa 1814) is on the banks of the St. Lawrence, right in the prime hunting area for white goose, it seems appropriate that this delicious recipe is one of the specialties of the house.

1	goose breast	1
3 Tbsps.	goose fat	45 mL
2 Tbsps.	Calvabec*	30 mL
$\frac{1}{2}$ cup	stock made from the goose carcass	125 mL
2-3	tarragon leaves	2-3
$2\frac{1}{2}$ oz.	heavy cream	70 mL
1 Tbsp.	butter	15 mL
	fresh chervil, to taste	
	fresh tarragon, to taste	

In a heavy skillet, heat the goose fat until it is very hot. Sauté the breast on the skin side until the skin is crisp. Sauté on the other side until browned, leaving the meat rare. Set aside in a warm place. Discard the cooking fat. Deglaze the pan with Calvabec until all the meat solids are dissolved. Flambé and add the stock. Shred the tarragon leaves and add. Over medium heat, reduce the sauce to half. Add the heavy cream, reheating gently. Whisk in the cold butter, a bit at a time, until the sauce is smooth. Be careful not to allow it to boil. Sprinkle with chervil. Pour the sauce onto a serving plate. Slice the breast into thin slices across the grain and lay on top of the sauce. Garnish with tarragon leaves.

Makes one serving. This recipe may be increased to make the number of servings needed.

Calvabec is a liqueur made in Quebec from apples. You may have to substitute Calvados because, as far as I know, Calvabec is not available outside Québec.

Wild Duck and Rice

MARIE MUSHRUSH, *Innkeeper*
HIGH BRASS HUNTING LODGE,
Winnipegosis, Manitoba

Marie Mushrush is an interesting lady. Originally from Ecuador, she and her husband now operate a waterfowl hunting lodge in the wilds of Manitoba and in the middle of their own, licensed, pheasant "shooting preserve." Most of Marie's recipes, understandably, use prepackaged foods, but you'll notice her Spanish flair coming through in them all.

4	ducks, breasts, and legs	4
2½ cups	water	625 mL
½ tsp. each	salt and freshly ground pepper	2 mL each
¼ cup	butter	50 mL
¼ cup	safflower oil	50 mL
2 cloves	garlic, crushed	2 cloves
2 cups	long grain rice	500 mL
1 pkg.	onion soup mix	1 pkg.
1 10½-oz. can	mushroom stems and pieces, drained	1 300-mL can
½ cup	onion flakes	125 mL
1 cup	water (second amount)	250 mL
1 cup	tomato juice	250 mL
2 Tbsps.	soy sauce	25 mL

The night before serving, prepare the ducks by cutting them apart into segments. Leave the breasts intact and remove the legs and thighs together. Soak in cold, salty water overnight. The next morning, rinse the duck pieces well, making sure that all feathers and pellets are removed. Reserve the breasts, legs and thighs. Refrigerate. Combine the backs and extra parts and the 2½ cups (625 mL) water. Season with salt and pepper and simmer, covered, for about 1½ hours. (You should have approximately 1½ cups [325 mL] of broth.) About 2 hours before serving, pat the duck dry with paper towels and slice the breasts diagonally ½ inch (1 cm) thick. In a heavy skillet, heat the butter and oil. Over medium heat, brown the duck breast slices, the legs and thighs with the crushed garlic.

In a heavy cast-iron or aluminum roaster, spread the raw rice. Sprinkle with half the onion soup mix. Arrange duck pieces over the rice. Pour the broth over and top with the remaining onion soup mix. Add the mushrooms, onion flakes, water, tomato juice and soy sauce. Bake at 350°F. (180°C), uncovered, for half an hour. Cover tightly and continue to bake 1½ hours. Check after 45 minutes and add more liquid if necessary. Marie serves the duck with a tossed green salad that has her own Creamy Dill Dressing (p. 40) over it.

Makes 6 servings.

TL'ELL RIVER LODGE AND FARM,
Tl'ell, Queen Charlotte Islands, B.C.

Muscovy Duck with Blue Potatoes, Red Cabbage and Local Wild Cranberries

🐾🐾🐾🐾🐾🐾🐾🐾🐾🐾🐾🐾🐾🐾🐾🐾🐾🐾🐾🐾🐾🐾🐾🐾🐾🐾🐾🐾🐾🐾🐾🐾🐾🐾🐾🐾🐾🐾🐾

CHRISTINE V. ZADORA-GERLOF, *Innkeeper*
TL'ELL RIVER LODGE AND FARM,
Tl'ell, Queen Charlotte Islands, B.C.

Blue potatoes have a definite blue tinge to their skin, but the inside is generally white. Potato growers in central and western Canada are just now beginning to grow them, but on P.E.I. and Newfoundland, older varieties such as MacIntyre and Blue Mac have been known for years. If you feel inclined, try the newest, and some say the best, variety — Caribe — in next year's garden. Your local Agriculture Canada office will gladly help you find the seed potatoes.

1 5-7 lb.	Muscovy duck	1 2.25- 3.1 kg
1½ tsps.	salt	7 mL
½-1 tsp.	freshly ground pepper	2-5 mL
2	cooking apples, unpeeled but cored	2
4	onions	4
1	small, red cabbage, shredded	1
1 cup	water	250 mL
⅓ cup	all-purpose flour	75 mL
	Wild Cranberry Sauce (p. 71)	
8-12	small, whole blue potatoes*, scrubbed and boiled until tender	8-12

Preheat the oven to 350°F. (180°C). Wash the duck and pat dry. Sprinkle 1 tsp. (5 mL) of the salt and all of the pepper inside and outside the duck. Fill the cavity with the apples and 2 of the onions. You can leave them whole or quarter them if you wish. Close the opening with a skewer. Pierce the skin all over with a fork to allow the fat to drain off. Set the duck on a rack in a roasting pan and cover. If you do not have a roasting rack, use mason jar rings. Roast for 20 minutes per pound, removing the cover for the final 30 minutes.

About 45 minutes before you wish to serve the duck, combine the red cabbage and the water in a large saucepan. Add the remaining $\frac{1}{2}$ tsp. (2 mL) salt. Chop the remaining onions and stir into the cabbage. Cover tightly and steam over low heat until most of the liquid has been absorbed and the cabbage is very tender.

When the duck is tender, remove it from the roasting pan and keep it warm while making the gravy. Pour all the drippings into a bowl. Return $\frac{1}{4}$ cup (50 mL) of the fat to the pan and discard the rest. You should have 1-1$\frac{1}{2}$ cups (250-375 mL) of duck stock. On top of the stove, heat the fat in the roaster. Stir in the flour and allow the mixture to bubble. Whisk in the duck stock. When the mixture is well thickened, add the hot, cooked red cabbage, and mix thoroughly. Correct the seasoning if necessary.

Carve the duck and arrange it on a hot platter surrounding a bowl of Wild Cranberry Sauce. Fill a large bowl with the red cabbage to serve over the steaming, boiled potatoes.

Makes 4 servings for hearty appetites.

· Red-skinned potatoes may be substituted.

Wild Cranberry Sauce

Wild cranberries grow in most of the coastal regions of Canada, from the soft, rain-forested Charlottes to the roadsides of Nova Scotia.

1 lb.	wild low-bush cranberries (domestic ones may be used instead)	450 g
1$\frac{3}{4}$ cups	granulated sugar	425 mL
$\frac{1}{2}$ cup	water	125 mL
$\frac{1}{2}$ cup	red wine	125 mL

Combine all the ingredients in a saucepan. Bring to a gentle boil. Cover and simmer for 10 minutes or until very tender. Allow to cool before serving.

Makes 3-4 cups (750 mL-1 L).

Chicken-in-the-pot Windsor Arms

MICHAEL BONACINI, *Chef*
THE WINDSOR ARMS,
Toronto, Ontario

2 3½-4 lb.	grain-fed chickens, with their livers	2 1.5-1.8 kg
¼ tsp.	finely chopped, fresh rosemary	1 mL
¼ tsp.	finely chopped, fresh thyme	1 mL
½ cup	chopped mushrooms	125 mL
½ tsp.	salt	2 mL
⅛ tsp.	freshly ground pepper	0.5 mL
1 clove	garlic, unpeeled	1 clove
2 pieces	ginger root, ½ in. (1 cm) square	2 pieces
2 sprigs	fresh rosemary	2 sprigs
2 sprigs	fresh thyme	2 sprigs
1	bay leaf	1
4 cups	chicken stock	1 L
2	small leeks, cut at an angle, ¼ in. (0.5 cm) thick	2
2-3	medium carrots, peeled and sliced diagonally	2-3
2 stalks	celery, thinly sliced diagonally	2 stalks
6 oz.	peeled pearl onions	175 g
2-3 Tbsps.	celery leaves, washed and finely chopped	25-45 mL

Dissect the chickens by first removing the legs; then detach the drumsticks and remove the thigh bones and skin. Remove the wings from the breasts and finally remove the breasts from the remaining carcasses. The bones and chicken necks can be used to make the stock.

Take the chicken wings and cut the tips off, forcing back the skin in order to turn the wing inside out and remove the finer bone. Set aside. Remove the thigh meat from the chicken leg. Combine the thigh meat with the chicken livers and pass it through a grinder or coarsely chop it in a food processor. In a small bowl, combine the liver mixture with the chopped rosemary, thyme, mushrooms, salt and pepper. Chill thoroughly. With wet hands, form the mixture into 8 small balls or dumplings. Set aside.

Make a bouquet garni by tying the garlic, ginger root, sprigs of rosemary, thyme and the bay leaf together in a cheesecloth bag. Bring the stock to a boil in a large saucepan. Add the bouquet garni, the leeks, carrots, celery and onions. Reduce the heat and simmer, covered, for 5-7 minutes. Add the chicken breasts, without the skin. Simmer together for 10 minutes or until the breasts are almost cooked.

Skim if necessary. Add the chicken dumplings and the chicken wings. Cover again and simmer for another 10-15 minutes or until the meat is cooked and the dumplings are firm. Taste the broth and correct the seasonings if required. To serve, place the dumplings, breasts and wings in individual soup bowls, spoon the broth and vegetables over the top. Sprinkle with celery leaves.

Makes 4 servings.

Breast of Chicken with Cumin and Peach Sauce

PAT HOGAN, *Executive Chef*
THE PILLAR AND POST,
Niagara-on-the-Lake, Ontario

J uicy, Niagara peaches complement the Asian flavor of this dish.

4	boneless chicken breasts	4
1 tsp.	salt	5 mL
$\frac{1}{2}$ tsp.	freshly ground pepper	2 mL
$\frac{1}{2}$ tsp.	ground cumin	2 mL
$\frac{1}{2}$ cup	egg wash	125 mL
3 Tbsps.	flour	45 mL
3 Tbsps.	clarified butter	45 mL
2	shallots, peeled and minced	2
2 Tbsps.	peach brandy	25 mL
$\frac{1}{2}$ cup	heavy cream (35%)	125 mL
2	peaches, peeled, pitted and sliced into 8 pieces	2
4 sprigs	mint	4 sprigs

Season the chicken with salt, pepper and cumin. Dip in egg wash, then in flour. Pan-fry in the clarified butter on low heat. When golden, add the shallots and peach brandy to deglaze the pan. Simmer slowly for 2-3 minutes. Remove the breasts while finishing the sauce and keep them warm. Increase the heat to reduce the sauce by half. Add the cream and continue cooking until thickened slightly. Taste and correct the seasonings, if necessary. Arrange the breasts on a hot serving dish, spooning the sauce over them. Garnish with peaches and mint sprigs.

Makes 4 servings.

Chicken in Curry Sauce

EVE AND MICHAEL CONCANNON, *Innkeepers*
MARQUIS OF DUFFERIN LODGE,
Port Dufferin, Halifax County, N.S.

2 Tbsps.	butter, margarine or chicken fat	25 mL
2	medium onions, diced	2
2	medium apples, peeled and chopped (Granny Smith preferred)	2
1 clove	garlic, crushed	1 clove
1 Tbsp.	medium curry powder	15 mL
2 Tbsps.	flour	25 mL
4 cups	chicken stock	1 L
1	bay leaf	1
1 tsp.	lemon juice	5 mL
$\frac{1}{3}$ cup	raisins	75 mL
8 halves	boneless, skinless chicken breasts	8 halves
2 Tbsps.	butter, margarine or chicken fat (second amount)	25 mL
	salt and pepper, to taste	

Curry Sauce

Melt the butter, margarine or chicken fat in a large saucepan and sauté the diced onions, apples and garlic until soft. Add curry powder and fry gently for a few minutes. Add flour and fry for another minute or so, stirring all the time to prevent burning. Pour on stock and bring to a boil, stirring frequently. Add the bay leaf, lemon juice and raisins. Check for seasoning, but remember curry flavor develops with cooking and keeping. Set aside.

Chicken

Preheat the oven to 325°F. (160°C) while you prepare the chicken. Rinse and dry the chicken breasts in paper towels. Sauté them very gently in butter, margarine or chicken fat for a few minutes on each side until lightly browned but not crisp or dry. Arrange them in a large casserole, season with salt and pepper and pour the curry sauce over, covering the chicken if possible with sauce. Bake, covered, in preheated oven for about 1 hour, or until the breasts are tender. Serve with rice and a mango chutney on the side.

Makes 4 generous servings.

Maple Chicken

ALEX AND JUDY RIDDELL, *Innkeepers*
CHÂTEAU BEAUVALLON,
Mont Tremblant, Québec

Perched beside a quiet lake, Château Beauvallon will help us all appreciate Québécois tradition and style. It's truly a taste of French Canada — from its food to its antiques.

1 3½-lb.	chicken	1 1.5-kg
	salt and pepper, to taste	
1 Tbsp.	oil	15 mL
2 Tbsps.	finely diced carrots	25 mL
2 Tbsps.	finely diced celery	25 mL
1½ Tbsps.	minced leek	20 mL
¼ cup	maple syrup, for basting	50 mL
(approx.)		(approx.)
⅓ cup	cider vinegar	75 mL
1 cup	chicken stock	250 mL
1½ Tbsps.	maple syrup (second amount)	20 mL
1 tsp.	butter	5 mL
1 tsp.	all-purpose flour	5 mL

Preheat the oven to 450°F. (230°C). Season the bird and tie it. Rub it with oil and place it in an open roasting pan. Roast for 10 minutes at 450° F. (230°C). Reduce heat to 350°F. (180°C) and continue to cook the chicken for about 30 minutes. Add the carrots, celery, and leek and rub the bird with maple syrup from time to time. Roast for another 30 minutes. At the end, the sauce will caramelize. Baste with the cider vinegar. Remove the chicken to a heat-proof platter and keep it warm while preparing the sauce.

To the roasting pan, add the chicken stock and the 1½ Tbsps. (20 mL) maple syrup. Stir over medium heat until the sauce begins to simmer. Cream together the butter and flour and add to the sauce to lightly thicken. Strain the sauce. Turn the oven on to 500°F. (260°C). Brush the chicken with a little sauce and place it in the oven for several minutes to glaze.* Pass the sauce separately.

Makes 4 servings.

*To save a little time, brush with a little extra maple syrup and glaze while you are completing the sauce.

STEAMERS STOP INN,
Gagetown, New Brunswick

Chicken (or Turkey) and Dumplings

ROBERT A. CORBETT, *Innkeeper*
STEAMERS STOP INN,
Gagetown, New Brunswick

This is one of the most popular dishes at the Steamers Stop Inn — perhaps because the boaters who tie up there have been out on the river all day and crave a substantial meal.

Chicken

1 4-6 lb.	boiling fowl	1 1.8-2.7 kg
	cold water	
3-4	carrots, peeled and chopped into 1 in. (2.5 cm) pieces	3-4
3 stalks	celery, sliced diagonally	3 stalks
2	medium onions, diced	2
2-3	broccoli stems, diced	2-3
1 cup	cubed turnip	250 mL
1-2	tomatoes, peeled and diced	1-2
1 tsp.	salt	5 mL
$\frac{1}{2}$ tsp.	freshly ground pepper	2 mL
$\frac{1}{2}$ tsp.	ground cumin	2 mL
$\frac{1}{2}$ tsp.	dried thyme	2 mL
2 tsps.	dried parsley	10 mL

Place the fowl in enough cold water to cover. Let cook, covered, for 2 to 3 hours. Remove the chicken and debone, leaving meat in fairly large pieces. Strain the broth. Return the meat and broth to pot. Bring to a boil and add the vegetables. Add salt, pepper and seasonings to taste. Cook until the vegetables can be pierced easily with a fork. Do not overcook. Meanwhile, prepare the dumplings.

Dumplings

1 cup	all-purpose flour	250 mL
1 Tbsp.	baking powder	15 mL
$\frac{1}{2}$ tsp.	salt	2 mL
1 Tbsp.	butter	15 mL
$\frac{1}{3}$ cup	milk	75 mL
(approx.)		(approx.)

Sift the flour, baking powder and salt together. Cut in the butter. Add milk to make a soft dough. Knead lightly. Turn onto a floured surface; divide into 6 rounds. Flatten slightly and drop into the boiling stew. Cook, covered, for 5 minutes. Remove the lid and cook for another 2 minutes. Test with a fork. Dumplings will triple in size.

Makes 6-8 hearty servings.

Marjorie's Rosemary Chicken

PIETER BERGIN AND JANET RODIER, *Innkeepers*
THE AMARYLLIS,
Rockport, Ontario

A dear friend of Pieter's, who also grew up on St. Lawrence summers, gave him this recipe to use when he was pressed for time.

6-8	chicken breasts, deboned	6-8
	freshly ground black pepper, to taste	
$1\frac{1}{2}$ tsps.	dried rosemary	7 mL
3 Tbsps.	vegetable oil	45 mL
$\frac{1}{4}$ cup	dry white wine	50 mL
$\frac{1}{2}$ cup	half-and-half cream (10%)	125 mL

Pound the chicken breasts between waxed paper until thin. Dust with ground pepper and crumbled rosemary on both sides.

In a heavy skillet, heat the oil over medium-high heat. Sauté the chicken until it is golden brown on each side and the meat is no longer pink. Remove from the pan and keep warm. Deglaze the pan with the white wine. Reduce the heat and stir in the cream, continuing to cook the sauce until bubbly and slightly thickened. Pour over the chicken.

Makes 6-8 servings.

Chicken Elizabeth

RON C. PHILLIPS, *Innkeeper*
BLOMIDON INN,
Wolfville, Nova Scotia

Between two old mountains, dipping down into the Bay of Fundy, lies a rich valley where most of Nova Scotia buys its produce. Indeed, the Annapolis region supplies most of the Maritimes.

Mud Creek, now known as Wolfville, is the home of Acadia University. Its streets were laid out centuries ago by a generous surveyor who allowed large, gracious lawns and deep lots. Further down the valley, Annapolis Royal and Granville Ferry pair up to be two of the most picturesque and historically important towns in the east. Much of the valley was logged over the years, thus creating the rolling acreages that we now know. The lumber was shipped out of Annapolis Royal where the ships still fight the 28-foot tides. In Granville Ferry, on Saturday mornings, there is a super little Farmers' Market. Go early because there are line-ups at the vegetable stalls.

Many of the old inns that grace the Maritimes were, at one time, the elegant homes of sea captains. Blomidon was built by one such man of the salt, Captain Rufus Burgess. The returning ships of his fleet would bring rare and beautiful woods from all over the world as ballast to grace Blomidon's vast interior. Even the plaster cornices and marble fireplaces were fashioned by Italian craftsmen. The entire inn is a showplace.

1	deboned chicken breast	1
1	square Swiss cheese, approx. 1 in. (2.5 cm) in diameter	1
1 tsp.	cooked spinach	5 mL
1 tsp.	snow crab meat	5 mL
	salt and freshly ground pepper, to taste	
	puff pastry (see p. 165)	

Preheat oven to 450°F. (230°C). Flatten chicken breast and slash partway through diagonally to tenderize. Place a square of Swiss cheese in middle of flattened breast. Add 1 rounded tsp. (5 mL) cooked spinach and 1 flat tsp. (5 mL) snow crab meat. Sprinkle with salt and pepper. Roll into a ball and wrap in a sheet of puff pastry, 6 in. x 6 in. (15 cm x 15 cm) and about $\frac{1}{4}$ in. (0.75 cm) thick. Place seam down on an ungreased cookie sheet. Braid a small piece of pastry to garnish, if desired. Bake in preheated oven at 450°F. (230°C) for 10 minutes; at 400°F. (200°C) for 5 minutes; and at 350°F. (180°C) for 15-20 minutes. Serve with Hollandaise Sauce (p. 117).

Makes 1 generous serving.

Chicken Dijonnaise

Mr. and Mrs. James T. Orr, *Innkeepers*
Sir Sam's Inn,
Eagle Lake, Haliburton, Ont.

This quick, elegant dish is especially good with freshly steamed asparagus and a big, tossed salad laced with Swiss Salad Dressing (p. 42). And how about a basketful of Grand Harbour Rolls (p. 153)?

8 4-oz.	chicken breasts, deboned and trimmed	8 115-g
	salt and freshly ground black pepper, to taste	
3 Tbsps.	butter	45 mL
$\frac{1}{4}$ cup	onion, finely minced	50 mL
2 Tbsps.	all-purpose flour	25 mL
$\frac{1}{4}$ cup	dry white wine	50 mL
$\frac{1}{2}$ cup	chicken stock	125 mL
$\frac{1}{4}$ cup	heavy cream (35%)	50 mL
2 tsps.	Dijon mustard	10 mL
$\frac{1}{4}$ cup	chopped walnuts	50 mL

Preheat the oven to 400°F. (200°C). Generously butter a 9 in. x 13 in. (3.5 L) glass baking pan. Lay out 4 of the chicken breasts in the baking pan so that they are flat and not touching. Lay out the next 4 directly on top of them. Lightly season with salt and pepper. Bake for 30 minutes. While the chicken is baking, prepare the sauce.

Melt the butter in a heavy saucepan, and when it is foaming, add the minced onions. Sauté over medium-low heat just until the onions are soft. Sprinkle the flour over the butter-onion mixture and cook gently until it begins to bubble, about 1 minute. Whisk in the wine, stock, cream and Dijon mustard, cooking until thickened. (The sauce should coat the back of a metal spoon.) Hold over very low heat until the chicken is baked. Pour the sauce over each serving of chicken and sprinkle with walnuts.

Makes 4 delicious servings.

Poulet Chasseur

🐝🐝

Mme MARTHE LEVER, *Innkeeper*
L'HAUT VENT,
Sutton, Québec

A tentative smile from another guest, and the ice is broken. Communication can be difficult if you speak only one language, but listen and appreciate the marvellous *culture Québécoise*. Soon you'll all be laughing!

The gentle sounds of warmth and love filter down to the guest quarters from Marthe Lever's large family. Mealtime is special, and the good feelings permeate the entire inn. L'Haut Vent was handcrafted by Marthe's son Mickey, and the old artistry of Québec's stone masons and woodworkers is evident throughout the inn. Guests return year after year.

6	whole chicken breasts	6
1	onion	1
1	green pepper	1
1 cup	fresh, sliced mushrooms	250 mL
3 cloves	garlic, minced	3 cloves
3 Tbsps.	cornstarch	45 mL
1	chicken bouillon cube	1
2 cups	peeled, chopped fresh or canned tomatoes	500 mL
1 tsp.	dried thyme, crushed	5 mL
$\frac{1}{2}$ tsp.	chili powder	2 mL
	salt and freshly ground pepper, to taste	

Preheat the oven to 350°F. (180°C). Bake the chicken with the skin on in a covered pan for 1 hour. Remove the chicken and skin and debone it; then set it aside. Skim the fat from the pan and use it to lightly sauté the onion, green pepper, mushrooms and garlic. Sprinkle the cornstarch over the vegetables and add the bouillon cube dissolved in 1 cup (250 mL) juice from the baking pan. Add the tomatoes. Stir in the thyme, chili powder, salt and pepper. Add the chicken pieces. Simmer on low heat for 15-20 minutes. Serve on a bed of rice with parsley and green beans.

Makes 6 servings.

Fish and Shellfish

GRAND HARBOUR INN
Grand Harbour, Grand Manan, N.B.

Fundy Scallops Parmesan

🐝🐝🐝

ALBERT AND GLORIA HOBBS, *Innkeepers*
GRAND HARBOUR INN,
Grand Harbour, Grand Manan, N.B.

Even on Grand Manan, right in the Bay of Fundy, the scallops are frozen, but for a slightly different reason than for most of us. The scallop fishermen drop off their 75-100 lb. catches all at once. So even the busiest innkeepers have to get moving and freeze most of them.

1 lb.	scallops, defrosted	450 g
1 cup	all-purpose flour	250 mL
1 tsp.	salt	5 mL
1	egg, beaten	1
	pinch of dill weed	
$\frac{2}{3}$ cup	dried bread crumbs	150 mL
$\frac{1}{3}$ cup	parmesan cheese	75 mL
$\frac{1}{3}$ cup	virgin olive oil	75 mL

Pat the scallops dry. Mix the flour and salt together in one bowl. Whisk the egg and dill weed together in another. And stir the crumbs and parmesan in still another. Dredge the scallops in the flour. Dip them into the egg and then coat them evenly with crumbs. Allow to sit for 10 minutes.

Heat the oil in a heavy skillet and sauté the scallops until they are golden. Serve without a sauce; just the vegetables of the day. *Makes 2-4 servings.*

Lobster Pie

🐝🐝🐝

DON, MARY AND JUDY CLINTON, *Innkeepers*
THE DUNDEE ARMS INN,
Charlottetown, P.E.I.

At the Dundee Arms, this is served in individual soup dishes with a salty, pastry topping.

Pastry

2 cups	all-purpose flour	500 mL
$\frac{1}{2}$ tsp.	salt	2 mL
$\frac{1}{2}$ tsp.	garlic salt	2 mL
1 Tbsp.	dried parsley	15 mL
$\frac{1}{8}$ tsp.	cayenne	0.5 mL
$\frac{1}{8}$ tsp.	black pepper	0.5 mL
$\frac{3}{4}$ cup	chilled shortening	175 mL
3-4 Tbsps.	ice water	45-50 mL

In a medium-sized bowl, stir together the flour, salt and seasonings. With a pastry cutter, cut in the shortening until the mixture is crumbly. Add the ice water, a spoonful at a time. Stir with a fork until the pastry holds together. Form into a ball, wrap with plastic or waxed paper and set aside.

Lobster Filling

4 qts.	mussels, in their shells	4 L
2 cups	dry white wine	500 mL
2 cloves	garlic, crushed	2 cloves
$\frac{1}{2}$ cup	butter	125 mL
1	medium onion, diced	1
$\frac{1}{4}$ cup	all-purpose flour	50 mL
8 oz.	nippy, old cheddar cheese, grated	225 g
	salt and freshly ground pepper, to taste	
2 lbs.	lobster meat*	900 g

Scrub the mussels and pull off the beards. Throw away any open ones. Soak in cold, salt water to cover for 1-2 hours. Drain. In a large saucepan, heat the white wine and garlic. Add the mussels; cover and steam until they open, 5-10 minutes. Discard any that do not open. Strain and reserve the delicious juices.

In another large saucepan, melt the butter. Add the onion and sauté briefly. Stir in the flour, heating until it bubbles. Add the reserved lobster and mussel juices and cook, stirring gently, until thickened. Add the cheese and stir until melted. Taste and season with salt and pepper, if desired. Add the lobster and cooked mussels. Pour into a large, buttered baking dish, about 10 in. x 15 in. (25 cm x 40 cm) or into 10 individual soup bowls.

On a floured board, roll out the pastry to a $\frac{1}{4}$ in. (6 mm) thickness. Cut into rounds or decorative shapes and top the casserole(s).

Bake in a preheated oven at 425°F. (220°C) for 10 minutes. Reduce the heat to 350°F. (180°C) and continue cooking for 20-25 minutes. The crust should be golden and the filling bubbly. The smaller individual onion soup dishes will take only 10 minutes at 350°F. (180°C). Serve this fabulous entrée with loaves of Maritime Brown Bread (p. 148), a large green salad, perhaps with Cream Cheese Dressing (p. 46), a steamed vegetable and a chilled bottle of white wine. *Makes 10 servings.*
This product is usually purchased frozen. Thaw it and then drain it well, reserving the juices.

Kluane Adventures Fish   Small Touches

After cleaning the freshly caught fish, place it, opened flat and with the backbone down, on a sheet of aluminum foil. Fill the fish with the following: $\frac{1}{2}$ in. (1 cm) of brown sugar, 4 heaping globs of butter, 3 or 4 large onion rings, liberal amounts of salt and pepper. (Lemon juice or slices may be added for extra flavor.) Wrap in aluminum foil and bake in hot coals for 30-40 minutes. When the fish is cooked and opened up, you can remove all the bones easily. (Doug Thomas, Gail and Bryant Jeeves, MacKintosh Lodge, Yukon)

MARQUIS OF DUFFERIN LODGE,
Port Dufferin, Halifax County, N.S.

Brian's Hebridean Poached Salmon

🐝🐝

EVE AND MICHAEL CONCANNON, *Innkeepers*
MARQUIS OF DUFFERIN LODGE,
Port Dufferin, Halifax County, N.S.

Eve writes that this recipe came from somewhere in the Hebrides via her brother-in-law, Brian. Note that the salmon may be served hot or, as the Concannons do, cold. Instructions are given for both.

1 5-6 lb.	whole salmon, cleaned, but with the head on	1 2.25- 2.75 kg
	enough dry white wine to cover the fish	
Per pound of fish:		Per 450 g of fish:
1 Tbsp.	wine vinegar	15 mL
1 Tbsp.	cooking oil	15 mL
1 tsp.	salt	5 mL
1 oz.	butter	28 g
2-3 sprigs	fresh rosemary	2-3 sprigs
2-3	bay leaves	2-3
2 Tbsps.	minced chives	25 mL
2 stalks	celery, sliced	2 stalks
1	lemon, sliced	1

Wash and scale the fish. If it is frozen, thaw it in a brine solution of 1 Tbsp. (15 mL) salt and 1 Tbsp. (15 mL) vinegar to every 2 cups (500 mL) cold water. Pat the fish dry. Prepare a baking pan large enough to hold the complete fish *flat* by lining it with heavy-duty aluminum foil — enough to cover and seal the fish completely when cooking. Place the whole fish on the foil and fold up the sides to form a "boat" for holding the liquid. Cover the fish with the wine and other liquid ingredients. Sprinkle with salt and dot with butter. Add the herbs, chives and celery. Cover the surface with lemon slices and fold the foil to seal the edges.

To serve hot

Bake in a preheated 350°F. (180°C) oven 8-10 minutes per pound (450 g). Lift from the cooking juices (these may be used for chowders) and lay on a hot platter. Remove the skin from the top side of the fish and decorate with fresh lemon slices. Serve immediately.

To serve cold

Bake the fish in a preheated oven at 350°F. (180°C) for 4-5 minutes per pound and allow the fish to cool, unwrapped, for at least 4 hours. Lift the salmon from the cooking liquids. Then refrigerate until thoroughly chilled.

Place the fish on a board. Remove the skin from the top side. Garnish with fresh lemon slices and cucumber. Surround with watercress and radish roses. Eve and Michael serve this dish as a salmon salad plate with mayonnaise (p. 41).

Makes 10-12 servings.

Orange Oven-poached Spring Salmon

FLORENCE AND BOB PEEL, *Innkeepers*
AGUILAR HOUSE,
Bamfield, Vancouver Island, B.C.

Aguilar comes from the Spanish word for eagle. And eagles do soar here!

Aguilar House is located at the northern end of the West Coast Hiking Trail and the 51,000-hectare Pacific Rim National Park. The Peels encourage their guests to explore the magnificent coastline and gentle rain forests near the inn. As one writer put it, "The setting at Aguilar is like a dream come true for lovers of seclusion."

This recipe is one that is served often, and Florence is known for its excellence.

8 lbs.	fresh spring salmon	3.6 kg
2 cups	fine bread crumbs	500 mL
	salt and freshly ground	
	black pepper, to taste	
2 tsps.	grated orange rind	10 mL
$\frac{1}{2}$ cup	orange juice	125 mL
$\frac{1}{4}$ cup	melted butter	50 mL

Preheat the oven to 375°F. (190°C). Cut the salmon into steaks. Mix the crumbs, salt, pepper and grated orange rind in a large bowl. Roll the fish in the seasoned crumbs. Place in a buttered baking dish. Mix the orange juice with the melted butter and spoon over the fish. Bake, covered, at 375°F. (190°C) for 20-35 minutes, or until the fish flakes easily.

Makes 10-12 servings.

Salmon in Cranberry Vinegar Sauce

SINCLAIR AND FREDRICA PHILIP, *Innkeepers*
PIA CARROLL, *Chef*
SOOKE HARBOUR HOUSE,
Whiffen Spit Beach, Vancouver Island, B.C.

Although this recipe was developed at Sooke, B.C., it would be equally at home in the Atlantic provinces where fresh salmon and wild Nova Scotian cranberries abound.

½ cup	unsalted butter, clarified	125 mL
2 small cloves	garlic	2 small cloves
2	small shallots, minced	2
4 8-oz.	salmon fillets	4 225-g
6 Tbsps.	cranberry vinegar*	90 mL
2 cups	fish stock	500 mL
1 cup	unsalted butter, room temperature	250 mL

Preheat the oven to 425°F. (220°C). In an oven-proof skillet, heat the butter, garlic and shallots over medium-high heat. Sauté the salmon fillets quickly on one side; turn fillets and add vinegar and stock. Sauté quickly, for less than 30 seconds. Cover skillet with foil and bake in the oven until the fish is cooked, about 5-10 minutes. Remove the fish carefully from the pan and keep warm. Reduce the pan juices over high heat to one-third. Decrease the heat to low and whisk in the unsalted butter, a spoonful at a time. Arrange the salmon on a warm platter. Cover with the sauce. *Makes 4 servings.*

*Cranberry Vinegar Place cranberries in a glass or ceramic bowl. Crush. Cover with rice vinegar (if available) or red wine vinegar. Cover the bowl with plastic wrap. Cut a small hole in the cover to allow the vinegar to breathe. Store in a cool place for 1-2 weeks. Strain and bottle.

Herbed Shrimp Diablo

JEAN AND GARY VEDOVA, *Innkeepers*
KETTLE CREEK INN,
Port Stanley, Ontario

Before dinner, treat yourself to the walking tour of Port Stanley's lovely old buildings — the walking tour guides are available from many of the downtown merchants. Or simply enjoy sunning yourself on the long, sandy beach.

Shrimp

1 lb.	raw shrimp	450 g
½ cup	butter	125 mL
¼ cup	sliced mushrooms	50 mL
¼ cup	sliced celery	50 mL
1	green pepper, sliced	1

Herb Seasoning

$\frac{1}{2}$ tsp.	chopped parsley	2 mL
1 tsp.	chives	5 mL
$\frac{1}{4}$ tsp.	dried tarragon	1 mL
$\frac{1}{4}$ tsp.	ground ginger	1 mL
$\frac{1}{2}$ tsp.	dry mustard	2 mL
$\frac{1}{8}$ tsp.	garlic powder	0.5 mL
$\frac{1}{4}$ tsp.	freshly ground black pepper	1 mL
1 tsp.	salt	5 mL
$\frac{1}{2}$ tsp.	paprika	2 mL
1	tomato, quartered	1
1 Tbsp.	lemon juice	15 mL
2 Tbsps.	brandy	25 mL

Shell and devein the shrimp. Set aside. Heat the butter in a frying pan. Add the mushrooms, celery and green pepper. Sauté for 1 minute. Remove from pan.

In a small bowl, combine the herb seasoning ingredients. Mix the shrimp with the herb seasoning. Add to the hot pan and sauté for 2 minutes. Add the vegetables, tomato and lemon juice. Simmer, covered, for 2 minutes. Heat the brandy, pour it over the Shrimp Diablo and flame. *Makes 2-3 servings.*

Halibut in Blue Cheese Sauce

FRANK LONGSTAFF AND JILL MALINS, *Innkeepers*
SHORECREST LODGE,
North Head, Grand Manan, N.B.

Because Frank and Jill would rather be bird-watching with their guests, they've invented a number of quick recipes that allow them to remain outdoors until the last possible moment.

$\frac{1}{4}$ cup	butter	50 mL
4 oz.	blue cheese, crumbled	115 g
1 tsp.	lemon juice	5 mL
1 lb.	fresh halibut fillets	450 g
$\frac{1}{2}$ tsp.	salt	2 mL
$\frac{1}{2}$ tsp.	freshly ground pepper	2 mL
$\frac{1}{2}$ tsp.	garlic powder	2 mL

In a small saucepan, melt the butter over low heat. Add the cheese and lemon juice, stirring until the cheese melts.

Lay the fillets in a 9 in. x 13 in. (3.5 L) buttered pan. Sprinkle with salt, pepper and garlic powder. Pour the sauce over evenly.

Preheat the oven to 450°F. (220°C). Bake the fish for 8-10 minutes, depending on thickness. Turn on the broiler and slide the fish under it. Broil until the sauce is golden and bubbling, about 4 minutes. *Makes 4 servings.*

Fillet of Sole with Crabmeat Stuffing

JIM AND DONNA LACEBY, *Innkeepers*
THE AMHERST SHORE COUNTRY INN,
Amherst, Nova Scotia

Donna and Jim Laceby moved to the beautiful seaside country near Amherst a few years ago. They have become true Nova Scotians and an integral part of their community's life. They regularly make a point of inviting their neighbors over to "test" Donna's magnificent creations. Imagine, having to force yourself to judge the delicacy of her Lobster Newburg or Fillet of Sole with Crabmeat Stuffing.

Donna's general menu is planned for a year in advance and when the first guests call to make reservations for dinner, Donna allows them to choose their favorite dishes from her sumptuous list for the entire dining room that night.

Stuffing

$\frac{1}{4}$ cup	butter	50 mL
$\frac{1}{2}$ cup	finely chopped onions	125 mL
2 cups	coarsely chopped, fresh mushrooms	500 mL
$\frac{1}{2}$ cup	fresh, snipped parsley	125 mL
6	Saltine crackers, crushed	6
	salt and freshly ground pepper, to taste	

Sauce

$\frac{1}{4}$ cup	butter	50 mL
$\frac{1}{4}$ cup	all-purpose flour	50 mL
2 cups	milk	500 mL
6 Tbsps.	dry white wine	90 mL
	salt and freshly ground pepper, to taste	

Fillets

6 6-8 oz.	fresh sole fillets	6 170-225 g
	salt and freshly ground pepper	
8 oz.	frozen crabmeat, thawed and drained	225 g
1 oz.	Swiss cheese, grated paprika	28 g

To make the stuffing, melt the butter, add the onions and sauté until tender, but not browned. Add the mushrooms and cook for 1 minute. Stir in the parsley, crackers, salt and pepper. Mix well. Correct seasonings, if necessary. Set aside.

To make the sauce, melt butter in a small saucepan. Add the flour, stirring and cooking for 2-3 minutes. Gradually add the milk. Cook until smooth and thickened. Whisk in the white wine. Continue to cook for 2 more minutes. Taste and season with salt and freshly ground pepper.

Preheat the oven to 350°F. (180°C). Rinse the sole fillets and pat dry. Sprinkle with a little salt and freshly ground pepper. Spread with one-sixth of the stuffing per fillet. Spread one-sixth of the crabmeat on top of the stuffing. Roll each fillet up. Place seam side down in a buttered 8 in. x 10 in. (20 cm x 25 cm) pan. Pour the sauce over the fish.

Bake for 40 minutes, basting well with the sauce several times. Slide the fish around from time to time to prevent sticking. Remove from the oven and spread Swiss cheese over the fillets. Sprinkle lightly with paprika. Return to the oven, just until the cheese melts. Serve immediately.

Makes 6 servings.

Deviled Fish

(Haddock, Halibut, Pollock or Cod)

ALBERT AND GLORIA HOBBS, *Innkeepers*
GRAND HARBOUR INN,
Grand Harbour, Grand Manan, N.B.

If you ever have a desperate need to unwind, Grand Manan is your answer! It is difficult to describe the feeling of stepping back into an earlier time when people did stop to smell the roses. When folks around you at supper are discussing with excitement the types of birds they've spotted that day, you know that something here is very different. Ornithologists the world over meet here to watch the birds, explore the wild, rocky terrain and savor Canadian hospitality.

1 Tbsp.	lemon juice	15 mL
$\frac{1}{4}$ tsp.	dry mustard	1 mL
$\frac{1}{2}$ cup	mayonnaise (p. 41)	125 mL
2 6-8 oz.	portions of fish fillets	2 170-225 g
	melted butter	
	paprika	

Mix the lemon juice and mustard; stir into the mayonnaise. Place fillets, skin side up, on a broiler pan; butter with a pastry brush. Broil until half done (1-2 minutes); flip and butter again. Broil only slightly. Spread mayonnaise mixture over the fish. Sprinkle lightly with paprika. Broil until golden brown. Serve on a hot plate.

Makes 2 servings.

THE AMARYLLIS,
Rockport, Ontario

St. Lawrence Fried Fish

🐾🐾🐾

PIETER BERGIN AND JANET RODIER, *Innkeepers*
THE AMARYLLIS,
Rockport, Ontario

A Thousand Islands shore dinner is a long tradition. All the ingredients are made ready, then the fire is built. The onions, potatoes and sometimes fresh corn from one of the farms along the river are roasted whole in the hot coals. An absolutely enormous cast-iron frying pan is brought out to fry a full pound of bacon. When the bacon is crisp, the bass and perch fillets are dipped in seasoned flour, then fried.

To have your own shore dinner, catch and fillet one bass or perch per person. The following recipe will give you enough of the flour/herb mixture to coat 8 to 10 small fish.

$\frac{1}{2}$ cup	all-purpose flour	125 mL
1 Tbsp.	crushed dill weed	15 mL
1 Tbsp.	crushed dried rosemary	15 mL
1 lb.	side bacon	450 g

Combine the flour and the herbs and set aside.

Over an open fire, in a very large cast-iron skillet, fry the bacon until crispy. Set aside or serve the bacon. Drain most of the drippings from the pan.

Roll the fresh fillets in the flour mixture. Lay gently into the hot pan and fry for 1 to 2 minutes on each side or until golden and encrusted with small bits of bacon. Serve with Fire-Baked Onions and Roasted Potatoes (p. 120). Finish your meal with a mug of Campfire Coffee.

Makes 8-10 servings depending on how skilled you are at fishing.

Campfire Coffee

In a large coffee pot, heat the water until boiling. Pull to the side of the fire and add 1 Tbsp. (15 mL) ground coffee per person. Allow it to steep over the coals, without boiling, for 4-5 minutes. Now comes the difference ... add a beaten egg and allow it to settle for 1 minute. This collects all the sediment and clarifies it wonderfully. Pour your coffee and enjoy it with the starlight.

Elizabethan Sole

LT. CDR. AND MRS. T. EDWARDS, *Innkeepers*
SEA HAVEN,
Annapolis Royal, Nova Scotia

Elizabeth is the Edwards' granddaughter who helped develop this recipe.

Sauce

3 Tbsps.	butter	45 mL
3 Tbsps.	all-purpose flour	45 mL
1 cup	fish stock	250 mL
1 3-oz. tin	lobster paste	1 75-g tin
¾ cup	half-and-half cream (10%)	175 mL
¼ cup	pear juice (drained from canned pears *or* pear nectar)	50 mL
1	diced pear, either fresh *or* canned	1

Sole

½ lb.	mushrooms, sliced	225 g
¼ cup	butter	50 mL
8	sole fillets, approximately 3 oz. (85 g) each	8
8	thin slices of ham	8
8	pear halves (if using canned, pat dry) watercress sprigs *and/or* pear slices, for garnish	8

To make the sauce, melt the butter in a heavy saucepan. Whisk in the flour and cook, bubbling, for about a minute. Still stirring, whisk in the stock, lobster paste, half-and-half cream and pear juice. Cook over medium heat until thickened. Stir in the diced pear. Taste and season with salt and pepper if needed. Keep warm over hot water.

Preheat the oven to 350°F. (180°C). In a small saucepan, sauté the mushrooms in the butter until they begin to brown. On each sole fillet, lay a slice of ham and one-eighth of the mushrooms. Place pear half in the center and roll. Secure with toothpicks. Stand upright in a buttered 9 in. (22 cm) square baking pan. Cover with half the sauce. Bake 20 minutes or until the fish flakes.

Pour the other half of the sauce onto a heated serving platter or individual plates. Arrange the sole on top, removing the toothpicks. Garnish with watercress and pear slices.

Makes 8 servings.

Acadian Jambalaya

ANNA AND PATRICK REDGRAVE, *Innkeepers*
THE GARRISON HOUSE INN,
Annapolis Royal, Nova Scotia

Cajun cooking has become quite trendy in North America. But it was in the Nova Scotian countryside where it began … in Acadia, where the tri-color flags are still flying.

When the British finally gained supremacy, they expelled the French Acadians from their lands and confiscated their properties. Cast adrift, the French found their way to the Mississippi Delta where their lilting language and excellent cooking blended with those of the Spanish and the Creoles. Even the word Jambalaya shows that mingling. "Jambon" and "à la" are French words for "ham" and "with," while "ya" is Creole for "rice."

2½ Tbsps.	chicken fat or lard	35 mL
⅔ cup	coarsely chopped, smoked ham	150 mL
½ cup	good, smoked pork sausage (e.g., Kielbasa)	125 mL
1½ cups	chopped onion	375 mL
1 cup	chopped celery	250 mL
¾ cup	chopped, green bell pepper	175 mL
½-¾ cup	uncooked chicken, cut in bite-sized chunks (boneless breast is a good choice)	125-175 mL
4	medium tomatoes, peeled and chopped	4
3 cloves	garlic, crushed or minced	3 cloves
¾ tsp.	Tabasco or Louisiana hot sauce	4 mL
2	bay leaves	2
1½ tsp.	salt	7 mL
1½ tsp.	black pepper	7 mL
2 tsps.	dried oregano	10 mL
2 tsps.	dried thyme	10 mL
¾ cup	tomato sauce	175 mL
2½ cups	seafood stock	625 mL
½ cup	chopped green onion	125 mL
2 cups	uncooked rice	500 mL
½ lb.	medium shrimp	225 g
¾ lb.	firm-fleshed fish (e.g., cod, haddock), cut into large chunks	340 g

Preheat the oven to 350° F. (180°C). In a large 4-6 qt. (5-7 L) saucepan, melt the fat over medium heat. (Anna uses big cast-iron pots.) Add the smoked ham and pork sausage and sauté about 5 minutes, stirring frequently. Add the onion, celery and peppers. Sauté until tender but still firm. Add the chicken. Raise the heat to high and cook 1 minute, stirring constantly. Add the tomatoes and cook until the chicken is tender, about 5 minutes, stirring frequently. Add the garlic, Tabasco and all the seasonings. Add the tomato sauce. Cook for a few minutes, stirring. Stir in the stock and bring to a boil. Then add the green onion and cook about 2 minutes, stirring occasionally. Add the rice, shrimp and fish; blend well and remove from the heat. Cover and bake for about 20-30 minutes. Remove bay leaves and serve immediately. *Makes 4 servings.*

Ling Cod Fillet with Shrimp Sauce

MARY ANN MCCREA-OKRAINEC AND BOB OKRAINEC, *Innkeepers*
DENMAN ISLAND GUEST HOUSE,
Denman Island, British Columbia

This is one of the house specialties expertly prepared by two innkeepers who know how close to Heaven the B.C. islands are.

1 lb.	shrimp	450 g
$\frac{1}{3}$ cup	butter	75 mL
$\frac{1}{3}$ cup	all-purpose flour	75 mL
$1\frac{1}{2}$ cups	milk	375 mL
$\frac{1}{3}$ cup	parmesan cheese	75 mL
1 tsp.	paprika	5 mL
8	large ling cod fillets	8
$\frac{1}{2}$-$\frac{3}{4}$ cup	dry white wine	125-175 mL
	parsley, for garnish	
	lemon pepper	
2-3 Tbsps.	butter	25-45 mL

Peel and devein the shrimp. In a heavy saucepan, melt the butter; stir in the flour. Add the milk gradually, stirring until thickened. Add the parmesan and paprika, stirring to dissolve the parmesan. Add the shrimp. Let the sauce simmer for a few minutes.

Arrange the cod fillets on a microwave-proof dish. Pour the wine over the fish. Sprinkle with parsley and lemon pepper to taste. Dab each fillet with butter. Cook in a microwave on a high setting for approximately 10 minutes. The fish will have to be turned, and the cooking time adjusted according to the thickness and size of fillets.

Arrange the cod on serving dishes; cover the fish with shrimp sauce. Garnish with fresh parsley. *Makes 8 servings.*

La Truite du Québec à la Mode
de l'Auberge
(Québec Trout Handfield)

CONRAD HANDFIELD, *Innkeeper*
ANDRÉ MORIZOT, *Chef des Cuisines*
L'AUBERGE HANDFIELD,
St-Marc sur le Richelieu, Québec

South of Montreal, on the historic Richelieu, you will find one of French Canada's best inns. Its joie de vivre enriches all of Canada, for Mr. Handfield has maintained the foods and surroundings of old Québec, all the while developing new and exciting recipes featuring local ingredients. He is on the leading edge with a handful of other special Canadian innkeepers.

4	pan-sized, fresh trout	4
1	carrot, peeled and chopped	1
1	onion, diced	1
1	bouquet garni*	1
	a few whole peppercorns	
2 Tbsps.	dry mustard	25 mL
2 cups	dry white wine	500 mL

Put the trout and all the remaining ingredients into a large covered saucepan. Bring the liquid to a boil and remove the saucepan from the heat. Keep it covered for 10 minutes. Arrange the trout on a warm platter. Make the following sauce and gently pour it over the fish.

Sauce

$\frac{1}{2}$ cup	butter	125 mL
$\frac{1}{2}$ cup	all-purpose flour	125 mL
3	egg yolks	3
	the strained cooking juices	
	from the trout	
$\frac{1}{2}$ cup	butter (second amount)	125 mL
1	lemon, juiced	1

In a saucepan, melt the first amount of butter. Stir in the flour and egg yolks. Whisk in the trout juices, little by little. Return to moderate heat. Bring to a simmer, stirring constantly. Remove from the heat when the sauce begins to bubble. Whisk in the second amount of butter, bit by bit. Then add the lemon juice. *Bon appétit!*

Makes 4 servings.

* Tie in a cheesecloth bag: fresh parsley, celery leaves, a bay leaf and grated nutmeg.

Barbecued Sturgeon (or Other Fish)

😃😃😃😃😃😃😃😃😃😃😃😃😃😃😃😃😃😃😃😃😃😃😃😃😃😃😃😃😃😃😃😃😃😃😃😃😃

Brush the fillets lightly with barbecue sauce (the Mesa Creek recipe is excellent, p. 118) and grill over medium coals. A sheet of oiled aluminum foil will help keep the fish from sticking. It takes only 4-5 minutes per side for each 1 in. (2.5 cm) of thickness. (Cécile and Emileen Morel, Manoir St-André, St-André, Québec)

Tranches d'Esturgeon au Four
(Baked Fillets of Sturgeon)

😃😃😃😃😃😃😃😃😃😃😃😃😃😃😃😃😃😃😃😃😃😃😃😃😃😃😃😃😃😃😃😃😃😃😃😃😃

CÉCILE AND EMILEEN MOREL, *Innkeepers*
MANOIR ST-ANDRÉ,
St-André, Quebec

The flesh of a sturgeon is very firm — much like a breast of chicken when cooked. It has no strong, "fishy" flavor, and hence it has become a favorite fish along this broad part of the St. Lawrence River.

2½ lbs.	sturgeon fillets, 1 in. (2.5 cm) thick	1 kg
⅔ cup	all-purpose flour	150 mL
1 tsp.	salt	5 mL
4 Tbsps.	butter	60 mL
3 Tbsps.	chopped onion	45 mL
3 Tbsps.	diced celery	45 mL
1⅔ cups	fresh bread cubes	400 mL
½ tsp.	salt (second amount)	2 mL
½ tsp.	freshly ground pepper	2 mL
1 tsp.	dried marjoram	5 mL

Preheat the oven to 450°F. (230°C). Sprinkle or dredge the sturgeon in the flour and salt (first amount). Arrange the fillets in a single layer in a buttered baking pan, about 9 in. x 13 in. (3.5 L).

In a saucepan, melt the butter and add the onion and celery. Stir, cooking gently, for 2-3 minutes. Toss in the bread cubes, salt, pepper and marjoram. Stir to combine thoroughly. Spread evenly over the slices of sturgeon. Bake 20-30 minutes. Serve with Hollandaise Sauce (p. 117).

Makes 6-8 servings.

THE HORSESHOE INN,
Cataract, Ontario

Fresh Rainbow Trout in Puff Pastry

❀❀

MAY DENREYER, *Innkeeper*
THE HORSESHOE INN,
Cataract, Ontario

Either rainbow trout or sole may be used in this recipe. They must be fresh; frozen fish tends to be watery.

2 lbs.	fresh rainbow trout or sole fillets	900 g
$\frac{1}{2}$ cup	lemon juice	125 mL
1 lb.	puff pastry (p. 165), freshly made or frozen	450 g
1-2 tsps.	dried tarragon leaves salt and freshly ground pepper, to taste	5-10 mL
2	egg yolks, beaten	2

Lay the fish in a flat dish. Add the lemon juice and soak for 15 minutes to an hour. Drain and pat dry thoroughly with paper towels.

On a lightly floured board, roll the puff pastry to $\frac{1}{2}$ in. (1 cm) thickness. Cut into 6 oval pieces. Sprinkle each with tarragon leaves. Divide the fillets among the 6 pieces of pastry. Shape the pastry around the fillets into the form of a fish. (May says that this takes practice.) Seal the seam with egg yolk. Flip the fish over so that the seam is on the bottom of each serving. Make a head at one end, the tail at the other and fins may be glued on with egg yolk. Scales can be simulated by gently pressing the tines of a fork along each "fish." Brush with egg yolk all over and let rest for 15 minutes to an hour.

Preheat the oven to 400°F. (200°C). Bake on ungreased baking sheets until golden brown, about 20-25 minutes. Serve with lemon slices.

Makes 6 servings.

Grouper Singapore-style

Helen and Eugene Kates, *Innkeepers*
Arowhon Pines,
Algonquin Provincial Park, Ont.

There are no grouper in Algonquin Park, and so Helen, with her usual style, sends a "rather large taxi" to Toronto's famous St. Lawrence Market to pick some up. It's only 200 miles! While they're at it, they buy the other special ingredients that Arowhon needs for that week — French cheeses, Greek olives, perfect produce and, of course, fresh fish. All winter long, Helen develops new recipes and finds sources of supply while her chefs are off perfecting their style in France. A truly world-class lodge!

Grouper Singapore-style is delicious on a bed of freshly cooked Chinese noodles with a mixture of stir-fried vegetables such as carrots, green and red peppers, snow peas, bok choy, bean sprouts and green onions.

Marinade Mixture

1½ cups	Japanese Superior Soy Sauce	375 mL
1½ cups	water	375 mL
2 oz.	dry sherry	50 mL
	fresh, finely chopped ginger root, to taste	
1 medium-sized clove	garlic, minced	1 medium-sized clove
¼ cup	sesame seeds	50 mL

Fillets

16 pieces	fresh grouper fillets	16 pieces
2-3 Tbsps.	peanut oil	25-45 mL

GARNISH fresh ginger root, cut into fine julienne strips; the green of green onions, cut into fine julienne strips.

Stir together the marinade. Lay the fish flat in a 9 in. x 13 in. (3.5 L) pan. Pour the marinade over and allow it to stand for 15 to 20 minutes only.

In a large skillet, heat the peanut oil. Pan-fry the drained fillets quickly, about 10 minutes per inch (2.5 cm). Turn gently to brown both sides after the first 3 or 4 minutes. Do not overcook.

Remove to a heated platter and garnish with the julienned ginger root and green onions.

Makes 8 servings.

Red Snapper with Clams in Wine Sauce

Mary Ann McCrea-Okrainec and Bob Okrainec, *Innkeepers*
DENMAN ISLAND GUEST HOUSE,
Denman Island, B.C.

Instead of dry white wine, Mary Ann uses a wine vinegar that she and Bob make from local plums and blackberries. The clams are dug locally.

12	clams, well scrubbed	12
½ cup	dry white wine or fruit vinegar	125 mL
1 Tbsp.	minced onion	15 mL
1 Tbsp.	minced celery	15 mL
1 8-10 oz.	fillet of red snapper	1 225-280 g
	pinch of garlic powder	
	pinch of paprika	
	pinch of parsley	

Cook the clams with wine, minced onion and celery in the microwave on high for 5 minutes, or until the clams have steamed open.

Place the snapper on a platter, sprinkling the spices over the fish. Pour the wine from the clams over the fish. Cook for 5 minutes on high, turning once. (The snapper may need to cook longer, depending on the thickness of the fillet.)

Arrange the clams around the red snapper. Cook for 1 minute on high and serve.

Makes 2 servings.

Sooke Harbour House Swimming Scallops in Champagne and Sweet Cicely Sauce

Sinclair and Fredrica Philip, *Innkeepers*
Pia Carroll, *Chef*
SOOKE HARBOUR HOUSE,
Whiffen Spit Beach, Vancouver Island, B.C.

These beautiful pastel bivalves flit away, butterfly fashion, from their predators.

40	swimming scallops	40
2 cups	heavy cream (35%)	500 mL
¾ cup	champagne	175 mL
½ cup	fish stock (don't substitute clam nectar; use more champagne if necessary)	125 mL

| 2 cloves | garlic, finely minced | 2 cloves |
| $\frac{1}{3}$ cup | finely chopped cicely leaf*
sweet cicely leaf and flower,
if available, for garnish* | 75 mL |

Scrub scallops under cold water and drain. Place the scallops, heavy cream, half of the champagne, the fish stock and the garlic in a large saucepan. Cover with a lid and bring to a boil. Allow the scallops to open while shaking the saucepan back and forth a few times. The scallops take approximately 4 minutes to cook. Remove them from the saucepan. On warm plates, arrange half of the scallop shells (with the meat in them) in a circular pattern. Keep warm.

Return the saucepan to a high heat, add the remaining champagne and stir the liquid until thickened — approximately 1 minute. (Be careful not to let the sauce become too thick.) Stir in the sweet cicely and pour the sauce over the scallops. Garnish with a sprig of sweet cicely leaf and serve. *Makes 2 servings.*

Sinclair notes that anise hyssop or fennel may be substituted if sweet cicely is not available.

Lobster Newburg

DONNA AND JIM LACEBY, *Innkeepers*
THE AMHERST SHORE COUNTRY INN,
Amherst, Nova Scotia

This has to be the best Lobster Newburg I have ever tasted.

4 cups	fresh lobster meat (if frozen, thaw and drain very well)	1 L
$\frac{1}{3}$ cup	butter	75 mL
$\frac{1}{2}$ cup	medium-dry sherry generous dash paprika generous dash nutmeg	125 mL
6	egg yolks	6
2 cups	heavy cream (35%)	500 mL

Cut the lobster into bite-sized pieces. Melt the butter in the top of a double boiler. Add the lobster meat; sauté it gently until it is heated through. Add the sherry, paprika and nutmeg. Heat it through again. Blend the egg yolks and heavy cream with a wire whisk. Add to the lobster. Heat gently until it is hot and the sauce begins to thicken. *Do not boil.* Serve immediately in individual side dishes with a rice pilaf.

If you wish to make this ahead, reheat very gently in a slow oven at 250°F.-300°F. (125°C-150°C) for 30-45 minutes. (Time depends on how completely the dish has been cooled.) Stir often and watch to make sure it doesn't overheat or the sauce will separate. *Makes 6 servings.*

SHORECREST LODGE,
North Head, Grand Manan, N.B.

Haddock Poached in Sherry

8888888888888888888888888888888888888888888888888

FRANK LONGSTAFF AND JILL MALINS,, *Innkeepers*
SHORECREST LODGE,
North Head, Grand Manan, N.B.

Coming from years of designing the out-trips for the Federation of Ontario Naturalists, Frank and Jill found a lovely old inn right on the Atlantic flyway. They are centering the activities of Shorecrest around their love of the outdoors, and guests truly benefit from their skills in bird- and whale-watching.

1½ lbs.	fresh haddock fillets*	675 g
½ tsp.	garlic powder	2 mL
1 tsp.	dried thyme	5 mL
½ tsp.	salt	2 mL
½ tsp.	freshly ground pepper	2 mL
1	large tomato, peeled and diced	1
1	medium onion, diced	1
2 Tbsps.	minced parsley	25 mL
½ cup	dry sherry	125 mL

Place the fish in a large skillet that has a cover. Sprinkle with garlic powder, thyme, salt and pepper. Cover with the tomato, onion and parsley. Pour in the sherry. Cover the skillet tightly and poach gently for 10 minutes or until the fish begins to flake. Remove the fish to a heated platter. Reduce the sauce a little and pour over the fillets. Serve with steamed rice.

Makes 6 servings.

Halibut or pollock may be substituted.

Les Fruits de Mer Gratinées
(Seafood au Gratin)

MME MARTHE LEVER, *Innkeeper*
L'HAUT VENT,
Sutton, Québec

Mme Lever makes this dish ahead and freezes it before baking.

$\frac{1}{4}$ cup	butter	50 mL
1 lb.	small, whole mushrooms	450 g
1-2	green onions, chopped	1-2
1 lb.	scallops	450 g
1 lb.	shrimp, cleaned and deveined	450 g
$\frac{1}{2}$ cup	dry white wine	125 mL
$1\frac{1}{2}$ lbs.	sole fillets	680 g
$\frac{1}{2}$ cup	all-purpose flour	125 mL
$2\frac{1}{2}$ cups	milk	625 mL
	salt and freshly ground pepper, to taste	
2 Tbsps.	minced parsley	25 mL
$\frac{1}{2}$-1 lb.	Swiss cheese, grated	225-450 g

Melt the butter in a skillet and sauté the mushrooms over medium heat until they begin to brown. Toss in the onions and stir until they begin to wilt. Remove from the heat and set aside.

In a covered saucepan, poach the scallops and shrimp in the white wine for 1-2 minutes. Remove with a slotted spoon. Cut the sole fillets into chunks and add them to the poaching liquid. Cover and poach for only 30 seconds — just until the fish begins to turn white. It must not be completely cooked. Remove with a slotted spoon and combine with the shrimp. Mix the flour with a little of the milk and whisk this into the hot liquid. Cook until thickened. Stir in the remaining milk, salt, pepper and parsley. Continue to cook until slightly thickened.

Divide the fish among 12 1-cup (250 mL) oven-proof ramekins which have been buttered or a 9 in. x 13 in. (3.5 L) buttered baking dish. Pour the warm sauce over the seafood. At this point, the dishes may be frozen for future dinners. Just cover tightly with plastic wrap and freeze. Thaw for 2-3 hours before topping the ramekins with lots of Swiss cheese and baking at 450°F. (220°C) for 20 minutes. Marthe serves this dish with steamed broccoli, cauliflower and rice.

Makes 12 servings.

Pia Carroll's Abalone Sautéed with Hazelnut and Lime Butter Sauce

SINCLAIR AND FREDRICA PHILIP, *Innkeepers*
PIA CARROLL, *Chef*
SOOKE HARBOUR HOUSE,
Whiffen Spit Beach, Vancouver Island, B.C.

P̲ia's genius with local specialties is matched by Sinclair's persistence in discovering them.

4	abalone in the shell (p. 44)	4
2	shallots, minced	2
1 clove	garlic, minced	1 clove
$\frac{1}{4}$ cup	apple cider vinegar	50 mL
$\frac{1}{2}$ cup	fish stock	125 mL
$\frac{1}{2}$ cup	dry white wine	125 mL
$\frac{1}{2}$ cup	cold unsalted butter	125 mL
	juice from $\frac{1}{2}$ lime	
$\frac{1}{3}$ cup	ground toasted hazelnuts	75 mL
$\frac{1}{4}$ cup	unsalted butter	50 mL
	(second amount)	
	thinly shredded red pickled ginger root (optional), for garnish*	

The abalone may be frozen first to tenderize the muscles. If the abalone are frozen, thaw them in the refrigerator. A large spoon easily removes them from their shells. Discard viscerae. Wash and scrub abalone to remove black coating from foot. Cut meat into $\frac{1}{8}$ in. (3 mm)-wide *vertical* slices (not steaks).

In a heavy saucepan, combine the shallots, garlic, vinegar, stock and wine. Bring to a boil and reduce over high heat until the amount remaining equals $\frac{1}{2}$ cup (125 mL). Strain. Return the liquid to the saucepan and over very low heat, add the butter, a teaspoonful at a time, whisking it in. This will become a smooth, velvety sauce. Add the lime juice and hazelnuts, stirring just to combine. Pia sometimes adds 1 cup (250 mL) of wild, trailing blackberries to the sauce at this point. Spoon onto heated plates.

In a sauté pan, heat the $\frac{1}{4}$ cup (50 mL) unsalted butter over medium-high heat. Add the abalone and cook briefly, 20-30 seconds on each side. Arrange on the individual plates by overlapping the slices. Garnish with pickled red ginger root shreds.

Makes 4 servings.

* *Red pickled ginger root is available at Oriental groceries.*

Lamb, Veal, Rabbit and Game

HEARN'S MANOR HOUSE
Indian Head, Saskatchewan

Shishlikee

စ္စ

AL AND BRENDA HEARN, *Innkeepers*
HEARN'S MANOR HOUSE,
Indian Head, Saskatchewan

Located in an English-style mansion house (circa 1889), Al and Brenda are true pioneers in the prairie provinces. There are no other real country inns except this one; at least, none that I could find. Shishlikee is served by Al and Brenda as a side dish. It is a variation of the Middle Eastern Sis Kebabi (Shish Kebab) and may be served as a main course with a rice pilaf, broiled or barbecued tomatoes and green peppers. Although it can be roasted in the oven in wintertime, it is at its best when barbecued.

3-4 lbs.	lean lamb, cut into $1\frac{1}{2}$-2 in. (4-5 cm) cubes	1.3-1.8 kg
2-3	Spanish onions, peeled and thinly sliced	2-3
2 tsps.	salt	10 mL
1-2 tsps.	freshly ground pepper	5-10 mL
1 cup	lemon juice	250 mL

In a container with a tight-fitting lid, layer the lamb, onions and seasonings. Pour the lemon juice over it all. Cover tightly. Shake well. Refrigerate. Keep this in the refrigerator for 2-3 days, shaking the lamb each morning and evening. Thread drained lamb onto skewers. Barbecue over medium coals until well browned.

Makes 6-8 servings.

Le Lapin en Civet au Luc

(Jugged Rabbit)

LUC INVERNIZZI, *Innkeeper*
L'AUBERGE LE RUCHER,
Val David, Québec

Luc is a Renaissance man. He seems to be able to turn his hand to almost anything he wishes. First, he built his inn; then he built his furniture. Now he develops recipes, cooks and survives Canadian winters in the south of France.

4 lbs.	rabbit, cut into 6 pieces	1.8 kg
4 cups	dry red wine	1 L
2 cups	water	500 mL
4	bay leaves	4

1	large onion, diced	1
1 sprig	fresh thyme	1
	or	
1 tsp.	dried thyme	5 mL
1 tsp.	dried rosemary	5 mL
12	whole peppercorns	12
$\frac{1}{2}$ cup	olive oil	125 mL
2 Tbsps.	all-purpose flour	25 mL
	salt and freshly ground	
	pepper, to taste	
$\frac{1}{4}$ cup	butter	50 mL
$\frac{1}{4}$ cup	all-purpose flour	50 mL
	(second amount)	
1 lb.	whole mushrooms	450 g

On the evening before serving, pat the rabbit dry. In a large casserole combine the wine, water, herbs and spices. Add the rabbit to the marinade and cover with plastic wrap. Refrigerate until needed. About 1-1$\frac{1}{2}$ hours before serving, heat the olive oil in a large, heavy stewing pot. (Luc suggests enameled cast-iron.) Remove the rabbit from the marinade and pat dry. Strain the marinade and reserve. Quickly sear the rabbit on both sides until golden. As the pieces brown, remove them and set aside. Sprinkle them with the 2 Tbsp. (25 mL) flour and season with salt and pepper. Add the strained marinade to the stewing pot and bring to a boil. Meanwhile, cream together the butter and flour to make a smooth paste (Beurre Manie, p. 17). Whisk this into the wine marinade a bit at a time until the sauce is the consistency of heavy cream. Return the rabbit to the stewing pot. Add the whole mushrooms. Cover and simmer on low heat for an hour. Luc serves the rabbit over butterfly (or bow-tie) noodles, surrounded by steamed carrots and cauliflower. Drizzle a little sauce over the noodles and pass the rest separately.

Makes 6 generous servings.

Caribou Burgers   *Small Touches*

In the far North, the long arm of the law has reached into the Yukon kitchen. Restaurants are not allowed to have wild game of any sort on the menu. Gail and Bryant Jeeves were kind enough to send recipes that they use personally, rather than at their establishment — Mackintosh Lodge. In each case, the name of the friend who gave them the recipe appears in the recipe foreword.

Gail gave me a few hints for substitutions when it comes to game. For moose, substitute beef; for caribou or sheep, use veal. Pork works well in place of bear. To reduce the gamey flavor of wild meat, marinate it in beer or milk for several hours before cooking.

To 1 lb. (450 g) of ground caribou, add 1 cup (250 mL) of finely crushed corn flakes, 1 tsp. (5 mL) salt, $\frac{1}{2}$ tsp. (2 mL) pepper, $\frac{1}{2}$ tsp. (2 mL) poultry seasoning and $\frac{1}{2}$ cup (125 mL) milk. Shape into 10 patties and fry in a heavy skillet that has been lightly greased. (To vary, use $\frac{2}{3}$ cup (150 mL) oatmeal in place of the corn flakes.) "Guaranteed to save your beef bills or moose mishaps." (Rev. John Watts, Gail and Bryant Jeeves, Mackintosh Lodge, Yukon)

Veal with Morels

&&&&&&&&&&&&&&&&&&&&&&&&&&&&&&&&&&&&&&&&&&&&&&&&&&&

ANDRÉ SCHWARZ, *Innkeeper*
THE POST HOTEL,
Lake Louise, Alberta

Morels are sometimes found growing wild in the damp woods of southern Canada. But morel pickers are a secretive lot; so most patches are fiercely guarded. If you can, use fresh morels. If you can't, use the dried variety, bought at a specialty food store.

1 oz.	dried morels	28 g
	or	
$\frac{3}{4}$ cup	slivered, fresh morels	175 mL
2 Tbsps.	unsalted butter	25 mL
$\frac{3}{4}$ cup	all-purpose flour	175 mL
3 Tbsps.	chopped onion	45 mL
2 Tbsps.	brandy	25 mL
$\frac{1}{4}$ cup	dry white wine	50 mL
1 cup	heavy cream (35%)	250 mL
2 tsps.	fresh lemon juice, or to taste	10 mL
	salt and freshly ground pepper, to taste	
$1\frac{1}{4}$ lbs.	veal, from leg or loin, cut into very thin scallops (about 18 scallops)	575 g
3 Tbsps.	light olive oil	45 mL

Cover the dried morels in hot water and soak them until they are soft — about 2 hours. Carefully lift the mushrooms from the liquid, leaving as much grit as possible behind. Discard the liquid or strain and reserve for another use. Rinse the mushrooms in two changes of cool water. Drain; slice lengthwise into very thin strips. Rinse again, drain well and set aside.

Make a Beurre Manie by mashing together 1 Tbsp. (15 mL) of the butter and 2 tsps. (10 mL) of the flour in a small bowl with a wooden spoon; when thoroughly blended, set aside.

Melt 1 Tbsp. (15 mL) butter in a noncorrodible, heavy skillet over medium-high heat. When the foam subsides, add the onion. Sauté, stirring frequently, until softened but not browned, about 1 minute. Add the reserved morels. Sauté, stirring 1 minute. Add brandy and ignite. Shake the pan until the flames are extinguished. Add the wine; increase the heat to high. Cook, uncovered, until the liquid is reduced to half. Add the cream to the skillet; heat it to boiling, then reduce the heat to medium. Whisk in the Beurre Manie, a little at a time, using only enough to thicken the sauce slightly, so that it coats the back of a metal spoon. Add the lemon juice, salt and pepper to taste. Remove from the heat, cover and keep warm.

Place the veal scallops between 2 sheets of waxed paper; pound each to $\frac{1}{8}$ in. (3 mm) thickness. Season the veal on both sides with salt and pepper. Spread the remaining flour on another sheet of waxed paper. Dip the veal, one piece at a time, into the flour, shaking off excess so that only a light dusting remains.

Heat a large, heavy skillet over medium-high heat until it is hot enough to evaporate a drop of water on contact. Add about $1\frac{1}{2}$ Tbsps. (20 mL) olive oil to the hot skillet, rotating to coat the bottom; heat until smoking. Increase the heat to high; add enough scallops to the skillet to fit in one layer without crowding. Sear until the undersides are browned. Turn scallops with tongs; sear on second sides until browned. Arrange the veal on a warmed serving platter; keep warm, covered with foil. Repeat until all the veal is sautéed, adding oil to the skillet as needed. Meanwhile, reheat the sauce, whisking contantly, over medium-high heat until heated through. Pour the sauce over the veal; serve it immdediately. *Makes 6 servings of 3 scallops each.*

Lamb Stew with Sherry

&&&&&&&&&&&&&&&&&&&&&&&&&&&&&&&&&&&&&&&&&&&&&&&&

JOHN AND EVA HEINECK, *Innkeepers*
THE SHERWOOD INN,
Glen Orchard, Muskoka, Ontario

$1\frac{1}{4}$ cups	dry sherry	300 mL
2 cloves	garlic	2 cloves
3 lbs.	deboned lamb (leg), cut into 2 in. (5 cm) pieces	1.3 kg
1 tsp.	salt	5 mL
$\frac{1}{2}$ tsp.	black pepper	2 mL
1 tsp.	ground caraway seeds	5 mL
4 Tbsps.	vegetable oil	60 mL
2	onions, sliced	2
2 Tbsps.	all-purpose flour	25 mL

Combine the sherry and garlic in a large mixing bowl. Add the pieces of lamb and mix well. Cover the bowl and leave the meat to marinate for 3 hours. Remove the lamb from the marinade. Drain well and dry the meat on paper towels. Reserve the marinade. Sprinkle the salt, pepper and caraway over the lamb. In a large saucepan heat the oil over moderate heat. Add the pieces of lamb and fry them for 3 to 5 minutes or until they are brown. Add the onions and fry for 3 minutes. Add the flour and mix it well with the lamb and onions. Pour over the reserved marinade and, stirring constantly, bring to a boil. Cover the saucepan and reduce the heat to low. Simmer the stew for at least 1 hour or until tender. *Makes 6 servings.*

Grilled Rabbit Tenderloin Pommery

✿✿

FREDY STAMM, *Chef*
THE MILLCROFT INN,
Alton, Ontario

Rabbit has long been used in Europe, but it is just lately becoming popular in Ontario. Fredy makes the following observations on purchasing it: "Fresh rabbits are best bought from a country abattoir or may be ordered from your butcher. The butcher will be glad to debone the rabbit and chop the bones on request, as butchering rabbit is fairly tricky. Fresh rabbit has beige-white flesh and the meat should be firm."

4	saddles of rabbit, deboned to make 8 fillets	4
$\frac{1}{2}$ oz.	unsalted butter	14 g
$\frac{1}{2}$ oz.	chopped shallots	14 g
7 oz.	dry white wine	200 mL
4 Tbsps.	Meaux mustard (old-fashioned mustard with coarsely ground seeds)	60 mL
7 oz.	rabbit stock (see below)	200 mL
14 oz.	heavy cream (35%)	400 mL
3 oz.	cool, sweet, unsalted butter salt and freshly ground pepper, to taste	75 g
1 oz.	finely chopped, shelled pistachio nuts peanut oil, as needed	28

Melt the $\frac{1}{2}$ oz. (14 g) of butter over low heat. Add the shallots and sweat gently until they are transparent. Deglaze the pan with the wine. Increase the heat and reduce to one-sixth the amount. Whisk in the mustard. Add the stock and reduce by three-quarters. Add the cream, slowly cooking the sauce until it coats the back of a wooden spoon. With a wire whisk, incorporate the cool butter a little at a time, never letting the sauce boil. Season with salt and pepper to taste.

At the last moment, stir in the pistachio nuts. Keep the sauce warm while you prepare the rabbit.

Salt and pepper the cleaned tenderloins. Turn them in peanut oil and grill them until they are medium-rare. Serve on top of the sauce which has been spooned onto heated plates.

Rabbit Stock

	the bones of the 4 saddles, chopped to the size of walnuts	
1	carrot	1
$\frac{1}{2}$	Spanish onion	$\frac{1}{2}$

$\frac{1}{4}$	celery root	$\frac{1}{4}$
1	bay leaf	1
1 sprig	fresh thyme	1 sprig
1	whole clove	1
	cold water to cover	

Place the chopped bones in a stock pot. Dice the vegetables into $\frac{1}{2}$ in. (1 cm) cubes. Add to the stock pot along with the seasonings. Cover with cold water and simmer for 2 hours or until the reduced liquid equals 7 oz. (200 mL). Strain through a cheesecloth and set aside. *Makes 7 oz. (200 mL).*

Leg of Lamb with Spinach, Ham and Ricotta Stuffing

ANDRÉ AND GEORGE SCHWARZ, *Innkeepers*
THE POST HOTEL,
Lake Louise, Alberta

André and his brother, George, are justifiably proud of their European-style kitchen. They were chosen, from a province full of fine chefs, to put together the restaurant in Alberta's pavilion at Expo 86.

1 6-lb.	leg of lamb, bone in	1 3-kg
3 oz.	cooked ham, diced into small cubes	100 g
5 oz.	well-drained, blanched spinach, chopped finely*	140 g
2 cloves	garlic, crushed	2 cloves
4 oz.	ricotta cheese	115 g
	salt, freshly ground pepper and grated nutmeg, to taste	
2	egg yolks	2
	dry bread crumbs, as needed	
$\frac{1}{2}$ cup	dry red wine	125 mL

Debone the leg of lamb or have the butcher do it for you. Set it aside.

To make the stuffing, combine in a large mixing bowl the ham, spinach, garlic and ricotta. Mix well. Taste and add salt, freshly ground pepper and nutmeg, as desired. Fold in the egg yolks and enough bread crumbs to bind the stuffing together loosely.

Preheat the oven to 375°F. (190°C). Fill the cavity with the stuffing and tie the opening together with butcher's string. Season the lamb with additional salt and pepper. Place it in an open roasting pan. Insert a meat thermometer at this stage of preparation. Roast for 15 minutes, then pour the red wine over. Continue to roast until the internal temperature is 140°F. (60°C), about 50 minutes. Baste frequently. Remove from the oven. Allow to rest 5 minutes before slicing.

Makes 6 generous servings.

The spinach may be fresh or frozen.

Medallions of Fresh Kid with Plums and Chanterelles

🐝🐝🐝🐝🐝🐝🐝🐝🐝🐝🐝🐝🐝🐝🐝🐝🐝🐝🐝🐝🐝🐝🐝🐝🐝🐝🐝🐝🐝🐝🐝🐝🐝🐝🐝🐝🐝🐝🐝

SINCLAIR AND FREDRICA PHILIP, *Innkeepers*
PIA CARROLL, *Chef*
SOOKE HARBOUR HOUSE,
Whiffen Spit Beach, Vancouver Island, B.C.

Much of the richness of Vancouver Island is displayed in this dish. All the ingredients are local!

2 lbs.	kid loin*	900 g
1½ cups	buttermilk	375 mL
2 sprigs	fresh rosemary	2 sprigs
2 sprigs	fresh lemon thyme	2 sprigs
2 tsps.	olive oil	10 mL
16	fresh, medium chanterelles (slice if too large)	16
12	Italian or Chinese plums, pitted and quartered	12
2 Tbsps.	brandy	25 mL
2 cups	lamb or beef stock	500 mL
1 Tbsp.	Dijon mustard	15 mL
1½ tsps.	fresh, chopped lemon thyme (second amount)	7 mL

Marinate the loin in the buttermilk with the rosemary and lemon thyme sprigs. Cover and refrigerate overnight.

The next day, discard the marinade and pat the loin dry with paper towels. Cut the loin into 18 slices (3 per person). Place the medallions (slices) between sheets of waxed paper and carefully flatten with a mallet.

Heat olive oil over high heat in a skillet. Sauté the medallions, browning the meat lightly on both sides, about 2-3 minutes. Keep it warm without cooking it further. Leave the burner on high. To the pan juices, add the chanterelles and plums. Sauté until the chanterelles are cooked, about 2-3 minutes. Add the brandy and flambé (light with a match), shaking the pan back and forth. Add the stock, mustard and lemon thyme and reduce until thickened. Arrange the medallions on heated plates and cover with the sauce.

Makes 6 servings.

Veal may be substituted for the fresh kid.

Savory Sauces

GARRISON HOUSE
Annapolis Royal, N.S.

Crème Fraîche

GARY BURROUGHS, *Innkeeper*
MARY COLTART, *Keeper of the Inn*
THE OBAN INN,
Niagara-on-the-Lake, Ontario

This is the classic soured cream which is used almost exclusively in French cooking. It is like yogurt in that it is left to ferment for a few hours, and one batch is the basis of the next.

1 cup	commercial sour cream	250 mL
1 cup	whipping cream	250 mL

Place the sour cream in a small bowl. With an electric beater at a low speed, gradually mix in the whipping cream, beating only until smooth. Pour the cream into a jar with a wide mouth and a tight-fitting lid. Cover and let it stand at room temperature until it is very thick, 8-12 hours. (Mary says that if she starts it after dinner, it has thickened by morning.) Stir lightly with a fork, cover and refrigerate at least 24 hours before using. When the cream is ready to use, it should be thick enough to dip out by the spoonful, like sour cream.

Makes 2 cups (500 mL).

Hot Mustard

GARY BURROUGHS,, *Innkeeper*
MARY COLTART, *Keeper of the Inn*
THE OBAN INN,
Niagara-on-the-Lake, Ontario

Mary serves this in a small bowl beside their pâté.

$\frac{1}{2}$ cup	dry mustard	125 mL
2 Tbsps.	flour	25 mL
3 Tbsps.	brown sugar	45 mL
$\frac{1}{3}$ cup	boiling water	75 mL
2 Tbsps.	cider vinegar	25 mL
3 Tbsps.	sherry	45 mL
1 tsp.	dried tarragon	5 mL

In a small bowl, stir together the mustard, flour and brown sugar. Slowly add the boiling water. Mix well until smooth. Cover and let stand for 30 minutes. Stir in the vinegar, sherry and tarragon. Pour into a covered jar. Date the jar and store in the refrigerator for a week before using.

Makes about 1 cup (250 mL).

GRAMMA'S HOUSE,
Port Saxon, Nova Scotia

Jean's Autumn Fruit Sauce

🐾🐾🐾

TED AND JEAN TURNER, *Innkeepers*
GRAMMA'S HOUSE,
Port Saxon, Nova Scotia

This delicious salt-free sauce is especially good with Baked Stuffed Pork Chops (p. 60).

$\frac{1}{2}$ cup	cider vinegar	125 mL
$\frac{1}{2}$ cup	brown sugar	125 mL
1 cup	raisins	250 mL
2	onions, peeled and chopped	2
4	apples, peeled and chopped	4
4	peaches, peeled and chopped	4
4	pears, peeled and chopped	4
6	whole cloves	6
1	cinnamon stick	1

Place the vinegar, sugar and raisins in a large kettle. Bring to a boil. Add the onions and fruit. Hang a tea ball containing cloves and cinnamon on the side of the kettle so that it enters the mixture, or tie the spices in a gauze bag. Simmer the sauce for about 1 hour or until fruit is soft. Remove the spices. Pour the sauce into a glass container and refrigerate.

Makes 3-4 cups (750 mL-1 L).

Dill Sauce

🐝🐝

ROBBIE AND SUE SHAW, *Innkeepers*
SHAW'S HOTEL,
Brackley Beach, Prince Edward Island

For many generations, the Shaws of Brackley Beach have been innkeepers. The original home, dating from 1866, can still be seen as part of the back of the lovely hotel which was expanded in the 1890s. Now the brother and sister team of Robbie and Sue Shaw have taken the reigns and the wonderful tradition continues with imagination and a *joie de vivre* only people who truly care about their guests can provide.

Sue reflects on her role as an innkeeper in these words: "You have to be a really giving type of person in this business. You just can't take all the time. I guess the best you can expect is to be successful. But what I really love is having people enjoy what I'm doing for them!

"There are no TVs and only one telephone in the lodge. It takes a day or so for some people to adjust, but they end up having a really good family experience. They discover each other, the kids aren't glued to the TV set and generally they head to the beach very early. We're up flipping eggs at sunrise."

1	egg, hard-cooked and mashed	1
1 cup	sour cream	250 mL
½ cup	plain yogurt	125 mL
1	green onion, minced	1
1 Tbsp.	lemon juice	15 mL
½ tsp.	salt	2 mL
⅛ tsp.	pepper	0.5 mL
	pinch granulated sugar	
1-2 Tbsps.	fresh dill weed	15-25 mL
	or	
1 Tbsp.	dried dill	15 mL
	green onions, pimentos, olives, watercress, lemon halves or wedges, cucumber slices, for garnish	

Combine the ingredients in the order given in a blender or food processor, or simply whisk them together. Store the sauce in the refrigerator. Serve this lovely Dill Sauce with The Little Inn's Pickerel Pâté (p. 17) or with any grilled or barbecued fish.

Makes about 1¾ cups (425 mL).

Sauce Citron Pour Anguille
(Lemon Sauce for Eel)

🐝🐝

CÉCILE AND EMILEEN MOREL, *Innkeepers*
MANOIR ST-ANDRÉ,
St-André, Québec

This simple sauce enhances any fish recipe. It's especially good with lobster!

$\frac{1}{3}$ cup	butter	75 mL
2 Tbsps.	chopped chives	25 mL
1 Tbsp.	lemon juice	15 mL
1 tsp.	lemon rind	5 mL
$\frac{1}{4}$ tsp.	salt	1 mL
$\frac{1}{4}$ tsp.	freshly ground pepper	1 mL

In a small pan, melt the butter. Add the chives, lemon juice and rind. Season with salt and pepper. Serve warm over grilled eel or fish.

Makes $\frac{1}{2}$ cup (125 mL).

Ginny's Wine Gravy

🐝🐝

JEAN AND PHIL CARDINAL, *Innkeepers*
THE BREADALBANE INN,
Fergus, Ontario

Usually I shy away from recipes that call for prepackaged ingredients. But the reputation of The Breadalbane and my own curiosity were too much. I tried this one, and it's great!

2 tsps.	Symington's Gravy Improver	10 mL
2 Tbsps.	powdered, mushroom soup	25 mL
$\frac{1}{2}$ cup	sherry or madeira	125 mL
$\frac{1}{4}$ cup	melted butter	50 mL
$\frac{1}{4}$ cup	water	50 mL

Combine the gravy mix with the soup mix. Using a rolling pin, crush the mixture finely. Add a little sherry to make a paste. In a saucepan over low heat, combine the gravy paste, melted butter, the remaining sherry and the water. Cook over low heat for 20 minutes, stirring often.

Makes about $\frac{3}{4}$ cup (175 mL).

Sooke Harbour House Chive and Watercress Sauce

🌸🌸🌸🌸🌸🌸🌸🌸🌸🌸🌸🌸🌸🌸🌸🌸🌸🌸🌸🌸🌸🌸🌸🌸🌸🌸🌸🌸🌸🌸🌸🌸🌸🌸🌸🌸

SINCLAIR AND FREDRICA PHILIP, *Innkeepers*
PIA CARROLL, *Chef*
SOOKE HARBOUR HOUSE,
Whiffen Spit Beach, Vancouver Island, B.C.

A special sauce for mild-tasting fish such as sole or cod.

¼ cup	dry white wine	50 mL
1 Tbsp.	finely minced shallots	15 mL
4 cups	fish stock	1 L
¾ cup	heavy cream (35%)	175 mL
1 Tbsp.	water	15 mL
½ cup	chopped chives	125 mL
⅓ cup	chopped watercress	75 mL
1 tsp.	unsalted butter	5 mL
3 Tbsps.	lemon juice	45 mL

In a small pan, bring the wine and shallots to a boil over high heat. Reduce heat and simmer until the shallots are tender and the wine is almost evaporated. Set aside.

In a large pot, bring the stock and cream to a boil. Cook, uncovered, until it has been reduced to a creamy consistency. Set aside.

In a blender or food processor, combine the water, chives, watercress and butter. Whirl together, then add the wine-shallot reduction and the stock-cream mixture. Process thoroughly. Stir in the lemon juice. *Makes about 2½-3 cups (625-750 mL).*

Derek's Shishkebab Marinade

🌸🌸🌸🌸🌸🌸🌸🌸🌸🌸🌸🌸🌸🌸🌸🌸🌸🌸🌸🌸🌸🌸🌸🌸🌸🌸🌸🌸🌸🌸🌸🌸🌸🌸🌸🌸

DEREK HILL AND BETSY JOHNSTON, *Innkeepers*
THE OLD NOTCH FARM INN,
Sutton, Québec

1½ cups	salad oil	375 mL
¾ cup	soy sauce	175 mL
¼ cup	Worcestershire sauce	50 mL
2 Tbsps.	dry mustard	25 mL
2 tsps.	salt	10 mL
1 Tbsp.	black pepper	15 mL
¼ cup	wine vinegar	50 mL
1 tsp.	dried parsley	5 mL
2 cloves	garlic, crushed	2 cloves
⅓ cup	lemon juice	75 mL

Put all the ingredients in the order given into a saucepan and bring to a boil. Simmer for 5 minutes. Store in glass jars in the refrigerator. *Makes 3½ cups (875 mL).*

Shishkebabs

Marinate steak for 24 hours before barbecuing. Thread pieces of meat onto long, metal skewers. On separate skewers, put mushrooms, green pepper chunks and cherry tomatoes. Brush with Derek's Marinade. Barbecue over hot coals. Derek uses maple wood.

Hollandaise Sauce

ꙮꙮꙮꙮꙮꙮꙮꙮꙮꙮꙮꙮꙮꙮꙮꙮꙮꙮꙮꙮꙮꙮꙮꙮꙮꙮꙮꙮꙮꙮꙮꙮꙮꙮꙮꙮꙮ

This is my own quick variation of the classic sauce. I like it because it requires very little attention and can be changed in so many ways.

½ cup	butter	125 mL
3	egg yolks	3
1½ Tbsps.	lemon juice	20 mL
2 tsps.	water	10 mL
¼ tsp.	salt	1 mL
	freshly ground white pepper, to taste	
½-1 tsp.	Dijon mustard	2-5 mL

Heat the butter in a small saucepan until it is bubbly but not browned. Put the egg yolks, lemon juice, water, salt, white pepper and mustard into the container of your blender or food processor. Blend on low speed for 5-10 seconds. While the machine is still running, pour the hot butter into the container in a slow, steady stream, until the blades are covered. Increase the speed to high and add the remaining butter. Serve immediately.

Makes 1 cup (250 mL).

Variations

Almond Hollandaise

Omit the mustard and add ¼ cup (50 mL) blanched almonds with the egg yolks. Whirl to finely chop the nuts and finish as above. Serve with fish or vegetables.

Caper Hollandaise

Add 2-3 Tbsps. (25-45 mL) drained capers to the completed sauce. Blend to chop slightly. Serve with grilled fish or chicken.

Mesa Creek Barbecue Sauce

DAVE AND LUCILLE GLAISTER, *Innkeepers*
MESA CREEK RANCH,
R.R. 1, Millarville, Alta.

Lucille says that she uses this sauce almost 365 days a year. She makes a big batch and seals it in sterilized jars.

1 15-oz.	bottle ketchup	1 520-g
1 10-oz.	bottle chili sauce	1 280-g
2 Tbsps.	liquid smoke*	25 mL
4 Tbsps.	salad oil	60 mL
$\frac{1}{4}$ cup	water	50 mL
$\frac{1}{4}$ cup	vinegar	50 mL
$\frac{1}{4}$ cup	brown sugar	50 mL
1	lemon, thinly sliced	1
	juice from a second lemon	
1	large onion, thinly sliced	1
1 tsp.	salt	5 mL
1 tsp.	dry mustard	5 mL
1 tsp.	paprika	5 mL

In a large saucepan, combine all the ingredients in the order given. Bring the sauce to a boil, stirring to prevent sticking. Ladle it into glass jars and seal. Store the jars in the refrigerator. This excellent sauce will keep for about 3 weeks. Use it on all kinds of beef dishes. Lucille even adds it to baked beans.

Makes about 4 cups (1 L).

*Available, bottled, in most supermarkets.

Vegetables

MESA CREEK RANCH
R.R. 1, Millarville, Alta.

P.E.I. Potatoes Romanoff

🌸🌸🌸🌸🌸🌸🌸🌸🌸🌸🌸🌸🌸🌸🌸🌸🌸🌸🌸🌸🌸🌸🌸🌸🌸🌸🌸🌸🌸🌸🌸🌸🌸🌸🌸🌸🌸🌸

CAPTAIN LARRY PECK, *Innkeeper*
VICTORIA VILLAGE INN,
Victoria-by-the-Sea, P.E.I.

From Canada's potato capital comes this super recipe.

5 lbs.	P.E.I. potatoes, peeled and quartered	2.25 kg
	water to cover	
$\frac{1}{4}$ cup	butter	50 mL
2	eggs, beaten	2
2 cups	cottage cheese	500 mL
2 cups	sour cream	500 mL
1 tsp.	salt	5 mL
$\frac{1}{2}$ tsp.	freshly ground pepper	2 mL
$\frac{1}{8}$ tsp.	garlic powder	0.5 mL
1 Tbsp.	dried parsley	15 mL
1 cup	grated, mild cheddar cheese	250 mL

In a large covered saucepan, cook the potatoes in the water until tender. Drain and mash with the butter. *Preheat the oven to 350°F. (180°C).* Beat in the eggs, cottage cheese, sour cream, salt and pepper, garlic powder and parsley. When creamy, spread in a well-buttered 9 in. x 13 in. (3.5 L) pan. Sprinkle with the cheese. Bake for 30 minutes or until the cheese is melted and golden. *Makes 8-10 servings.*

Cucumber with Dill Weed or Mint Flakes

Anne serves this frequently when her full days at the newspaper begin to overflow. It's a quick lift to a bland vegetable.

Peel a cucumber and remove the seeds. Slice it or cut balls out with a melon scoop. Cook gently in boiling, salted water. Place in a colander and cool under water. Drain. Reheat in butter mixed with dill weed or mint flakes, to taste. (Anne Wanstall and Aileen Adams, Bayberry House, Granville Ferry, Nova Scotia)

Fire-baked Onions and Roasted Potatoes

Serve this recipe with St. Lawrence Fried Fish (p. 90) as a part of a Thousand Islands shore dinner.

Remove the stem and root end — but do not peel — one medium-sized cooking onion per person. Scrub one or two medium potatoes per serving. Wrap individually in heavy foil and throw them into the fire among some of the hot glowing coals, or roast them on the grill next to the frying pan. Turn them often with tongs. When soft to the touch, remove them and keep them warm. Each guest unwraps his own and butters them. Pass grated, old cheddar cheese to be sprinkled on the onions. (Pieter Bergin, The Amaryllis, Rockport, Ontario)

&&&&&&&&&&&&&&&&&&&&&&&&&&&&&&&&&&&&&&&&&&&&

GARY BURROUGHS, *Innkeeper*
MARY COLTART, *Keeper of the Inn*
THE OBAN INN,
Niagara-on-the-Lake, Ontario

8	medium potatoes	8
3	medium leeks	3
2 Tbsps.	butter	25 mL
1 clove	garlic, crushed	1 clove
2 cups	grated Swiss cheese	500 mL
3	eggs	3
1⅓ cups	milk	325 mL
1 tsp.	salt	5 mL
¼ tsp.	freshly ground black pepper	1 mL
½ tsp.	grated nutmeg	2 mL
¼ cup	grated Swiss cheese (second amount)	50 mL

Peel the potatoes and cook in boiling, salted water until tender. Drain, cool and cut into slices about ⅛ in. (3 mm) thick. Slice the leeks lengthwise and wash thoroughly, being careful to remove all the sand. Trim the roots and most of the green off. Cut into thin slices. Heat the butter in a large, heavy skillet over medium heat and add the garlic and the leeks. Turn heat to low and stir until leeks are tender, about 10 minutes.

Preheat the oven to 375°F. (190°C). Butter a 2-qt. (2 L) casserole. Layer in it one-third of the potatoes, one-half of the leeks and 1 cup of the cheese. Repeat, ending with the final one-third of the potatoes. Beat together the eggs, milk, salt, pepper and nutmeg. Pour over the layers. Sprinkle with cheese. Bake until set and lightly browned on top, about 25 minutes.

Makes 8 servings.

Ranch Style Onions for Hot Dogs, Hamburgers and Steak Sandwiches

Slice 6-8 medium onions into vertical quarters; then slice thinly lengthwise. Heat 2-3 Tbsps. (25-45 mL) oil in an electric frying pan or skillet. Add the onions and toss gently until they are all coated with oil. Sprinkle in 1 Tbsp. (15 mL) paprika, ¼ tsp. (1 mL) ground cumin, salt and pepper. Cover and braise slowly on very low heat, adding water if necessary. Cook for about 10 minutes. Add additional seasoning if desired. (Mary Bond, Black Cat Guest Ranch, Hinton, Alberta)

MacNeill Manor,
Chester, Nova Scotia

Armadillo Potatoes

🐾🐾🐾

Doris Hall and George Evans, *Innkeepers*
MacNeill Manor,
Chester, Nova Scotia

Another winner from this small, very busy inn!

8-10	medium-sized potatoes	8-10
$\frac{1}{4}$-$\frac{1}{2}$ cup	melted butter	50-125 mL
1 clove	garlic, minced	1 clove
1 Tbsp.	grated parmesan cheese	15 mL
1 tsp.	oregano	5 mL
	sour cream	
	chives, minced	

Preheat oven to 425°F. (220°C). Wash and scrub the potatoes. Score the top of each potato with a series of shallow, parallel slashes. Place them in a lightly oiled baking dish and bake in the oven. In a small bowl, mix the melted butter, garlic, parmesan cheese and oregano. While the potatoes are baking, brush with small amounts of the butter mixture. Bake for 45 minutes or until they are done when tested with a fork. Serve with sour cream and chives. *Serves 8-10.*

Cinnamon-Honeyed Carrots

🐾🐾🐾

Pieter Bergin and Janet Rodier, *Innkeepers*
The Amaryllis,
Rockport, Ontario

The Amaryllis is a Victorian houseboat, and she has no pretentions. Floating snuggly beside her own island in the river, she does have a library full of old books, comfortable chairs, cozy, albeit a bit saggy beds and the most hospitable host on this part of the St. Lawrence River. The word *gentleman* was coined for Pieter. An environmentalist and one-time vegetarian, he is a superb cook. Although he now teaches skiing at a European Club Med in the wintertime and leads a typical bachelor's carefree life, he has also worked for such renowned agencies as UNESCO. His roots run deeply through the Frontenac Axis's granite islands. Under the oak, amongst the blueberries and wintergreen, he calls himself at home in *"mon pays"* — "my land."

Serve this as a part of your Thousand Islands Shore Dinner (p. 90) or simply as a wonderful way of jazzing up fresh carrots.

3-4 cups	sliced carrot coins	750 mL-1 L
2 Tbsps.	butter or oil	25 mL
2 Tbsps.	honey	25 mL
$\frac{1}{4}$ tsp.	cinnamon	1 mL
$\frac{1}{2}$ tsp.	vanilla	2 mL
1 Tbsp.	water	15 mL

Steam the carrots until tender. Heat the butter in a heavy skillet over low heat. Add the carrots and toss to coat with the butter. In a small bowl, stir together the honey, cinnamon, vanilla and water. Pour this mixture over the carrots, mixing well. Cover and keep warm until serving.

Makes 6 servings.

Champignons Farcis
(Stuffed Mushrooms)

CÉCILE AND EMILEEN MOREL, *Innkeepers*
MANOIR ST-ANDRÉ,
St-André, Québec

The Morels use freshly smoked St. Lawrence eel from their own smoke-house in this recipe.

$\frac{1}{3}$ cup	flaked, smoked eel	75 mL
$\frac{1}{3}$ cup	bread crumbs	75 mL
1 clove	garlic, minced	1 clove
1 Tbsp.	melted butter	15 mL
12	large mushrooms	12
	salt and freshly ground pepper, to taste	
	chopped parsley	

Preheat the oven to 400°F. (200°C). In a small bowl mix the eel, crumbs, garlic and butter. Remove the stems from the mushrooms and dice finely. Add to the eel stuffing. Season with salt, freshly ground pepper and chopped parsley. Mound the stuffing into the hollow of each mushroom. Place on a lightly greased baking sheet. Bake 10 minutes or until the crumbs are golden brown.

Makes 4-6 servings as a side dish or appetizer.

Tofu or Tempeh Stroganoff

🐾🐾

RESA LENT, *Innkeeper*
THE DESERT ROSE INN AND CAFÉ,
Elora, Ontario

Tofu, also known as bean cake, is what a nutritionist might call a "super food." It is very high in protein and calcium and has no cholesterol. Tempeh is simply a stronger-flavored tofu.

1 lb.	tofu or tempeh	450 g
½ cup	tamari *or* soy sauce	125 mL
3 cloves	garlic, minced	3 cloves
1 tsp.	ground cumin	5 mL
	salt and freshly ground pepper, to taste	
2 Tbsps.	vegetable oil	25 mL
1	medium onion, thinly sliced	1
4 cups	sliced mushrooms	1 L
¼ tsp.	ground nutmeg	1 mL
¼ tsp.	cinnamon	1 mL
¼ cup	dry white wine	50 mL
1 cup	plain yogurt (or a mixture of yogurt and sour cream)	250 mL

Cut the tofu or tempeh into small cubes. Combine with soy sauce, garlic, cumin, salt and pepper. Stir gently and allow to marinate for 30 minutes. In a large, heavy pot, heat the oil and sauté the onions until soft. Add the mushrooms. Drain the tofu, reserving the marinade. Add to the onion mixture. Season with nutmeg and cinnamon. Cook, covered, on low heat for 15 minutes. Add marinade, if necessary, to keep the mixture moist. Gently stir in the wine and yogurt. Taste and correct seasonings if necessary. Reheat without boiling. Serve over your choice of noodles. Resa prefers fettucine or rice.

Makes 6 servings.

Small Touches   Green Beans with Savory

🐾🐾

Another of Anne's quickies — this recipe will add the finishing touch to a meal. Cook tender, green beans gently in chicken stock. Drain. Sprinkle with summer savory and mix in butter to taste. (Anne Wanstall and Aileen Adams, Bayberry House, Granville Ferry, Nova Scotia)

Marmalades, Jellies and Relishes

THE WHITMAN INN
Caledonia, Nova Scotia

Cora's Chow

Bruce and Nancy Gurnham, *Innkeepers*
The Whitman Inn,
Kempt, Queen's County, N.S.

Nancy writes: "Cora was the lady for whom our house was built. She lived here until her death 12 years before we bought it. The house was vacant and, we think, waiting for us until we found it in 1981. Cora loved this place as much as I do. We care about flowers and trees. I even have her recipe cigar box. This is known as Cora's Chow here in Kempt. It has a 'zing' to it you don't usually find in chow. The recipe is figured on the basis of 4 quarts ($4\frac{1}{2}$ L); increase as desired. I got this recipe from Miriam DeLong, Cora's daughter-in-law and my Canadian mom."

4 qts.	vegetables, cut to desired size (cauliflower, onions, green and red peppers, green tomatoes, etc.)	4.5 L
1 cup	pickling salt	250 mL

Sprinkle the vegetables with salt and cover with boiling water. Allow them to sit overnight. In the morning, drain and cover them with hot water. Heat through, but do *not* boil. Drain again.

Prepare the Pickling Solution as follows:

4 cups	cider vinegar	1 L
5 cups	brown sugar*	1.25 L
3 tsps.	cinnamon	15 mL
$1\frac{1}{2}$ tsps.	whole cloves	7 mL
3 tsps.	whole allspice	15 mL
4 oz.	pkg. pickling spice	115 g

In a separate saucepan, heat together the vinegar and sugar. Divide the spices into 3 cheesecloth bags and add these to the vinegar and brown sugar. Boil the syrup. Add the drained vegetables and simmer for 15 minutes. Remove the spice bags and seal the chow in sterilized jars. *Makes 4 quarts (4.5 L).*

For a less sweet chow, use 4 cups (1 L) brown sugar.

Red Onion Marmalade

Lisa Whitely, *Innkeeper*
Mark Bussieres, *Chef*
The Benmiller Inn,
R.R. 4, Goderich, Ont.

More like a chutney than a marmalade, Red Onion Marmalade is delicious with roasted meats or grilled sausages. The Benmiller serves it with their pâté.

8 cups	sliced, red onions	2 L
4 cups	sliced, MacIntosh apples, cored and peeled	1 L
2 Tbsps.	butter	25 mL
3 Tbsps.	granulated sugar	45 mL
$1\frac{1}{2}$ tsps.	salt	7 mL
$\frac{1}{2}$ tsp.	ground cloves	2 mL
$\frac{1}{2}$ tsp.	cinnamon	2 mL
$\frac{1}{3}$ cup	cider vinegar	75 mL
$\frac{1}{2}$ cup	apple cider	125 mL
2 Tbsps.	fancy molasses (not blackstrap)	25 mL

To prepare the onions, peel them and slice them lengthwise into fairly thick strips. Peel and slice the apples as you would for a pie.

In a heavy covered saucepan, combine the onions and butter. Cover and steam on low heat for 10 minutes. Add the sugar, salt, cloves, cinnamon, vinegar, apple cider and molasses. Continue cooking until the onions are quite soft, about 20-25 minutes. Add the apples and cook for another 10 minutes, until they begin to break up. Remove from the heat and ladle into hot, sterilized glass jars. Seal and store in a cool, dark place.

Makes approximately 3 pint (3 500-mL) jars.

Rhubarb Relish

LESLIE LANGILLE, *Innkeeper*
BOSCAWEN INN,
Lunenburg, Nova Scotia

8 cups	finely chopped onions	2 L
4 cups	boiling water	1 L
8 cups	diced rhubarb	2 L
3 cups	cider vinegar	750 mL
5 cups	granulated sugar*	1.25 L
2 tsps.	salt	10 mL
1 tsp.	black pepper	5 mL
2 tsps.	ground cloves	10 mL
2 tsps.	cinnamon	10 mL

Scald the cut-up onions in the boiling water. Drain and set the onions aside. To help prevent sticking, rub the bottom of a large kettle with a good shortening before adding the ingredients. Combine all the ingredients in the kettle. Cook until quite thick. Stir to keep from sticking. Store in sterilized jars. This is great with fish or pork.

Makes 4-5 pint (4-5 500-mL) jars.

*More sugar may be needed if rhubarb is particularly sour.

Hot Apple Chutney

DEBORAH HERTZBERG, *Innkeeper*
DEBORAH'S,
Sooke, Vancouver Island, B.C.

4 oz.	fresh ginger root	115 g
4 cups	malt vinegar	1 L
4 lbs.	demerara sugar	1.8 kg
$\frac{1}{2}$ lb.	dark raisins	225 g
2 Tbsps.	salt	25 mL
1 oz.	dried chili powder	28 g
1 tsp.	cayenne pepper	5 mL
2 oz.	garlic (two full bulbs)	56 g
4 lbs.	tart, crisp apples, peeled, cored and diced finely	1.8 kg

Peel the ginger root and dice coarsely. Blend with some of the vinegar. In a large preserving kettle, make a syrup of the remaining vinegar and sugar. Add the ginger and vinegar, raisins and seasonings. Bring to a rolling boil, then add the apples. Cook, uncovered, over medium heat until dark colored and soft, stirring occasionally. Leave overnight. Next morning, reheat to boiling, stirring constantly. Cook for 5-10 minutes longer. Pour into sterilized jars. Seal with melted paraffin wax. *Makes 10 4-oz. (125-mL) jars.*

Bread-and-Butter Pickles

ISOBEL AND DAN MACAULAY, *Innkeepers*
INVERARY INN,
Baddeck, Nova Scotia

16 cups	cucumbers, sliced, not peeled	4 L
8	onions, sliced	8
$\frac{1}{3}$ cup	coarse pickling salt	75 mL
5 cups	granulated sugar	1.25 mL
3 cups	white vinegar	750 mL
$1\frac{1}{2}$ tsps.	turmeric	7 mL
$1\frac{1}{2}$ tsps.	celery seed	7 mL
3 tsps.	mustard seed	15 mL

Place the cucumbers and onions in a large kettle and sprinkle them with salt. Leave them for 3 hours or overnight. Drain off the brine and rinse the vegetables once. In another kettle, bring the sugar, vinegar and spices (tied in a cheesecloth bag) to a boil; boil for 8-10 minutes. Pour this mixture over the vegetables. Bring this to a boil, stirring occasionally for uniform cooking. Ladle into sterilized jars, seal and store in a cool, dark place. *Makes 5 pint (500-mL) jars.*

Seville Orange Marmalade

DEBORAH HERTZBERG, *Innkeeper*
DEBORAH'S,
Sooke, Vancouver Island, B.C.

A true Seville marmalade — bittersweet and very British.

8 cups	water	2 L
2 lbs.	Seville oranges (about 7 or 8)	900 g
2	lemons	2
8 cups	granulated sugar	2 L

In a large covered kettle, bring the water, whole oranges and lemons to a boil. Simmer, covered, for about 1-1½ hours or until the fruit can be pierced easily with a knife. Remove the fruit to a separate dish to cool, leaving the juice in the kettle. Cut the fruit into quarters or eighths. Remove the seeds and add them to the juice. Boil the seeds and juice for 10 minutes. Strain; then discard the seeds. Cut the fruit up finely, in small chunks or thin slices. Add to the juice. Bring the mixture to a boil, uncovered, then add the sugar. Boil hard for 25-30 minutes, until the jelly stage has been reached.* Stir frequently to keep from sticking or boiling over. Pour into sterilized jars and seal with melted paraffin wax.

Makes 6-8 pint (500-mL) jars.

Pumpkin Marmalade

JULIE SIMMONS, *Innkeeper*
THE SILVER FOX INN,
Summerside, P.E.I.

9 cups	prepared diced pumpkin*	2.25 L
2	large oranges, seeded and ground	2
1	lemon, seeded and ground	1
4 cups	granulated sugar	1 L

Place the diced pumpkin, ground oranges and lemon with the sugar in a large, open kettle. Let these ingredients sit overnight to draw out the juices. In the morning, place on high heat and boil hard for about 10 minutes. Lower heat to medium and continue cooking until thickened to desired consistency, about 45 minutes. Stir frequently to prevent sticking. Pack in sterile jars, pressing down with a spoon to remove air bubbles. Seal. Store in a cool, dark place.

Makes approximately 4 pint (500-mL) jars.

* *To prepare the pumpkin, peel it, remove the seeds and dice it into ¼ in. (0.5 cm) cubes.*

Spiced Grape Jelly

உ உ

JULIE SIMMONS, *Innkeeper*
THE SILVER FOX INN,
Summerside, P.E.I.

Silver foxes brought brief but massive wealth to the island in the early 1900s. In 1911, a single pelt sold for $20,000. Charlie Dalton, who began as a poor trapper in the 1880s, was eventually made lieutenant governor, partly because of his efforts in the silver fox industry.

$6\frac{1}{2}$ cups	granulated sugar	1.6 L
$\frac{1}{4}$ tsp.	ground cinnamon	1 mL
$\frac{1}{4}$ tsp.	ground cloves	1 mL
$\frac{1}{4}$ tsp.	ground allspice	1 mL
3 cups	water	750 mL
1 12-oz.	frozen grape juice	1 341-mL
can	concentrate, thawed	can
1	bottle liquid pectin	1

Sterilize 10 8-oz. (250 mL) jelly jars and lids. Leave them in simmering water until ready to fill.

In a large kettle, combine the sugar and spices. Stir in the water. Cook, stirring constantly, over high heat to dissolve the sugar. Bring to a full rolling boil, stirring constantly. Boil hard 1 minute, stirring. Stir in the thawed concentrate and the pectin. Return to a full rolling boil for 1 minute. Remove from the heat and skim with a large spoon. Ladle into the hot jelly jars.

Cover immediately with melted paraffin wax, or if you are using Mason type jars, simply seal with the lids. When the wax has hardened, put on the lids.

Makes ten 8-oz. (250-mL) jars.

*JELLY TEST Dip a metal spoon into the boiling hot syrup. Lift the spoon and let the mixture run off the edge of the spoon. When two drops form, then flow together into a sheet, the jelly is done. Remove it from the heat immediately.

Muffins, Biscuits, Quick Breads and Granola

SILVER FOX INN
Summerside, P.E.I.

THE RAM'S HEAD INN,
Rossland, British Columbia

Puffy French Toast

DOREEN AND DAVE BUTLER, *Innkeepers*
THE RAM'S HEAD INN,
Rossland, British Columbia

The cooking aromas drift from the inn's kitchen before an exciting day of downhill skiing. New snow has fallen, sunlight slants through the dense pine forest and 2,800-foot mountains silently challenge us to conquer them. And after a breakfast like this one we all need the exercise!

1 cup	all-purpose flour	250 mL
1½ tsps.	baking powder	7 mL
½ tsp.	salt	2 mL
1 cup	milk	250 mL
2	eggs	2
8 slices	good, wholesome bread (We like Anadama, p. 150.) good-quality cooking oil, as needed	8

In a medium-sized bowl, stir together the flour, baking powder and salt. Mix in the milk and eggs, stirring until the batter is smooth. Cut the bread slices in half. In a large frying pan, heat ½ in. (1 cm) of oil until hot. Dip the bread into the batter. Fry until golden on both sides. Drain on paper towels. Sprinkle with icing sugar before serving. Garnish with sliced oranges or top with a fruit that is in season.

Doreen makes a delicious syrup by combining:

¼ cup	Grand Marnier	50 mL
1 cup	maple syrup	250 mL

Makes 6-8 servings.

Whitman Inn Baking Mix

BRUCE AND NANCY GURNHAM, *Innkeepers*
THE WHITMAN INN,
Kempt, Queen's County, N.S.

This type of recipe is often the secret of the better-organized inns. They use a basic formula on which they can expand for many dishes and baked goods.

3 cups	white, unbleached, steel-ground flour	750 mL
$1\frac{1}{2}$ Tbsps.	baking powder	20 mL
1 tsp.	salt	5 mL
$\frac{3}{4}$ cup	butter (margarine only if you must)	175 mL

Blend until well mixed in a food processor. Make multiple batches in just minutes and store, sealed, on the shelf for 2-3 weeks or in the refrigerator indefinitely. Great for pancakes, muffins and biscuits. Use in any of the following recipes.

Makes $3\frac{1}{2}$ cups (825 mL) baking mix.

Whitman Inn Berry Muffins

BRUCE AND NANCY GURNHAM, *Innkeepers*
THE WHITMAN INN,
Kempt, Queen's County, N.S.

6 cups	Whitman Inn baking mix	1.5 mL
$1\frac{1}{3}$ cups	granulated sugar	325 mL
1 tsp.	cinnamon	5 mL
2 cups	milk	500 mL
2	eggs	2
2 cups	wild, Nova Scotia blueberries or low-bush cranberries *	500 mL

Preheat the oven to 425°F. (220°C). Combine the dry ingredients and set aside. Combine the milk and the eggs and stir into the dry mixture. Blend well. Fold in the blueberries and combine to distribute them throughout the batter. Do not over-mix at this point. Spoon into greased muffin tins and bake for 18-20 minutes.

Makes 2 dozen large muffins.

If using low-bush cranberries, omit cinnamon and increase sugar to $2\frac{1}{2}$ cups (625 mL).

Refrigerator Bran Muffins

❀❀❀

P.M. "CHARLIE" HOLGATE, *Innkeeper*
CAMELOT INN,
Musquodoboit Harbour, N.S.

These muffins are a godsend to Charlie, who is not only an innkeeper but a devoted and helpful friend to many.

5 cups	natural bran	1.25 L
2 cups	boiling water	500 mL
$1\frac{1}{2}$ cups	shortening, (room temperature)	375 mL
3 cups	granulated sugar	750 mL
4	eggs	4
5 cups	sifted all-purpose flour	1.25 L
3 Tbsps.	baking soda	45 mL
1 Tbsp.	salt	15 mL
1 quart	buttermilk	1 L
3 cups	bran flakes	750 mL
2-3 cups	raisins or chopped dates	500-750 mL

Combine the bran and boiling water (mixture is fairly dry). Beat the shortening, sugar and eggs; mix into the bran and cool. Sift the flour before measuring, then sift again with the soda and salt. Add to the bran mixture alternately with buttermilk, combining after each addition. Fold in the bran flakes and fruit. Turn the batter into a large bowl or jars. Cover and refrigerate. Leave at least one day before using. Keeps up to 1 month. To bake, scoop batter into well-greased muffin pans and fill three-quarters full. Bake at 375°F. (190°C) for 20-30 minutes, depending upon the size of the pans. *Makes 4-6 dozen.*

Dundee Bran Muffins

❀❀❀

DON, MARY AND JUDY CLINTON, *Innkeepers*
THE DUNDEE ARMS INN,
Charlottetown, P.E.I.

Buttermilk muffins at their best!

$\frac{1}{3}$ cup	all-bran	75 mL
$\frac{1}{3}$ cup	boiling water	75 mL
$\frac{1}{3}$ cup	shortening, melted	75 mL
$\frac{3}{4}$ cup	brown sugar	175 mL
2	eggs, beaten	2

1½ cups	buttermilk	375 mL
2 cups	all-purpose flour	500 mL
2 tsps.	baking soda	10 mL
1 tsp.	salt	5 mL
1¾ cups	bran flakes	425 mL
1 cup	raisins (optional)	250 mL

Preheat the oven to 400°F. (200°C). In a small bowl, soften the all-bran in the boiling water. Cream together the shortening and the brown sugar in a large mixing bowl. Add the beaten eggs and buttermilk. Mix well. Add the softened all-bran, stirring well. Stir together the flour, soda and salt. Add to the liquid ingredients. Finally, fold in the bran flakes and raisins. Do not over-mix.* Bake in greased muffin tins for 20 minutes. Cool on rack.

Makes about 1½ dozen.

Mixture can be refrigerated until ready to use.

Breakfast Muffins

GERALD AND HELEN SHAW, *Innkeepers*
NORTHERN WILDERNESS LODGE,
Plaster Rock, New Brunswick

This basic muffin recipe lends itself to numerous variations. Simply add two cups (500 mL) of your favorite fruit: blueberries, raspberries, chopped apple, peaches or whatever your heart desires.

¾ cup	all-purpose flour	175 mL
1½ cups	whole wheat flour	375 mL
1 tsp.	salt	5 mL
1 tsp.	baking powder	5 mL
1 tsp.	baking soda	5 mL
1 Tbsp.	granulated sugar	15 mL
½ cup	vegetable oil	125 mL
½ cup	liquid honey	125 mL
1 cup	buttermilk *or* sour milk	250 mL
1	egg, beaten	1

Preheat oven to 400°F. (200°C). In a large bowl, combine the flours, salt, baking powder, baking soda and sugar. In a separate bowl, whisk together the oil, honey, buttermilk and egg. Pour into the dry ingredients, stirring until moistened. Fill well-greased muffin tins two-thirds full. Bake for 20 minutes.

Makes 12-15 muffins.

Oatmeal Muffins

🐾🐾🐾

GORDON AND EVELYN BURNHAM, *Innkeepers*
WESTWAY INN,
Plympton, Digby County, N.S.

½ cup	brown sugar, packed	125 mL
⅓ cup	shortening	75 mL
1	egg	1
1 cup	buttermilk	250 mL
1 cup	quick-cooking oats	250 mL
1 cup	all-purpose flour	250 mL
1 tsp.	baking powder	5 mL
1 tsp.	salt	5 mL
½ tsp.	baking soda	2 mL
½ cup	raisins	125 mL

Preheat the oven to 400°F. (200°C). Cream together the brown sugar and shortening; add the beaten egg and buttermilk. Stir together the dry ingredients and add to the sugar-shortening mixture, stirring just until the flour is moistened. Add the raisins. The batter should be slightly lumpy. Fill greased muffin tins about two-thirds full. Bake for 20-25 minutes. *Makes 12 muffins.*

Fruit Muffins

🐾🐾🐾

RICHARD HILL AND RON FRIEND, *Innkeepers*
YELLOW POINT LODGE,
Ladysmith, Vancouver Island, B.C.

A versatile treat!

3 cups	all-purpose flour	750 mL
1 cup	granulated sugar	250 mL
4 tsps.	baking powder	20 mL
1 tsp.	salt	5 mL
½ cup	butter or margarine	125 mL
2	eggs	2
1 cup	milk	250 mL
2 cups	blueberries *or* raspberries *or* blackberries *or* other fruit	500 mL

Preheat the oven to 400°F. (200°C). In a large bowl, stir the dry ingredients together. Cut in the butter or margarine with a pastry blender or two knives. Beat the eggs into the milk and add to the dry mixture, mixing just until moist. Add the fruit. Fill well-greased muffin tins two-thirds full. Bake 20-30 minutes.

Makes 12 jumbo-sized muffins.

BLACK CAT GUEST RANCH,
Hinton, Alberta

Crustless Breakfast Quiche

😈😈😈😈😈😈😈😈😈😈😈😈😈😈😈😈😈😈😈😈😈😈😈😈😈😈😈😈😈😈😈😈😈😈😈😈😈

MARY AND JERRY BOND,
BLACK CAT GUEST RANCH,
Hinton, Alberta

¼ lb.	salt pork, bacon or ham	115 g
¾ cup	all-purpose flour	175 mL
¼ tsp.	salt	1 mL
¼ tsp.	baking soda	1 mL
2 cups	milk	500 mL
6	eggs	6
4	green onions, minced	4
¼ cup	chopped green pepper	50 mL
6	mushrooms, sliced	6
½ cup	grated cheddar or Swiss cheese	125 mL

Preheat the oven to 400°F. (200°C). Cut the pork into ½ in. (1 cm) pieces and place in 2 heavy cast-iron frying pans. Bake in the oven until crispy, 10-15 minutes. Stir together the flour and salt in a large bowl. Dissolve the baking soda in the milk, then whisk into the flour. Beat in the eggs, one at a time, combining thoroughly. In a small bowl, toss together the onions, green pepper, mushrooms and cheese. Pour the egg mixture into the hot pans when the pork is crisp. Top with the vegetable-cheese mixture. Return to the oven and continue to bake at 400°F. (200°C) for about 30 minutes, or until a knife comes out clean when inserted in the center. *Makes 6-8 servings.*

Small Touches   *Pieto's French Toast*

😈😈😈😈😈😈😈😈😈😈😈😈😈😈😈😈😈😈😈😈😈😈😈😈😈😈😈😈😈😈😈😈😈😈😈😈

Dip thin slices of dark, rye bread into a mixture of egg and milk. Fry them in butter or oil until golden and top with fresh blueberries. Pour a little maple syrup over each serving and pass cream as well. The final touch is done at the table. Light a small ladle full of Grand Marnier and pour it, still flaming, over each dessert. (Pieter Bergin, The Amaryllis, Rockport, Ontario)

Summer Breakfast Pancakes Small Touches

Over each serving of pancakes, pour a little maple syrup, sprinkle with fresh, wild raspberries and let your guests help themselves to rich farm cream. (Mary Bond, Black Cat Guest Ranch, Hinton, Alberta)

Tobique Pancakes

GERALD AND HELEN SHAW, *Innkeepers*
NORTHERN WILDERNESS LODGE,
Plaster Rock, New Brunswick

The Tobique River flows through the mountains of northern New Brunswick and is famous for its excellent salmon fishing. Numerous trout streams also abound. Gerald makes these pancakes "the size of bread and butter plates."

2 cups	all-purpose flour	500 mL
$\frac{1}{4}$ cup	granulated sugar	50 mL
$4\frac{1}{2}$ tsps.	baking powder	22 mL
1 tsp.	salt	5 mL
2	eggs, lightly beaten	2
2 cups	milk	500 mL
$\frac{1}{4}$ cup	melted butter or margarine	50 mL
2-3 Tbsps.	oil or shortening for frying	25-45 mL

Sift or stir together the flour, sugar, baking powder and salt in a large mixing bowl. Combine the eggs, milk and butter. Add to the dry ingredients, whisking together to just combine the ingredients, leaving no dry areas.

Heat some of the oil in a heavy skillet. Fry the pancakes until bubbles break all over the surface. Flip and continue to cook until golden on the under side.

Serves 4-6 hungry fishermen.

Blueberry Pancake Syrup Small Touches

Combine 2 cups (500 mL) blueberries, 1 cup (250 mL) granulated sugar and $\frac{1}{2}$ cup (125 mL) water in a saucepan. Boil until the berries are soft, then put them through a sieve or food mill. Seal in a pint jar (500 mL). Use over pancakes, waffles or biscuits. (Rosalie Washington, Gail and Bryant Jeeves, Mackintosh Lodge, Yukon)

Whitman Inn Pancakes

✿✿✿

BRUCE AND NANCY GURNHAM, *Innkeepers*
THE WHITMAN INN,
Kempt, Queen's County, N.S.

3 cups	Whitman Inn baking mix	750 mL
$\frac{1}{4}$ cup	granulated sugar	50 mL
4	eggs, well beaten	4
$1\frac{1}{3}$-$1\frac{1}{2}$ cups	milk, to reach desired thickness	325-375 mL

In a large mixing bowl, stir together the baking mix and sugar. Combine the eggs and milk and add to the dry ingredients. Mix only until no dry spots remain. Cook on a greased skillet. Flip when the top is covered with bubbles. Continue to fry until golden.

Makes 4-6 servings.

Queen's County Scrambled Eggs

✿✿✿

BRUCE AND NANCY GURNHAM, *Innkeepers*
THE WHITMAN INN,
Kempt, Queen's County, N.S.

1 Tbsp.	butter, in slivers	15 mL
1-2	chopped Egyptian onions (winter onions)	1-2
4	eggs, well beaten	4
1 tsp.	minced parsley generous pinch of summer savory or a minuscule pinch of winter savory	5 mL
2 Tbsps.	cold water	25 mL
$\frac{1}{2}$ tsp.	salt	2 mL

In a non-stick skillet, melt the butter. Sauté the onions lightly. Whisk together the eggs, parsley, summer savory, cold water and salt. Pour into the skillet and stir over medium heat until the eggs are set.

Makes 2-3 servings.

Basic Quick Bread Mix

🦋🦋🦋

GORDON AND EVELYN BURNHAM, *Innkeepers*
WESTWAY INN,
Plympton, Digby County, N.S.

2¼ cups	all-purpose flour	550 mL
2¼ cups	whole wheat flour	550 mL
¾ tsp.	salt	3 mL
2 Tbsps.	baking powder	25 mL
1 cup	shortening	250 mL

Blend the ingredients in a food processor until fine. Or cut the shortening into the sifted, dry ingredients with a pastry cutter, then rub lightly between the hands until it reaches the consistency of fine corn meal. Use in any of the following recipes.

Biscuits

3 cups	Basic Quick Bread Mix	750 mL
¾ cup	milk	175 mL

Preheat the oven to 450°F. (230°C). Put the mix into a bowl; make a well in the middle. Add the milk and stir with a fork. Turn out onto a floured board. Knead 6 times. Roll to ½ in. (1.5 cm) thickness and cut into 2 in. (5 cm) rounds. Place on a greased baking sheet and bake for 15 minutes.

Makes 12-18 biscuits.

Fruit-Filled Coffeecake

This rich, sweet coffeecake could easily be used as a dessert.

2 cups	Basic Quick Bread Mix	500 mL
3 Tbsps.	granulated sugar	45 mL
1	egg, beaten	1
½ cup	milk	125 ml
⅔ cup	marmalade *or* apricot *or* berry jam	150 mL
¼ cup	brown sugar	50 mL
½ cup	raisins	125 mL
¼ tsp.	cinnamon	1 mL

Preheat the oven to 350°F. (180°C). Combine the basic mix and granulated sugar. Stir in the egg and milk. Add the liquid to the dry ingredients and mix thoroughly. Spread half of the dough in a well-greased 8 in. (2 L) pan. Spread the marmalade or jam on the dough. Mix the brown sugar, raisins and cinnamon. Sprinkle on top of the marmalade. Drop remaining dough by spoonfuls around edge of pan. Bake for 40 minutes. Remove from the oven and, with a sharp knife, loosen the edges. Slice and serve warm from the pan or invert the coffeecake onto a serving plate.

Makes 4 servings.

Small Touches   Maple Butter

Blend 1 lb. (450 g) softened butter with $\frac{1}{2}$ cup (125 mL) strong maple syrup. Serve on fresh, hot muffins or biscuits. (Ted and Jean Turner, Gramma's House, Port Saxon, Nova Scotia)

Banana Bread

BRUCE AND NANCY GURNHAM, *Innkeepers*
THE WHITMAN INN,
Kempt, Queen's County, N.S.

This is an excellent and versatile recipe. Vary it by adding nuts or raisins; it can even be made into muffins.

4	large, very ripe bananas	4
1	egg	1
1 cup	granulated sugar	250 mL
3 Tbsps.	cooking oil or melted butter	45 mL
2 cups	all-purpose flour	500 mL
1 tsp.	baking powder	5 mL
1 tsp.	baking soda	5 mL
$\frac{1}{2}$ tsp.	salt	2 mL

Preheat the oven to 350°F. (180°C). Mash the bananas well. Beat the egg, sugar and oil together. Stir into the mashed bananas and beat well. Sift the dry ingredients together and add them to the batter. Mix well. Pour into a greased 9 in. x 5 in. x $2\frac{1}{2}$ in. (2 L) loaf pan and bake for about 1 hour, or until a testing needle comes out clean. This freezes very well and tastes even better after being frozen. Serve chilled, thinly sliced, with butter.

Makes 1 loaf.

Gerald's Biscuits

🐾🐾

GERALD AND HELEN SHAW, *Innkeepers*
NORTHERN WILDERNESS LODGE,
Plaster Rock, New Brunswick

A delicious home-style biscuit!

2 cups	all-purpose flour	500 mL
4 tsps.	baking powder	20 mL
$\frac{1}{2}$ tsp.	salt	2 mL
1 Tbsp.	granulated sugar	15 mL
$\frac{1}{2}$ cup	shortening	125 mL
$\frac{2}{3}$ cup	milk	150 mL
1	egg, slightly beaten	1

Preheat the oven to 450°F. (230°C). Combine the flour, baking powder, salt and sugar in a large bowl. Cut in the shortening with a pastry blender until the texture is like coarse crumbs. Stir the milk and egg together. Make a well in the center of the dry ingredients and pour in the milk-egg mixture. With a fork, combine the liquid and dry ingredients. Turn out onto a lightly floured board. Knead several times, then roll or pat to a 1 in. (2.5 cm) thickness. Cut into rounds and arrange about 1 in. (2.5 cm) apart on a greased baking sheet. Bake for 10-12 minutes or until just beginning to turn golden.

Makes eighteen $1\frac{1}{2}$ in. (4.5 cm) biscuits.

Mary's Scones

🐾🐾

GARY BURROUGHS, *Innkeeper*
MARY COLTART, *Keeper of the Inn*
THE OBAN INN,
Niagara-on-the-Lake, Ont.

4 cups	all-purpose flour	1 L
2 tsps.	cream of tartar	10 mL
1 tsp.	baking soda	5 mL
$\frac{1}{2}$ tsp.	salt	2 mL
$\frac{1}{2}$ cup	butter	125 mL
$1\frac{1}{2}$-2 cups	milk	375- 500 mL
1 cup	raisins	250 mL

Preheat oven to 450°F. (230°C). Stir the flour, cream of tartar, soda and salt together in a large bowl. With a pastry cutter, blend in the butter until it looks like coarse meal. Stir in the milk all at once, adding more only if the dough is dry and crumbly. Add the raisins with the milk. Turn out onto a floured board and knead 5 or 6 times. Pat into a circle about $\frac{3}{4}$ in. (2 cm) thick. Cut into small biscuit shapes and arrange about 1 in. (2.5 cm) apart on a greased baking sheet. Bake 12-15 minutes or until golden brown.

Makes 12-16 scones.

Different Drummer Granola

&&&&&&&&&&&&&&&&&&&&&&&&&&&&&&&&&&&&&&&&&&&&&&&

ELINOR AND TED PHILIPS, *Innkeepers*
THE DIFFERENT DRUMMER,
Sackville, New Brunswick

Antiques and peaceful gardens provide the perfect finale after a day of bird-watching in New Brunswick's famous Tantramar Marsh wetlands. Built in 1899, The Different Drummer is furnished with period furniture and good books.

$\frac{1}{2}$ cup	oil	125 mL
1 cup	margarine	250 mL
2 Tbsps.	molasses	25 mL
1 Tbsp.	vanilla	15 mL
1 cup	brown sugar	250 mL
1 cup	honey	250 mL
$\frac{1}{2}$ tsp.	salt	2 mL
2 lbs.	old-fashioned, slow-cooking, rolled oats	900 g
$\frac{1}{2}$ cup	sesame seeds	125 mL
1 cup	chopped almonds	250 mL
2 cups	wheat flakes	500 mL
1 cup	5-grain cereal	250 mL
1 cup	coconut	250 mL
1 cup	sunflower seeds	250 mL
1 cup	raisins	250 mL

Preheat the oven to 300°F. (150°C). Melt together the oil, margarine, molasses, vanilla, brown sugar, honey and salt. Cool slightly, then mix well with all the remaining ingredients, except raisins. Bake for about 1 hour at 300°F. (150°C), stirring every 7 minutes or so. Cool in a bowl on a rack and stir in raisins.

Makes 14-16 cups (3.5-4 L).

Maple Granola

Ronald C. Phillips, *Innkeeper*
Bread and Roses,
Annapolis Royal, Nova Scotia

Bread and Roses takes its name from a poem by James Oppenheim, written in 1912, in response to the women textile workers' strike in Lawrence, Massachusetts. The marching women carried a banner saying, "We want bread and roses, too." This lovely Victorian mansion provides both — delicious food and quiet, nineteenth-century elegance.

5 cups	rolled oats	1.25 L
1 cup	soy flour	250 mL
1 cup	skim milk powder	250 mL
1 cup	wheat germ	250 mL
1 cup	coconut	250 mL
1 cup	chopped nuts *or* soy nuts	250 mL
1 cup	sunflower seeds	250 mL
$1\frac{1}{3}$ cups	oil	325 mL
$\frac{2}{3}$ cup	maple syrup (second grade is fine)	150 mL
1 cup	raisins	250 mL

Preheat the oven to 325°F. (160°C). In a large, oiled roasting pan, toss together all the dry ingredients thoroughly. Mix together the oil and maple syrup in a small bowl; then pour it over the dry ingredients. Stir to combine well with a wooden spoon. Bake, uncovered, for 1 hour, stirring every 10 minutes. When the granola is golden and crispy, remove it from the oven and toss in the raisins. (Other dried fruits could be added at this point as well.) Allow to cool, stirring several times. Package in plastic bags or in an airtight container.

Makes 12 cups.

Yeast Breads and Rolls

THE DUNDEE ARMS INN
Charlottetown, P.E.I.

Charlottetown Rye Bread

🌸🌸

DON, MARY AND JUDY CLINTON, *Innkeepers*
THE DUNDEE ARMS INN,
Charlottetown, P.E.I.

An excellent dark rye bread!

1 cup	milk	250 mL
2 Tbsps.	shortening	25 mL
2 Tbsps.	brown sugar	25 mL
$\frac{1}{3}$ cup	molasses	75 mL
1 Tbsp.	salt	15 mL
1 Tbsp.	caraway seeds	15 mL
$\frac{1}{2}$ cup	warm water	125 mL
1 tsp.	granulated sugar	5 mL
2 Tbsps.	active dry yeast	25 mL
(2 pkgs.)		(2 pkgs.)
2 cups	all-purpose flour	500 mL
2 Tbsps.	cocoa	25 mL
4 cups	dark rye flour	1 L

Bring the milk to a boil in a small saucepan. Remove from the heat and stir in the shortening, brown sugar, molasses, salt and caraway. Set aside to cool to lukewarm. In a large bowl, stir together the warm water and white sugar. Sprinkle the yeast over the water. Let it stand 5-10 minutes, until puffy. Add the milk-shortening mixture to the yeast, stirring well. Beat in the white flour, cocoa and rye flour. This will make a stiff dough. Knead on a floured board for 1-2 minutes. Cover and let the dough relax for 10 minutes. Knead for another 5 minutes.

Place the dough in a well-greased bowl and cover. Let the bread rise until it is double in bulk. Punch down and divide into 2 loaves. Either place the dough in greased loaf pans or shape it into the more traditional long loaves and place on greased baking sheets. Slash the tops on an angle. Cover and let rise until again doubled in size. *Preheat the oven to 375°F. (190°C).* Bake the rye bread for 45 minutes. Remove from the pans and lightly brush the tops with butter if desired. Let cool.

Makes two loaves.

Dill Bread

╭

(decorative border)

P.M. "CHARLIE" HOLGATE, *Innkeeper*
CAMELOT INN,
Musquodoboit Harbour, N.S.

This bread is deliciously different!

$\frac{3}{4}$ cup	warm water	175 mL
2 tsps.	granulated sugar	10 mL
2 Tbsps.	active dry yeast	25 mL
(2 pkgs.)		(2 pkgs.)
2 cups	cream-style cottage cheese	500 mL
$\frac{1}{4}$ cup	butter	50 mL
$\frac{1}{4}$ cup	finely chopped onion	50 mL
2 tsps.	salt	10 mL
2	eggs, lightly beaten	2
2 Tbsps.	dried dill weed or dill seed	25 mL
5 cups	all-purpose flour	1.25 L
1	egg white	1
1 Tbsp.	water	15 mL
	sliced onion, as needed	

Measure the warm water into a large bowl. Add the sugar and yeast. Let it stand for 10 minutes until puffed. Stir well. Press the cottage cheese through a sieve (or use cuisinart). In a saucepan, heat the butter and suet; add the onion and stir until golden, approximately 5 minutes. Add the cottage cheese, onion-butter mixture, salt, eggs, dill and half the flour to yeast. Beat until smooth. Add the remaining flour, first with a spoon and later mixing by hand. Knead the dough on a floured surface until smooth, approximately 8 minutes. Gather it into a ball. Grease or oil a large bowl; put in the dough; then turn the greased side to the top. Cover with a damp cloth and let the dough rise in a warm place until double, about 1$\frac{1}{2}$ hours. Punch down. Divide into 2 pieces. Grease two 9 in. x 5 in. (2 L) loaf pans. Shape dough into 2 loaves and place in pans. Beat egg white with 1 Tbsp. (15 mL) water. Brush over the tops of the loaves. Lay the onion rings or slices on top of loaves. Let rise until double, about 1 hour. *Bake in a preheated oven at 350°F. (180°C) for 45-50 minutes.*

Makes two loaves.

Maritime Brown Bread

LINDA L'AVENTURE AND CECILIA BOWDEN, *Innkeepers*
THE COMPASS ROSE,
North Head, Grand Manan, N.B.

Wholesome brown bread, well laced with molasses, seems to smack of the East Coast. The dough for this bread is very soft and bakes into moist, delicious loaves.

1 cup	rolled oats	250 mL
2 tsps.	salt	10 mL
2 Tbsps.	lard	25 mL
½ cup	molasses	125 mL
2½ cups	boiling water	625 mL
1	yeast cake	1
	or	
1 Tbsp. (1 pkg.)	active dry yeast	15 mL (1 pkg.)
½ cup	warm water	125 mL
5-5½ cups	white flour	1.25- 1.375 L

In a large mixing bowl, stir together the rolled oats, salt, lard and molasses. Stir in the boiling water until the lard dissolves. Cool to lukewarm. Add the yeast to ½ cup (125 mL) warm water, stirring to dissolve. Add to the oatmeal mixture. Stir in the flour, a cupful at a time. Turn onto a floured board, kneading until smooth, 4-5 minutes. Wash and grease the mixing bowl.

Return the dough to the bowl. Cover and allow it to rise in a warm, draft-free place until doubled in bulk, about 1½ hours. Punch down and shape into 2 loaves. Place in 2 well-greased 9 in. x 5 in. (2 L) loaf pans. Allow to rise a second time. *Preheat the oven to 350°F. (180°C).* When the loaves have doubled, bake for 30-40 minutes or until golden brown. *Makes two fragrant loaves.*

Beer Bread

FRANK AND JULIA LOLICH, *Innkeepers*
NORTHERN LIGHTS LODGE,
Likely, British Columbia

From one of the remote inns deep in the mountainous interior of the province, a recipe for beer bread.

1 Tbsp. (1 pkg.)	active dry yeast	15 mL (1 pkg.)
½ cup	warm water	125 mL
1 tsp.	granulated sugar	5 mL
12 oz.	beer	375 mL

2 Tbsps.	butter	25 mL
1 Tbsp.	granulated sugar	15 mL
$1\frac{1}{2}$ cups	cold water	375 mL
$8\frac{1}{2}$ cups	all-purpose flour	2125 mL
2 tsps.	salt	10 mL

Dissolve the yeast in the warm water and 1 tsp. sugar; let the mixture stand about 10 minutes, until foamy. In a medium-sized saucepan heat the beer to the boiling point (it will boil over if it gets too hot). Add the butter and 1 Tbsp. sugar (15 mL); then add cold water. Mix the beer mixture and the yeast together and pour over the flour and salt. Beat well with an electric mixer or by hand until all the flour is absorbed. Do not knead, or knead very lightly, just until mixed. Dough should be the consistency of a drop biscuit. Cover the bowl with a damp cloth and let the dough rise until double.

Turn it onto a floured surface and form into rolls or put into loaf pans. Let rise again until double. Bake at 350°F. (180°C) until brown (about 25-30 minutes). Brush with butter when taken from oven. Makes three $9\frac{3}{4}$ x $5\frac{3}{4}$ x $2\frac{1}{2}$ in. (2 L) loaves.

Gramma's House Herb Bread

🐾🐾🐾🐾🐾🐾🐾🐾🐾🐾🐾🐾🐾🐾🐾🐾🐾🐾🐾🐾🐾🐾🐾🐾🐾🐾🐾🐾🐾🐾🐾🐾🐾🐾🐾🐾

TED AND JEAN TURNER, *Innkeepers*
GRAMMA'S HOUSE,
Port Saxon, Nova Scotia

To be in the home of an exceedingly happy couple who work together as a perfect team is a rare and special experience. Ted and Jean Turner have had a lifetime of shared interests and Gramma's House — which was indeed Jean's grandmother's — was a warm and joyful place to come home to after our travels.

Jean has executive organizational skills. She serves dinner to any guest who wishes it (i.e., all of them) and sometimes an outsider or two is able to slip into the group as well. While we were waiting for dinner, my sons and I meandered down some of the backroads around Port Saxon, ending up at a beach that stretched as far as our eyes could see; miles of white Atlantic sand, with no one else on it.

This is a fine-textured loaf. Slice it thinly and enjoy it with a good cheddar.

1 cup	warm water	250 mL
$\frac{1}{4}$ cup	granulated sugar	50 mL
1 Tbsp.	active dry yeast	15 mL
1 Tbsp.	Kraft Italian dressing	15 mL
1	egg, beaten	1
1 tsp.	herb mixture*	5 mL
$3\frac{1}{2}$ cups	all-purpose flour	875 mL

Place the lukewarm water, sugar and yeast in a mixing bowl. Let the mixture stand for 10 minutes. Add the dressing, egg and herb mixture. Stir well. Add flour and knead thoroughly. Let rise in warm place until doubled in bulk. Punch down and shape into a long loaf and place on a greased pan. Let rise until doubled. *Bake for 30 minutes in a pre-heated 350°F. (180°C) oven. Makes one long, French-style loaf.*

*HERB MIXTURE Combine equal parts of savory, tarragon, rosemary, basil and garlic salt. This mixture can be stored in a jar, ready for use.

Anadama Bread

🐾🐾🐾

GORDON AND EVELYN BURNHAM, *Innkeepers*
WESTWAY INN,
Plympton, Digby County, N.S.

This is the old Nova Scotian yarn about Anadama Bread that Gordon Burnham related. It appears that a certain couple were not getting along too well. In fact, their marriage was downright rocky! He would come home, dog-tired, from a hard day's work and all she would feed him was cornmeal mush. Then one day he returned to find his wife, Anna, gone and on the table a pot of cold, glutinous mush. He was famished and tired but pulled himself together and baked a batch of cornmeal bread, all the while muttering "ANNA-DAMN-'ER."

1 cup	milk, scalded	250 mL
1 cup	boiling water	250 mL
1 cup	yellow cornmeal	250 mL
3 Tbsps.	shortening	45 mL
½ cup	molasses	125 mL
2 tsps.	salt	10 mL
2 Tbsps.	active dry yeast	25 mL
(2 pkgs.)		(2 pkgs.)
1 tsp.	granulated sugar	5 mL
½ cup	lukewarm water	125 mL
5½-6 cups	all-purpose flour	1.3-1.5 L

Stir the hot milk and boiling water into the cornmeal. Add the shortening, molasses and salt. Let the mixture stand until lukewarm. Mix the yeast, sugar and lukewarm water; allow it to stand for 10 minutes; then add to the cornmeal mixture, along with part of the flour, to make a batter. Beat well. Knead in the rest of the flour. Place the dough in a greased bowl, turning the dough to grease it on all sides. Cover and let it rise in a warm place for about 1½ hours or until double in bulk. Shape it into loaves. Allow it to rise again for 45 minutes or until doubled. Bake for 40-50 minutes in a *preheated oven at 350°F.-375°F. (180°C-190°C).*

Makes four small loaves.

RITA'S INN,
Ganges, Saltspring Island, B.C.

Sweet Coconut Koulitch

🐞🐞🐞🐞🐞🐞🐞🐞🐞🐞🐞🐞🐞🐞🐞🐞🐞🐞🐞🐞🐞🐞🐞🐞🐞🐞🐞🐞🐞🐞🐞🐞🐞🐞🐞🐞

RITA DODS, *Innkeeper*
RITA'S INN,
Ganges, Saltspring Island, B.C.

Before taking over her inn, Rita and her family were Saltspring Island's bakers.

$\frac{1}{2}$ cup	milk	125 mL
$\frac{1}{3}$ cup	granulated sugar	75 mL
1 tsp.	salt	5 mL
$\frac{1}{2}$ cup	butter *or* margarine	125 mL
2 Tbsps.	active dry yeast	30 mL
(2 pkgs.)		(2 pkgs.)
$\frac{1}{2}$ cup	lukewarm water	125 mL
2 tsps.	granulated sugar	10 mL
2	eggs, well beaten	2
$1\frac{1}{2}$ cups	desiccated coconut	375 mL
$4\frac{1}{2}$ cups	all-purpose flour	1.125 L
	Confectioners' Icing (p. 154)	

In a small saucepan, scald the milk until steaming. Combine with the $\frac{1}{3}$ cup (75 mL) sugar, salt and butter in a small bowl. Let cool to lukewarm. Dissolve the yeast and 2 tsps. (10 mL) sugar in the lukewarm water. Let stand 10 minutes until puffy. Stir well. Stir milk mixture, well-beaten eggs and coconut into the yeast. Add 2 cups (500 mL) of the flour and beat until smooth. Blend in the remaining flour by hand.

Knead on a lightly floured surface until smooth. Place in a greased bowl. Let rise in a warm place until double in bulk. Punch the dough down. Let rest for 10 minutes. Cut into 6 equal pieces and knead each one. Shape into long, slender rolls and place in a greased 9 in. x 13 in. (3.5 L) pan or place 2 pieces of dough into each of 3 9 in. x 5 in. (2 L) loaf pans. Let rise about 1 hour or until almost double. *Bake in a preheated oven at 375°F. (190°C) for 20-25 minutes*. Remove and let cool on a rack. Drizzle with Confectioners' Icing.

Makes six small, slender loaves or three double ones.

THE COMPASS ROSE,
North Head, Grand Manan, N.B.

Lobster Rolls

🐾🐾🐾🐾🐾🐾🐾🐾🐾🐾🐾🐾🐾🐾🐾🐾🐾🐾🐾🐾🐾🐾🐾🐾🐾🐾🐾🐾🐾🐾🐾🐾🐾🐾🐾🐾🐾

LINDA L'AVENTURE AND CECILIA BOWDEN, *Innkeepers*
THE COMPASS ROSE,
North Head, Grand Manan, N.B.

No collection of Atlantic coast recipes would be complete without these delicious rolls. Even truckstops serve them.

Rolls

2 Tbsps.	active dry yeast	25 mL
$\frac{1}{2}$ cup	lukewarm water	125 mL
$1\frac{1}{2}$ tsps.	granulated sugar	7 mL
$2\frac{1}{2}$ cups	warm water	625 mL
$\frac{1}{2}$ cup	oil	125 mL
1 tsp.	salt	5 mL
$\frac{1}{2}$ cup	granulated sugar	125 mL
7-8 cups	all-purpose flour	1.75-2 L

Place the yeast, $\frac{1}{2}$ cup (125 mL) warm water and $1\frac{1}{2}$ tsps. (7 mL) sugar in a large mixing bowl. Stir lightly and let sit for 10 minutes. Add the rest of the ingredients, except the flour, and allow to sit for another 5 minutes or until a little foamy. Add the flour gradually, stirring with a wooden spoon. When too stiff to stir easily, turn out onto a floured surface and add more flour gradually, kneading after each addition. Continue only until the dough stops sticking to your hands. Wash and grease the bowl. Roll the dough in the bowl to grease all sides. Cover and put it in a warm place until doubled in bulk. Make into oblong rolls and place on greased cookie sheets. Let them rise until double. *Bake in a preheated oven at 375°F. (190°C).* Slice and butter like a hot dog roll. *Makes 3-4 dozen.*

Filling

2 cups	coarsely chopped, cooked lobster	500 mL
$\frac{1}{2}$ cup	chopped celery	125 mL
2 Tbsps.	minced green onion	25 mL
2 Tbsps.	finely diced green pepper	25 mL
1 Tbsp.	finely minced parsley	15 mL

$\frac{1}{2}$-$\frac{3}{4}$ cup	mayonnaise (p. 41)	125-
		175 mL
	salt and freshly ground	
	pepper, to taste	

To complete the Lobster Rolls, prepare the filling as follows. The amount may be varied with the number of people you're serving. In a small bowl, mix the chopped, cooked lobster, chopped celery, green onion, green pepper, parsley and mayonnaise to moisten. Season with salt and pepper. Fill the rolls, leaving them open-faced. Place them on a baking sheet and broil until bubbly. *Makes 6-8 rolls.*

Grand Harbour Rolls

AL AND GLORIA HOBBS, *Innkeepers*
GRAND HARBOUR INN,
Grand Harbour, Grand Manan, N.B.

Grand Harbour Inn has its original guest book dating from 1905-1915 when it operated as Harbour View House. A recent inscription, however, is one of Al's favorites: a lady asked if she could take the cook home please. In fact, the cook ought to be in many of our kitchens because he loves fresh herbs and uses very little salt.

Grand Manan has been known as the Bermuda of the North. Al has harvested his cauliflower during the second week in June — about the same time the rest of Canada is planting theirs. It's wonderful to see an inn almost completely enclosed by gardens.

2 Tbsps.	active dry yeast	25 mL
(2 pkgs.)		(2 pkgs.)
$\frac{1}{3}$ cup	maple *or* pancake syrup	75 mL
2 cups	warm water	500 mL
1 tsp.	salt	5 mL
1	egg, well beaten	1
3 Tbsps.	melted, clarified butter	45 mL
$5\frac{1}{2}$-6 cups	white, unbleached flour	1375-
		1500 mL

In a large mixing bowl, combine the yeast, syrup and warm water. Allow it to puff for about 10 minutes. Stir in the salt, egg and melted butter. Beat in the flour, a cupful at a time until it is difficult to stir. Turn the dough out onto a floured surface. Wash and oil the bowl.

Knead the dough 5-6 minutes until it is smooth and elastic. Cover it with a damp towel and allow it to rise in a warm place; *or* cover it with plastic wrap, weigh it down with a plate and refrigerate for up to a week.

Shape the dough into rolls. Place on a greased baking sheet. Allow them to rise until doubled in bulk. *Bake in a preheated oven at 425°F. (220°C) for 15-20 minutes. Makes 3-4 dozen.*

Variations: Al brushes the unbaked rolls with an egg wash made of 1 beaten egg combined with 3-4 Tbsps. (45-60 mL) milk. Then he sprinkles them with sesame or poppy seeds. Or sometimes, he works $1\frac{1}{2}$ cups (375 mL) finely grated old cheddar into the dough before allowing it to rise.

Hot Cross Buns

Rita Dods, *Innkeeper*
Rita's Inn,
Ganges, Saltspring Island, B.C.

Rita has lost count of how many dozens of Hot Cross Buns she has baked — probably many hundreds.

2 cups	milk	500 mL
$\frac{3}{4}$ cup	granulated sugar	175 mL
1 Tbsp.	salt	15 mL
$1\frac{1}{2}$ cups	raisins	375 mL
$1\frac{1}{2}$ Tbsps.	active dry yeast	20 mL
$\frac{1}{2}$ cup	lukewarm water	125 mL
2 tsps.	granulated sugar (second amount)	10 mL
2	eggs	2
$\frac{1}{2}$ cup	shortening	125 mL
7 cups (approx.)	all-purpose flour	1.75 L (approx.)
1 Tbsp.	cinnamon	15 mL

In a large heavy saucepan, scald the milk; add the sugar, salt and raisins. In a small bowl, sprinkle the yeast over the lukewarm water in which the sugar has been dissolved. Let stand for 10 minutes. Add the beaten eggs, shortening and yeast to the milk mixture, which is now lukewarm. Add about 6 cups of flour and beat until it becomes a smooth sponge. Stir in the cinnamon with the final cup of flour.

Add the last of the flour gradually, kneading well after each addition — just until the dough stops sticking to your hands.

Turn out onto a floured surface; let the dough rest for 10 minutes. Knead until smooth. Place the dough in a large, well-greased bowl; turning the dough to grease its entire surface. Put it in a warm place and let it rise until double in bulk, $1-1\frac{1}{2}$ hours. Shape into buns, flatten slightly and place on a greased pan. Make a cross on the top of each one with scissors. Let them rise in a warm place until doubled, $1-1\frac{1}{2}$ hours. *Bake in a preheated oven at 375°F. (190°C) until golden brown, 20-25 minutes.*

While still warm, drizzle with a thin Confectioners' Icing made by mixing together the following:

2 cups	icing sugar	500 mL
1 tsp.	vanilla	5 mL
2-3 Tbsps.	milk or cream	25-45 mL

Makes 40-50 buns.

Cakes

YELLOW POINT LODGE,
Ladysmith, Vancouver, Island B.C.

Tomato Juice Cake

❀❀

RICHARD HILL AND RON FRIEND, *Innkeepers*
YELLOW POINT LODGE,
Ladysmith, Vancouver Island, B.C.

This is one of the recipes that were burned in the 1985 fire. Millie and Bernice, two of the cooks, found a copy and sent it. No doubt it will be on their new menu.

2 cups	all-purpose flour	500 mL
1 cup	granulated sugar	250 mL
1 tsp.	baking powder	5 mL
1 tsp.	ground cloves	5 mL
	pinch of salt	
$\frac{2}{3}$ cup	butter *or* margarine	150 mL
1	egg	1
1 cup	tomato juice	250 mL
1 cup	raisins *or* currants	250 mL
1 cup	chopped walnuts	250 mL

Preheat the oven to 350°F. (180°C). In a large bowl, combine the dry ingredients. Cut in the butter or margarine with a pastry blender or 2 knives until fine. Beat the egg in the tomato juice and mix into the dry ingredients. Beat well with an electric mixer. Add fruit and nuts. Stir. Bake in a well-greased 9 in. x 9 in. (22 cm x 22 cm) pan for about 1 hour. Serve with or without icing. *Makes 9 servings.*

Old-Fashioned Gingerbread

❀❀

FRANK AND GLORIA ARRIS, *Innkeepers*
EVELEIGH HOTEL,
Evandale, New Brunswick

The St. John River has a few old inns left at its river ferry crossings. Step into the earlier part of this century when you bake this cake.

1 cup	butter	250 mL
1 cup	granulated sugar	250 mL
2	eggs	2
2 cups	molasses	500 mL
5 cups	all-purpose flour	1.25 L
1 Tbsp.	baking soda	15 mL
1 tsp.	salt	5 mL
2 tsps.	cinnamon	10 mL
2 tsps.	ground ginger	10 mL
1 tsp.	ground cloves	5 mL
2 cups	hot water	500 mL

Preheat the oven to 325°F. (160°C). Cream the butter and sugar till light and lemon colored. Add the eggs and molasses and continue beating. Stir together the flour, soda, salt and spices; blend with the first mixture, mixing until no dry spots remain. Add the hot water. Beat well. Line 3 8 in. (2 L) pans with waxed paper. Divide the batter between the pans and bake for about 55 minutes, or until a testing needle comes out clean. The batter doubles on baking. Serve with whipped cream. *Makes three 8 in. (2 L) cakes.*

Partridgeberry Spice Cake

CHRISTINE AND PETER BEAMISH, *Innkeepers*
THE VILLAGE INN,
Trinity, Newfoundland

Christine suggests that if you don't have a ready source of partridgeberries, you might find them under another name. In some parts of Canada they are called mountain cranberries, in others they are named creeping cranberries. A further substitute is the plain low-bush cranberry which is available across the country at Thanksgiving and Christmas. These are larger than partridgeberries and should be chopped coarsely for this recipe.

Warm from the oven, this golden loaf hardly needs even a touch of butter. Pour yourself a steaming cup of coffee and slice off a thick slab of berry-laden cake for a mid-morning treat.

1 cup	butter, softened	250 mL
1 cup	granulated sugar	250 mL
1	egg	1
$\frac{1}{2}$ cup	water	125 mL
1 cup	raisins	250 mL
$\frac{1}{2}$ cup	chopped walnuts	125 mL
$1\frac{3}{4}$ cups	all-purpose flour	425 mL
$\frac{1}{4}$ tsp.	salt	1 mL
1 tsp.	baking soda	5 mL
1 tsp.	baking powder	5 mL
1 tsp.	cinnamon	5 mL
$\frac{1}{2}$ tsp.	ground cloves	2 mL
1 cup	partridgeberries	250 mL

Preheat the oven to 350°F (180°C). Grease an $8\frac{1}{2}$ in. x $4\frac{1}{2}$ in. (1.5 L) loaf pan thoroughly. Line it with waxed or brown paper and grease lightly again. In a large mixing bowl, cream together the butter and the sugar. Add the egg and the water and continue to beat until it is light and fluffy. Stir in the raisins and walnuts.

In a separate bowl, stir together the flour, salt and spices. Add to the creamed mixture, folding gently to barely combine. Sprinkle in the berries and mix until no dry spots remain. Pour into the prepared pan and bake for 1 hour or until high and golden. Remove from the oven and cool for 5 minutes in the pan. Remove from the pan, and set on a wire rack to cool. Let the loaf stand for another 30 minutes before removing the paper. *Makes one $8\frac{1}{2}$ in. x $4\frac{1}{2}$ in. (1.5 L) loaf.*

Pineapple Cake

FRANK AND JULIA LOLICH, *Innkeepers*
NORTHERN LIGHTS LODGE,
Likely, British Columbia

The interior of British Columbia is extremely remote: some highways are open only in the summertime; shops and most of the day-to-day amenities we take for granted are often unavailable. That's why I've included this recipe that calls for a mix. It's very moist and the ingredients can be kept on hand for those days when the planes or the all-terrain vehicles carrying groceries don't arrive.

Cake

1	two-layer, yellow *or* white cake mix	1
2	eggs*	2
2 cups	crushed pineapple, with juice	500 mL

Frosting

$\frac{1}{4}$ cup	butter	50 mL
$\frac{1}{4}$ cup	granulated sugar	50 mL
$\frac{1}{4}$ cup	canned evaporated milk	50 mL
1 cup	desiccated coconut *or* finely chopped nuts	250 mL

Preheat the oven to 325°F. (160°C). Put the dry cake mix into the mixing bowl. Add the eggs and crushed pineapple. Beat 2 minutes at medium speed. Pour into a greased 9 in. x 13 in. (3.5 L) baking pan and bake for 45 minutes. To make the frosting, place the butter, sugar and canned milk in a saucepan and boil over medium heat for 2 minutes. Add the nuts or coconut. Pour the topping over the cake while the cake is still warm. (The cake is best iced right in the pan.)

Makes one 9 in. x 13 in. (3.5 L) cake.

*When using a cake mix that calls for 3 eggs and oil, use the 3 eggs and the amount of oil prescribed on the package and proceed as above.

Desert Rose Carrot Cake

Resa Lent, *Innkeeper*
The Desert Rose Inn and Café,
Elora, Ontario

This is probably one of Resa's best-known desserts. She has made hundreds of these moist cakes for the prestigious St. John's-Kilmarnock antique sale.

3 cups	unbleached, white flour	750 mL
1½ cups	demerara sugar	375 mL
1 Tbsp.	baking soda	15 mL
1 Tbsp.	cinnamon	15 mL
4	eggs	4
1½ cups	vegetable oil	375 mL
2 Tbsps.	vanilla	25 mL
1 cup	puréed, *cooked* carrots	250 mL
1 cup	crushed pineapple, drained	250 mL
1 cup	flaked coconut	250 mL
1 cup	walnut pieces	250 mL

Preheat the oven to 350°F. (180°C). In a large bowl of a mixer, combine the flour, sugar, soda and cinnamon. Begin beating and add the eggs, one at a time, and the oil. Continue mixing for 2-3 minutes on medium speed. Add the vanilla, carrots, pineapple, coconut and walnuts. Mix gently. Overbeating will dry the cake. Grease and flour a 9 in. x 13 in. (3.5 L) cake pan or 2 8 in. (1.2 L) round layer pans. Bake for 30-40 minutes for the layers, 60 minutes for the larger rectangular pan, or until a knife inserted comes out clean. Cool for 10 minutes in the pans. Loosen around the edges and turn out onto a serving plate. Ice with Cream Cheese Icing and decorate with walnuts, orange slices or strawberry halves, if desired.

Makes one 9 in. x 13 in. (3.5 L) cake.

Cream Cheese Icing

¼ cup	butter	50 mL
1 4-oz. pkg.	cream cheese	1 113-g pkg.
3 cups	icing sugar	750 mL
2-3 tsps.	milk	10-15 mL
1 tsp.	vanilla	5 mL

Have the butter and cream cheese at room temperature. Cream them together until fluffy. Add the sugar. Thin with milk and vanilla. Continue beating until smooth and creamy. This amount will ice your rectangular cake. For the layer cake, you should increase the amounts slightly.

Makes enough icing for the rectangular cake above.

AUBERGE HISTORIQUE 1867,
Sutton, Québec

Dreamy Chocolate Sponge Cake

MADELEINE FOREST, *Innkeeper*
AUBERGE HISTORIQUE 1867,
Sutton, Québec

1 cup	all-bran	250 mL
¾ cup	milk	175 mL
½ cup	butter, softened	125 mL
½ cup	granulated sugar	125 mL
2	eggs, beaten	2
1 cup	self-rising flour	250 mL
3 squares	semi-sweet chocolate, melted	3 squares

Filling

½ cup	heavy cream (35%)	125 mL
4 squares	semi-sweet chocolate, melted (second amount)	4 squares
½ cup	whole almonds, toasted	125 mL

Preheat the oven to 350°F. (180°C). Grease and flour or line with waxed paper two 8 in. (20 cm) cake pans. Place the all-bran and milk in a bowl and leave until the milk is absorbed. Cream the butter and sugar until light and fluffy, then gradually beat in the eggs. Fold in the softened all-bran and flour. Gently stir in the 3 melted squares of chocolate. Pour mixture into the pans and bake for about 20-25 minutes or until a wooden pick inserted near the center comes out clean. Turn out onto cake racks and let cool. Spread the remaining chocolate on top of both layers. Allow to cool, but not set. Whip the cream and spread over the chocolate on one layer; top with the second layer of cake and chill. Decorate with whole toasted almonds on top of the cake. *Makes 8 servings.*

Mincemeat Cake

DOROTHEA DEAN, *Innkeeper*
DELPHINE LODGE,
Wilmer, British Columbia

Dorothea uses many different fillings for this soft, moist cake, from cherry to a European-style cottage cheese.

3 cups	all-purpose flour	750 mL
1½ cups	butter *or* margarine	375 mL
1	egg	1
2	egg yolks	2
1 Tbsp.	table cream (18%)	15 mL
1 cup	icing sugar	250 mL
1 Tbsp.	baking powder	15 mL
	grated rind of 1 lemon	
2¾ cups	mincemeat or other	675 mL
	cooked pie filling	

Preheat the oven to 350°F. (180°C) or 325°F. (160°C) for glass pie plate. Place the flour in a large bowl. Cut in the butter or margarine until the mixture resembles fine corn meal. Beat together the egg, 2 egg yolks and the cream; add to the flour mixture. Mix fast as the flour will absorb them quickly. Sift in the icing sugar and baking powder. Add the lemon rind. Stir and then knead quickly and lightly. Divide the soft, buttery dough into 2 parts, one larger than the other. Roll out the larger part on a floured surface to fit a 9 in. (22 cm) pan with a 1 in. (2.5 cm) or less rim (a flan pan is perfect), being sure to extend the dough about ½ in. (1.5 cm) above the edge of the pan. Add the mincemeat or other cooked pie filling. Roll out the other part of the dough to make the upper crust. Fold the edge of the bottom crust over the outside of the top crust. Prick with a fork and bake for about 1 hour or less, until yellow, not brown. Watch carefully as the crust bakes quickly. The crust is cake-like, moist and light. *Makes 6-8 servings.*

Blueberry Cake

DAVID EVANS, *Innkeeper*
LISCOMBE LODGE,
Liscomb Mills, Nova Scotia

A lovely, moist cake with a shiny surface — a real treat for brunch.

2 cups	all-purpose flour	500 mL
1 cup	granulated sugar	250 mL
½ tsp.	salt	2 mL
1 Tbsp.	baking powder	15 mL
⅓ cup	oil	75 mL
2	eggs	2
1 cup	milk	250 mL
2 cups	Nova Scotia blueberries	500 mL

Preheat the oven to 350°F. (180°C). Grease and flour a 9 in. x 13 in. (3.5 L) baking pan. In a large mixing bowl, stir together the flour, sugar, salt and baking powder. With an electric beater, mix in the oil and add the eggs, one at a time. While still mixing, add the milk. Continue beating and fold in the blueberries. Pour into the prepared pan. Bake 50-60 minutes or until done when tested with a toothpick. Allow to cool for 10-15 minutes before removing from the pan. Ice with a vanilla butter frosting, if desired, or simply serve in large, berry-studded slices. *Makes one 9 in. x 13 in. (3.5 L) cake.*

Cachette Framboise
(Wild Raspberry Cake)

✿✿✿

MME. MARTHE LEVER, *Innkeeper*
L'HAUT VENT,
Sutton, Québec

Wild Raspberries grow all around L'Haut Vent.

Fruit Base

1 quart	wild raspberries *or* blueberries	1 L
$\frac{1}{2}$ - $\frac{2}{3}$ cups	sugar*	125- 150 mL
2-3 Tbsps.	water**	25-45 mL

Topping

$\frac{1}{3}$ cup	shortening *or* butter	75 mL
$\frac{3}{4}$ cup	granulated sugar	175 mL
2	eggs, beaten	2
$\frac{1}{3}$ cup	milk	75 mL
1 tsp.	vanilla	5 mL
$1\frac{1}{3}$ cups	all-purpose flour	325 mL
2 tsps.	baking powder	10 mL
$\frac{1}{8}$ tsp.	salt	0.5 mL

Preheat the oven to 350°F. (180°C). Grease or butter a 10 in. (25 cm) square pan. Spread the fruit evenly on the bottom of the pan. Sprinkle the fruit with sugar and with water, if needed. In a large bowl, cream the shortening and sugar. Beat in the eggs and milk. Add the vanilla. Sift in the dry ingredients and beat well. Spread over the fruit base. Bake for 50-55 minutes. Invert and cut into squares. Serve with a little table cream (18%) or half-and-half (10%).

Makes 6-8 servings.

The amount of sugar will vary according to taste and the sweetness of the berries.
**Water is needed only if berries are dry.*

Pies and Tarts

THE VILLAGE INN,
Trinity, Newfoundland

Partridgeberry Pie

๛๛๛

CHRISTINE AND PETER BEAMISH, *Innkeepers*
THE VILLAGE INN,
Trinity, Newfoundland

The story goes that the Newfie Bullet, a train of character, but of no great speed, used to climb the hills at such a slow pace that the passengers would get off at the front of the train with their little pails and pick partridgeberries until they could clamber back on near the caboose with full containers. Unfortunately, the old Bullet has long since retired so we have neither the joy of picking berries nor of travelling through life at that leisurely gait.

This recipe is more like a jam tart than a deep-dish pie. It is made with a short, biscuit-like dough which Christine also uses to bake Raisin Buns at the inn.

Filling

2 cups	partridgeberries (no substitutes this time, please)	500 mL
2 cups	granulated sugar	500 mL

Crust

3 cups	all-purpose flour	750 mL
6 tsps.	baking powder	30 mL
$\frac{2}{3}$ cup	granulated sugar	150 mL
$\frac{1}{4}$ tsp.	salt	1 mL
$\frac{3}{4}$ cup	butter	175 mL
1	egg	1
$\frac{3}{4}$ cup	milk	175 mL

Preheat the oven to 375°F. (190°C). To make the filling, combine the berries and the sugar in a small heavy saucepan. Crush a little to release the juices and cook over medium heat until the berries begin to burst. Stir often to prevent sticking. Simmer for 5-7 minutes to thicken. Remove from the heat and allow to cool while you are making the crust.

To make the crust, stir or sift together the flour, baking powder, sugar and salt. With a pastry cutter, cut in the butter until the mixture has the texture of fine crumbs.

Stir together the egg and the milk. Add it to the dry ingredients and stir to combine. Shape into a ball and roll on a floured surface to $\frac{1}{4}$ in. (0.5 cm) thickness.

Line a 9 in. (22 cm) pie plate with the dough, reserving one-third of it for the lattice top. Pour in the filling and roll the remaining dough out and cut into strips about $\frac{1}{2}$ in. (1 cm) wide. Lay the strips on top of the filling to form a lattice. Bake for 15 minutes or until beginning to brown. Remove from the oven and allow to cool before serving. Christine says that it is super with vanilla ice cream or lightly sweetened whipped cream.

Makes one 9 in. (22 cm) tart.

Flaky Pastry

❀❀❀

PAT HOGAN, *Chef*
THE PILLAR AND POST,
Niagara-on-the-Lake, Ontario

5¼ cups	pastry flour	1.3 L
¾ cup	butter, chilled	175 mL
¾ cup	shortening, chilled	175 mL
1 tsp.	salt	5 mL
1 tsp.	granulated sugar	5 mL
½ cup	ice water	125 mL

Measure the flour into a large mixing bowl. With a pastry blender, cut in the butter and shortening until you have pea-sized pellets. Stir the salt and sugar into the ice water. Make a well in the center of the flour. Add the water, all at once. With a fork, stir until the water has been completely absorbed. Gather into a ball and chill for 20 minutes before rolling on a floured board. *Makes enough pastry for 5 9-in. (22 cm) single-crust or 2 10-in. (25 cm) double-crust pies.*

Dad's Puff Pastry

❀❀❀

This recipe was developed by my father, Glenn MacDonald. He was a baker and loves to experiment. Although it is not a true French Puff Pastry, it is much quicker and quite a bit easier to make. Throughout the book, there are recipes which call for Puff Pastry. Either make your own, using Dad's recipe, or buy it frozen from your local supermarket. Small bakeries will often sell it fresh by the pound. Since it freezes well, you may want to stock up.

1 cup	unsalted butter	250 mL
1 cup	all-purpose flour	250 mL
1 cup	cake and pastry flour	250 mL
1 tsp.	salt	5 mL
½ cup (approx.)	ice water	125 mL

Allow two-thirds of the butter to become soft. Combine the flours and the salt in a large mixing bowl. With a pastry cutter, blend in the one-third of hardened butter until the mixture resembles fine crumbs. With a fork, add the ice water, using only enough to hold the mixture together. Gather the dough into a ball and turn out onto a lightly floured board. Roll it into a rectangle about ¼ in. (6 mm) thick.

Spread two-thirds of the dough with one-quarter of the softened butter. Fold the unbuttered third over the center third. Fold the remaining third over so that it covers the first. You will now have three layers of dough with butter between each layer. Turn the dough one-quarter of the way around on the board and repeat the process. Cover in plastic wrap and chill for 45 minutes. Repeat the process, chilling once more, until all the butter is used. Cover tightly with plastic wrap and store in the refrigerator. If you freeze it, make sure that it is unthawed in the refrigerator. *Makes 1 lb. (450 g).*

THE PILLAR AND POST,
Niagara-on-the-Lake, Ontario

Apple Frangipane Tart

❀❀❀

PAT HOGAN, *Chef*
THE PILLAR AND POST,
Niagara-on-the-Lake, Ontario

Purchase the almond paste from a delicatessen or pastry shop.

6¼ oz.	almond paste	175 g
1 cup	granulated sugar	250 mL
¾ cup	butter	175 mL
1	egg white, from a small egg	1
¾ cup	cake and pastry flour	175 mL
4	eggs	4
1 10-in.	unbaked pie shell (p. 165)	1 25-cm
6-8	cooking apples, peeled and thinly sliced	6-8

Preheat the oven to 300°F. 150°C). In a mixing bowl, cream together the almond paste, sugar, butter and egg white. Add the cake flour, a few spoonfuls at a time, still beating. Now, beat in the eggs, one at a time. Continue to beat for 3 minutes. Fill the pie shell. Arrange the apple slices, slightly overlapping, in concentric circles. Bake for 1 hour. Allow to cool before slicing. Serve with lightly sweetened whipped cream if desired.

Makes one 10-in. (25 cm) pie.

Brandy Cream Pie

❀❀❀

LINDA L'AVENTURE AND CECILIA BOWDEN, *Innkeepers*
THE COMPASS ROSE,
Grand Manan, New Brunswick

Pure, unadulterated decadence!

1	10-in. (25 cm) baked pie shell (p. 165)	1
	or	
1	10-in. (25 cm) graham wafer crust	1
1 Tbsp.	unflavored gelatin	15 mL
$\frac{1}{2}$ cup	cold water	125 mL
6	egg yolks	6
1 cup	granulated sugar	250 mL
2 cups	heavy cream (35%)	500 mL
$\frac{1}{2}$ cup	brandy *or* rum	125 mL
	shaved, semi-sweet chocolate, for garnish	

In a small saucepan, soak the gelatin in the cold water. Let stand for 5 minutes. *Slowly* heat until it is dissolved and begins to boil. Meanwhile, in a medium bowl, whip the egg yolks with the sugar until light and lemony in color. Slowly pour the hot gelatin into the egg-yolk mixture, beating well. Whip the cream in a large bowl until stiff. Fold in the egg yolk and gelatin mixture. Flavor with the brandy. Cool thoroughly. Pour into the prepared pie shell. Garnish with chocolate curls. Chill until serving time. *Makes 8 servings.*

Butter Tarts

GARY BURROUGHS, *Innkeeper*
MARY COLTART, *Keeper of the Inn*
THE OBAN INN,
Niagara-on-the-Lake, Ontario

If you enjoy golden, oozing, butter tarts, this is your recipe! Add raisins or nuts to each tart shell, if you wish.

	pastry for 12 deep tart shells (see p. 165)	
$\frac{1}{2}$ cup	butter	125 mL
$1\frac{1}{2}$ cups	brown sugar	375 mL
$\frac{1}{4}$ cup	granulated sugar	50 mL
$\frac{1}{4}$ cup	corn syrup	50 mL
1 Tbsp.	vinegar	15 mL
1 tsp.	vanilla	5 mL
3	eggs	3

Preheat the oven to 375°F. (190°C). Line the tart tins with the pastry. (Paper muffin tin liners make removal of the tarts easier.) In a saucepan, melt the butter. Add the brown and white sugar, corn syrup, vinegar and vanilla. Bring to a simmer, stirring to prevent burning. Remove from the heat. Beat in the eggs, 1 at a time. Fill the tart shells three-quarters full. Bake, watching constantly, for 12-15 minutes or until golden brown. *Makes 12 tarts — enough for 2 to 4 afficionados.*

Ogre Canyon Saskatoon Pie

MARY AND JERRY BOND, *Innkeepers*
BLACK CAT GUEST RANCH,
Hinton, Alberta

A true Alberta wilderness lodge, Black Cat has leased 460 acres of Crown Land in the foothills of the Rockies. There are game trails, old logging roads and seismic lines all over the property.

In 1985, the Bonds had their best crop of Saskatoon berries ever. They pick them wild in the picturesque Ogre Canyon. Mary freezes them by just packing them, 4 or 6 cupfuls at a time, in small bags and storing them in the freezer.

4 cups	Saskatoon berries	1 L
½ cup	fruit juice (Mary uses raspberry juice in season *or* orange juice)	125 mL
1 cup	granulated sugar	250 mL
3 Tbsps.	all-purpose flour	45 mL
	dash of grated nutmeg	
	dash of salt	
1 Tbsp.	butter	15 mL
	pastry for a double-crust, 9-in. (22 cm) pie (p. 165)	

Preheat the oven to 425°F. (220°C). In a medium-sized bowl, stir together the berries and juice. Combine the sugar, flour, nutmeg and salt separately. Mix into the berries, stirring well. Pour into the prepared pie shell. Dot with butter. Cover with the top crust, pinching the edges together to seal. Cut small holes with a thimble for steam vents. Bake at 425°F. (220°C) for 15 minutes. Reduce the heat to 350°F. (180°C) and bake until nicely browned and the juice begins to bubble through the holes. *Makes 6 servings.*

Tarte Sucre

(Québec Sugar Pie)

JOHN PARKER, *Innkeeper*
ROLLANDE THISDÈLE, *Chef*
PARKER'S LODGE,
Val David, Québec

Sugar Pie is probably as old as Québec itself. Originally made with ground maple sugar, it gave the active men and women energy, and perhaps comfort too, through the long winters. It's almost like fudge in a crust and would be best served after a light meal, or perhaps at an *après-ski* party.

1 8-in.	unbaked double-crust pie shell (p. 165)	1 20-cm
2 Tbsps.	all-purpose flour	25 mL
2 cups	brown sugar	500 mL
1 cup	heavy cream (35%)	250 mL

Preheat the oven to 400°F. (200°C). Rub the sides and bottom of the pie shell with some of the flour. This seals the crust. Gently tip any excess into the brown sugar. Mix the remaining flour with the brown sugar. Spread it evenly in the pie crust. Pour the heavy cream over the brown sugar, gently pulling a small spoon back and forth a few times to mix it a little. Wet the edges of the pastry with cold water and top with the upper crust. Pinch, trim and flute the edges. Cut several steam vents in the top to prevent the filling from boiling over. Brush with a little milk. Bake for 35-40 minutes or until golden brown. Cool before serving. *Makes 6-8 servings.*

Buttermilk Pie

꿈꿈꿈꿈꿈꿈꿈꿈꿈꿈꿈꿈꿈꿈꿈꿈꿈꿈꿈꿈꿈꿈꿈꿈꿈꿈꿈꿈꿈꿈꿈꿈꿈꿈꿈꿈

TED AND JEAN TURNER, *Innkeepers*
GRAMMA'S HOUSE,
Port Saxon, Nova Scotia

Coasting down the French Shore, south of Annapolis Royal, the brightly painted shingles of Acadian homes cluster about each inlet. Their blue, white and red flags flap proudly in the salt breezes and long lines of drying wash billow in the sunshine.

Turning inland across to Yarmouth and Gramma's House at Port Saxon, the landscape suddenly changes. Large boulders are strewn across the fields and freshwater lakes sparkle. Great blueberry country! Down the backroads, wild creeping cranberries line each ditch. Blackberries and chokecherries abound, while the natives can show you Indian Pear.

The south shore, or Lighthouse Route, as the Nova Scotians call it, is a long band of salt-washed beaches and secluded bays. Craftspeople are finding these areas, so that a visit can easily be tied together with shopping, antique-hunting and sampling local specialties such as Buttermilk Pie, a favorite of Ted and Jean's guests.

4	eggs	4
1 cup	granulated sugar	250 mL
$\frac{1}{4}$ cup	all-purpose flour	50 mL
2 cups	buttermilk	500 mL
$\frac{1}{2}$ tsp.	salt	2 mL
$\frac{1}{8}$ tsp.	grated nutmeg *or* mace	0.5 mL
1	unbaked pastry shell for 9.-in. (22 cm) pie (p. 165)	1

Preheat the oven to 375°F. (190°C). Beat the eggs. Whisk in the remaining ingredients, beating after each addition. Pour into the unbaked pie crust. Bake for 45-50 minutes, until the center is firm. *Makes one 9-in. (22 cm) pie.*

MACKINTOSH LODGE,
Mile 1,022, Haines Junction, Yukon

Mock Cherry Pie

🐝🐝🐝

SANDY BREMMER, GAIL AND BRYANT JEEVES, *Innkeepers*
MACKINTOSH LODGE,
Mile 1,022, Haines Junction, Yukon

Sandy writes that, "This is an unusual way to use cranberries. Along with the raisins, they make a tangy pie filling amazingly like cherries. Fabulous with ice cream."

1½ cups	granulated sugar	375 mL
4 Tbsps.	flour	60 mL
½ tsp.	salt	2 mL
1 cup	water	250 mL
3 cups	low-bush cranberries, washed	750 mL
1 cup	scalded raisins	250 mL
½ tsp.	almond extract	2 mL
	pastry for 1 9-in. (22 cm) double-crust pie (p. 165)	

In a medium saucepan, mix together the sugar, flour and salt. Stir in the water. Slowly bring to a boil, stirring constantly. Add the cranberries and the raisins. Bring back to a boil and simmer, stirring constantly for 5 minutes. Remove from the heat and add the almond extract. Allow to cool while you *preheat the oven to 475°F. (240°C)*. Pour into the prepared pie shell. Cover with the top crust, pinching the edges together to seal. Trim off the excess pastry and flute the edges. Cut several slits in the top to allow the steam to escape. Bake at 475°F. (240°C) for 15 minutes. Reduce the heat to 375°F. (190°C) and continue to bake for 30 minutes or until the crust is lightly browned and the filling is bubbling.

Makes 6 servings.

Nova Scotia Blueberry Pie

P.M. "Charlie" Holgate, *Innkeeper*
Camelot Inn,
Musquodoboit Harbour, N.S.

Always a big winner at Camelot Inn dinners!

Filling

¼ cup	flour	50 mL
	or	
2 Tbsps.	cornstarch	25 mL
⅔ cup	granulated sugar	150 mL
4 cups	blueberries, fresh or frozen	1 L
2 Tbsps.	lemon juice	25 mL
1	9-in. (22 cm) unbaked deep-dish pie shell (p. 165)	1 1

Topping

½ cup	flour	125 mL
⅓ cup	brown sugar, packed	75 mL
¼ - ½ tsp.	cinnamon	1-2 mL
¼ cup	butter	50 mL

Preheat the oven to 425°F. (220°C). Mix the flour or the cornstarch with the white sugar and blueberries. Stir in the lemon juice. Pour the berry mixture into the unbaked shell.

To make the topping, mix the flour, brown sugar and cinnamon together. Cut in the butter finely. Pack down lightly over the berry mixture. Bake at 425°F. (220°C) for 20 minutes. Reduce the heat to 350°F. (180°C) for approximately 45-50 minutes, for frozen berries. If using fresh blueberries, cooking time will be 10-15 minutes less. Serve warm or cold with ice cream or whipped cream.

Makes one 9-in. (22 cm) pie.

Rich Lemon Butter

P.M. "CHARLIE" HOLGATE, *Innkeeper*
CAMELOT INN,
Musquodoboit Harbour, N.S.

Charlie always doubles this recipe. It keeps for at least two weeks. Having small, baked tart shells on hand means instant dessert. Good on graham wafers for little ones.

2	lemons	2
	grated rind of 1 of the lemons	
1 cup	granulated sugar	250 mL
$\frac{1}{4}$ cup	butter	50 mL
3	eggs	3

Use the juice of 2 lemons and the grated rind of 1 of them. Mix ingredients together and cook in the top of a double boiler over boiling water until the mixture is as thick as honey. Pour into a jar, cover and refrigerate.

Makes $1\frac{1}{2}$ cups (375 mL).

Cookies and Squares

THE UNION HOTEL,
Normandale, Ontario

Almond Shortbread

RUTH AND HAL PEETS, *Innkeepers*
THE UNION HOTEL,
Normandale, Ontario

Many inns featured in this book are registered historical properties. The Union Hotel at Normandale is a unique and important survivor of those nineteenth-century inns which still remain in the province of Ontario.

Built in the 1830s, when the Van Norman foundry was at its zenith on Lake Erie's northern shore, the Union Hotel has been blessed by fate. From 1870 until 1971, when Ruth Peets purchased it, there had been no real modernization. Ruth and Hal have restored the hotel with imagination and care, leaving as many of the original features as possible: the door pulls and hinges, the lovely pine floors, the huge old windows, the graceful bannisters and the old pine trim. They even reconstructed the two-storey sunporch. The restoration has been a real labor of love.

The original version of this recipe came from Ruth's mother's old 1920 I.O.D.E. cookbook.

$\frac{1}{2}$ cup	butter, room temperature	125 mL
$\frac{1}{2}$ cup	shortening, room temperature	125 mL
6 Tbsps.	icing sugar	90 mL
1 cup	unblanched almonds, chopped finely	250 mL
2 cups	all-purpose flour	500 mL

Preheat the oven to 350°F. (180°C). Cream together the butter, shortening and icing sugar. Add the almonds and the flour. Mix thoroughly. Form into 1-in. (2.5 cm) balls and place on a lightly greased cookie sheet. Gently flatten each cookie with a glass dipped in water, then in granulated sugar.* Bake for 8-10 minutes, until just barely golden at the edges. Place on a rack and sprinkle with icing sugar while still warm. Cool completely before storing.

Makes 3-4 dozen.

A tumbler with a design on the bottom will give very attractive cookies.

May's Sesame Cookies

MAY DENREYER, *Innkeeper*
THE HORSESHOE INN,
Cataract, Ontario

This is May's recipe for a delicious and *very easy* shortbread type of cookie.

2 cups	all-purpose flour	500 mL
$\frac{1}{2}$ cup	brown sugar	125 mL
$\frac{1}{2}$ cup	granulated sugar	125 mL
$\frac{1}{4}$ tsp.	salt	1 mL
1 tsp.	baking powder	5 mL
1 cup	butter, softened	250 mL
1	egg	1
$\frac{1}{2}$ cup	chopped walnuts (optional)	125 mL
1 cup	sesame seeds	250 mL

Combine all the ingredients except the sesame seeds, in order, in a food processor. Process until well mixed. Chill 1 hour. When ready to bake, *preheat the oven to 350°F. (180°C)*. Roll the dough into small balls and set on waxed paper. Put the sesame seeds on a plate and press each ball flat onto the sesame seeds, coating both sides with as many seeds as possible. Place on baking sheets. The cookies spread very little, so you can put lots of them on each pan. Bake 8-10 minutes or until golden.

Makes 2 dozen cookies.

Caramel Cuts

GARY BURROUGHS, *Innkeeper*
MARY COLTART, *Keeper of the Inn*
THE OBAN INN,
Niagara-on-the-Lake, Ontario

$\frac{1}{2}$ cup	butter	125 mL
1 cup	brown sugar	250 mL
1	egg	1
$\frac{3}{4}$ cup	all-purpose flour	175 mL
1 tsp.	baking powder	5 mL
1 tsp.	vanilla	5 mL
1 cup	sultana raisins	250 mL

Preheat the oven to 350°F. (180°C). Melt the butter over low heat in a heavy pan. Add the brown sugar, stirring to dissolve. Remove from the heat. While still warm, beat in the egg. Stir the flour and baking powder together. Add to the sugar mixture, along with the vanilla and raisins. Pour into a greased 9 in. (22 cm) square baking pan. Bake for 30 minutes.

Makes about 2 dozen squares.

Chocolate Macaroons

🐝🐝🐝🐝🐝🐝🐝🐝🐝🐝🐝🐝🐝🐝🐝🐝🐝🐝🐝🐝🐝🐝🐝🐝🐝🐝🐝🐝🐝🐝🐝🐝🐝🐝🐝🐝🐝🐝🐝

LINDA L'AVENTURE AND CECILIA BOWDEN, *Innkeepers*
THE COMPASS ROSE,
North Head, Grand Manan, N.B.

Because the climate of Grand Manan is quite moderate in the winter, many birds stay over. Brant geese, loons and many northern gulls call this home. And in the summertime, the Arctic terns nest on the island before beginning their incredible flight back to the Antarctic for winter. Local fishermen will take visitors out to view the self-assured little puffins, the noisy seals and even the odd pod of whales. It is in local lore that the largest Great White Shark ever caught was hauled in off Grand Manan. It was said to be 37 feet long.

Linda serves these macaroons with afternoon tea.

1 cup	coconut	250 mL
2 squares	unsweetened chocolate, melted	2 squares
	or	
2 Tbsps.	cocoa	25 mL
2	egg whites	2
$\frac{3}{4}$ cup	granulated sugar	175 mL
$\frac{1}{8}$ tsp.	salt	0.5 mL
	hazelnuts (optional)	

Preheat the oven to 350°F. (180°C). Mix the coconut with either chocolate or cocoa. In a separate bowl, beat the egg whites until stiff. Beat in the sugar, a spoonful at a time, and the salt. Stir into the coconut mixture. Drop by tablespoonfuls onto a baking sheet lined with parchment or brown paper. If you like, press whole nuts into the cookies. Bake until done, about 10-15 minutes. *Makes 2-3 dozen.*

Chocolate Bars

🐝🐝🐝🐝🐝🐝🐝🐝🐝🐝🐝🐝🐝🐝🐝🐝🐝🐝🐝🐝🐝🐝🐝🐝🐝🐝🐝🐝🐝🐝🐝🐝🐝🐝🐝🐝🐝🐝🐝

GARY BURROUGHS, *Innkeeper*
MARY COLTART, *Keeper of the Inn*
THE OBAN INN,
Niagara-on-the-Lake, Ontario

Could a recipe be any faster?

$\frac{1}{2}$ cup	butter	125 mL
$1\frac{1}{2}$ cups	crushed digestive biscuits	375 mL
1 cup	raisins	250 mL
1 7-oz. pkg.	semi-sweet chocolate chips	1 196-g pkg.
1 15-oz. tin	sweetened, condensed milk	1 300-mL tin

Preheat the oven to 350°F. (180°C). In a medium-sized saucepan, melt the butter over low heat and combine with the digestive biscuits and raisins. Pat into a greased 9 in. (22 cm) square pan. Sprinkle with chocolate chips and pour the condensed milk over them. Spread evenly. Bake for 30 minutes. Let cool, then cut.

Makes one 9 in. (22 cm) pan.

Scottish Oatcakes

🐝🐝

ISOBEL AND DAN MACAULAY, *Innkeepers*
INVERARY INN,
Baddeck, Nova Scotia

Cape Breton is a virgin part of Canada where the wide rivers provide fine Atlantic salmon and the secluded fishing villages are as ruggedly beautiful as any in the Highlands of Scotland. In fact, the original settlers hailed from the Highlands. Steep cliffs, unexpected sandy coves and spectacular scenery provide a backdrop for the excellent foods available at the Inverary Inn. Your appetite, whetted by lots of fresh sea air, will be further teased by the fragrant chowders and home-baked breads.

Pick out your best tartans and practice your Scottish brogue while you whip up a batch of oatcakes.

$\frac{1}{2}$ tsp.	baking soda	2 mL
$\frac{1}{2}$ cup	hot water	125 mL
3 cups	rolled oats	750 mL
2 cups	all-purpose flour	500 mL
1 cup	brown sugar	250 mL
$\frac{1}{2}$ tsp.	salt	2 mL
1 cup	lard or shortening	250 mL

Preheat the oven to 400°F. (200°C). Dissolve the baking soda in hot water; set aside. In a large bowl, stir together the rolled oats, flour, brown sugar and salt. Work in the lard with your fingers. Add the water-baking soda mixture, a little at a time, until the dough is of rolling consistency. Sprinkle a little oatmeal on the surface you will be rolling the dough on. Dust the rolling pin with flour. Roll to about $\frac{1}{4}$ in. (6 mm) thickness. Cut in squares. Bake on lightly greased cookie sheet for 10-12 minutes.

Makes 3-4 dozen.

Oban's Shortbread

GARY BURROUGHS, *Innkeeper*
MARY COLTART, *Keeper of the Inn*
THE OBAN INN,
Niagara-on-the-Lake, Ontario

A wonderful hostess gift at Christmastime.

1 lb.	butter	450 g
1 cup	brown sugar	250 mL
1	egg yolk	1
3½ cups	all-purpose flour	875 mL
½ cup	cornstarch	125 mL
¼ tsp.	baking powder	1 mL

Preheat the oven to 350°F. (180°C). Cream the butter and sugar together until light and fluffy. Add the egg yolk and continue beating. Stir together the flour, cornstarch and baking powder. Add to the creamed mixture, beating until no dry spots remain. Pat into circles on ungreased baking sheets. Decorate the top as desired and score. Bake for 25-35 minutes, watching carefully. Cool on racks. Wrap tightly and store. May be frozen, or simply kept in an airtight container.
Makes 3-4 rounds.

Ginger Sugar Cookies

BRUCE AND NANCY GURNHAM, *Innkeepers*
THE WHITMAN INN,
Kempt, Queen's County, N.S.

¾ cup	butter	175 mL
1¼ cups	granulated sugar	300 mL
1	egg	1
¼ cup	molasses	50 mL
2 cups	all-purpose flour	500 mL
2 tsps.	baking soda	10 mL
1 tsp.	ground ginger	5 mL
1 tsp.	cinnamon	5 mL
½ tsp.	ground cloves	2 mL
½ tsp.	salt	2 mL

Preheat the oven to 375°F. (190°C). In a large mixing bowl, cream together the butter and 1 cup (250 mL) of the sugar, beating until fluffy. Add the egg and molasses, blending well. Stir together the flour, soda, spices and salt. Mix into the creamed mixture. Knead the dough lightly. Pinch off small pieces and roll into little balls. Place on a well-greased baking sheet and flatten slightly. Sprinkle with the reserved ¼ cup (50 mL) sugar. Bake for 8-10 minutes.

Makes 3-4 dozen cookies.

Desserts and Dessert Sauces

THE OBAN INN,
Niagara-on-the-Lake, Ontario

Chocolate Amaretto Cheesecake

DON, MARY AND JUDY CLINTON, *Innkeepers*
THE DUNDEE ARMS INN,
Charlottetown, Prince Edward Island

This recipe was the star of my Stewart clan tasting night. It's smooth and rich and creamy!

Crust

1 7-oz. pkg.	chocolate wafers	1 200-g pkg.
$\frac{1}{4}$ cup	butter, melted	50 mL

Filling

4 8-oz. pkgs.	cream cheese, softened	4 250-g pkgs.
1 cup	granulated sugar	250 mL
$\frac{1}{8}$ tsp.	salt	0.5 mL
4	eggs	4
1 cup	sour cream	250 mL
4 tsps.	lemon juice	20 mL
$\frac{1}{2}$ cup	Amaretto	125 mL

Chocolate Topping

1 cup	granulated sugar (second amount)	250 mL
3 Tbsps.	cocoa	45 mL
6 Tbsps.	cornstarch	90 mL
1 cup	water	250 mL
2 Tbsps.	Amaretto (second amount)	25 mL

Preheat the oven to 350°F. (180°C). Grind or crush the chocolate wafers and combine them with the melted butter. Press into a 10 in. (25 cm) spring-form pan. Bake for 5 minutes. Allow to cool while you are preparing the filling.

Reduce the oven heat to 300°F. (150°C). Set a pan of water in it on the lower rack for moisture. In a large bowl, beat together the softened cream cheese, white sugar and salt until smooth. Add the eggs, one at a time. Beat well after each addition, scraping the bowl. Add the sour cream, lemon juice and Amaretto (no tasting!), beating together thoroughly. Pour into the prepared crust. Bake at 300°F. (150°C) for 1$\frac{1}{2}$ hours. Turn the oven off to allow the cheesecake to set and to cool.

While the cheesecake is cooling, prepare the chocolate topping. This is a very thick sauce. Combine the sugar, cocoa and cornstarch in a small, heavy saucepan. Stir in the water and the Amaretto. Cook, stirring constantly, over medium heat until thickened. Cool before using.

Remove the cheesecake from the oven. Spread with the chocolate topping. Chill until serving time. Garnish with fresh fruit slices, such as strawberries, or whipped cream and toasted almonds.

Makes 12-15 servings.

Blueberry Buckle

🏵🏵🏵

CAPTAIN LARRY PECK, *Innkeeper*
VICTORIA VILLAGE INN,
Victoria-by-the-Sea, P.E.I.

$\frac{1}{4}$ cup	shortening	50 mL
$\frac{1}{2}$ cup	granulated sugar	125 mL
2	eggs	2
$\frac{1}{2}$ cup	milk	125 mL
$1\frac{1}{2}$ cups	all-purpose flour	375 mL
2 tsps.	baking powder	10 mL
$\frac{1}{2}$ tsp.	salt	2 mL
$\frac{1}{2}$ tsp.	grated nutmeg	2 mL
$\frac{1}{4}$ tsp.	ground cloves	1 mL
2 cups	fresh P.E.I. blueberries	500 mL

Topping

$\frac{1}{3}$ cup	granulated sugar	75 mL
$\frac{1}{3}$ cup	all-purpose flour	75 mL
$\frac{1}{2}$ tsp.	cinnamon	2 mL
$\frac{1}{4}$ cup	butter, softened	50 mL

Preheat the oven to 350°F. (180°C). Cream the shortening and the sugar together. Whip in the eggs and milk. In a separate bowl, stir together the flour, baking powder, salt, nutmeg and cloves. Add to the egg mixture, mixing only until there are no dry spots left. Spread in a 9 in. (22 cm) square pan. Sprinkle the blueberries evenly all over. In a small bowl, mix the topping ingredients together until crumbly. Sprinkle over the blueberry layer. Bake for 45-55 minutes or until golden. Serve warm with sweetened whipped cream or table cream.

Makes one 9 in. (22 cm) square pan.

KETTLE CREEK INN,
Port Stanley, Ontario

Figgy Duff with Molasses Coady

🐾🐾🐾

CHRISTINE AND PETER BEAMISH, *Innkeepers*
THE VILLAGE INN,
Trinity, Newfoundland

This is an old, old recipe. It is in reality a bread pudding but made with the locally available ingredients of the days of the rum runners — especially molasses.

Although originally made from the strong blackstrap molasses, I tried it with the lighter fancy variety and found it to be just as Christine says . . . "great for people who like a starchy pudding." And believe it or not, it *is* surprisingly good!

Figgy Duff

2 cups	soaked bread cubes (see below)	500 mL
1 cup	raisins	250 mL
$\frac{1}{2}$ cup	molasses	125 mL
1 tsp.	ground ginger	5 mL
1 tsp.	ground allspice	5 mL
1 tsp.	cinnamon	5 mL
$\frac{1}{4}$ tsp.	salt	1 mL
$\frac{1}{4}$ cup	melted butter	50 mL
1 tsp.	baking powder	5 mL
1 Tbsp.	hot water	15 mL
$\frac{1}{2}$ cup	all-purpose flour	125 mL

Molasses Coady

1 cup	molasses	250 mL
$\frac{1}{4}$ cup	water	50 mL
5 Tbsps.	butter	75 mL
1 Tbsp.	vinegar	15 mL

To make the pudding, soak trimmed white or brown bread cubes in water for a few minutes. Squeeze out the excess water and measure out 2 cups (500 mL). In a large bowl, combine the bread with the raisins, molasses, ginger, allspice, cinnamon and salt. Stir well and pour in the melted butter. Dissolve the baking powder in the hot water and add to the mixing bowl along with the flour. Stir to combine and pour into a well-greased pudding mold or basin. Cover with waxed paper and tie on securely with a string. Cover again with a piece of cotton cloth and tie once more. Lower into a deep pot that has 2-3 in. (5-7.5 cm) boiling water in it. Cover tightly and steam for 2 hours. When ready to serve, invert it on a large flat plate and slice into thin wedges. Serve with Molasses Coady.

To make Molasses Coady, combine the molasses, water, butter and vinegar in a small, heavy saucepan. Bring to a boil and simmer for 10 minutes. Serve while still warm.

Makes 10 man-sized servings.

Grape Nuts Puff Pudding

WARREN J. "BUD" MILLER, *Innkeeper*
MILFORD HOUSE,
R.R. 4, Annapolis Royal, N.S.

This is a very special, old-fashioned Nova Scotia dessert with a lemony custard base and a cake-like top.

½ cup	butter	125 mL
2 cups	granulated sugar	500 mL
4 Tbsps.	all-purpose flour	60 mL
4	eggs, separated	4
2 cups	milk	500 mL
6 Tbsps.	Grape Nuts cereal	90 mL
2	lemons, grated rind and juice	2

Preheat the oven to 375°F. (190°C). Cream together the butter, sugar and flour. Whisk together the egg yolks, milk, Grape Nuts, lemon juice and grated rind. Add to the creamed mixture. Mix thoroughly. Fold in the egg whites, beaten stiff. Bake in a large, ungreased casserole, set in a pan of hot water, for approximately 1 hour. When pudding is done, it will have a tender, golden crust on top. It can be served warm with whipped cream.

Makes 8-10 servings.

Chocolate Sundae Pudding

WARREN J. "BUD" MILLER, *Innkeeper*
MILFORD HOUSE,
R.R. 4, Annapolis Royal, N.S.

You are able to glimpse another side of Nova Scotia's personality at Milford House. Instead of open surf, clear crystalline lakes sparkle. Each cottage has its own private dock and guests are encouraged to canoe, swim and fish all day long. At the evening meal, any fish (mainly yellow perch and brown trout) are served to whoever caught them. Milford House was built by wealthy American fishermen in the 1800s. The only real changes to it that I can imagine are that the trees have grown and a tennis court has been added. "Bud" Miller or as the brochure says, Warren J. Miller, is a tall, slim country gentleman who looks much younger than his calendar years. He grew up at Milford House and knows the history of each cabin.

Home cooking, and lots of it! That's Bud's philosophy.

1 cup	sifted, all-purpose flour	250 mL
$\frac{1}{2}$ tsp.	salt	2 mL
2 tsps.	baking powder	10 mL
2 Tbsps.	cocoa	25 mL
$\frac{2}{3}$ cup	granulated sugar	150 mL
2 Tbsps.	melted butter	25 mL
$\frac{1}{2}$ cup	milk	125 mL
1 tsp.	vanilla	5 mL
1 cup	chopped walnuts or pecans (optional)	250 mL

Topping

$\frac{1}{4}$ cup	granulated sugar	50 mL
3 Tbsps.	cocoa	45 mL
$\frac{1}{2}$ cup	brown sugar	125 mL
$\frac{1}{2}$ tsp.	salt	2 mL
1 tsp.	vanilla	5 mL
1 cup	boiling water	250 mL

Preheat the oven to 350°F. (180°C). Sift together the flour, salt, baking powder, 2 Tbsps. (25 mL) cocoa and sugar. Stir in the butter, milk, vanilla and nuts. Pour into a buttered or oiled casserole. Make the topping by simply stirring together the granulated sugar, 3 Tbsps. (45 mL) cocoa, brown sugar, salt and vanilla. Spread evenly over the batter. Gently pour the boiling water over everything. Do not mix in. Bake, uncovered, for 30 minutes. Cover and continue to bake for an additional 30 minutes. Serve warm with ice cream.

Makes 3-4 servings.

Maple Walnut Mousse

🐝🐝

EVE AND MICHAEL CONCANNON, *Innkeepers*
MARQUIS OF DUFFERIN LODGE,
Port Dufferin, Halifax County, N.S.

1 Tbsp.	gelatin	15 mL
¼ cup	cold water	50 mL
2	eggs	2
½ cup	milk	125 mL
1 cup	maple syrup	250 mL
1 cup	whipping cream (35%)	250 mL
¼ cup	chopped walnuts	50 mL
(or more)		(or more)
	walnut pieces, for garnish	

Soak the gelatin in cold water. Beat eggs with milk and syrup and put into the top of a double boiler over gently boiling water. Stir together and cook until mixture starts to thicken, whisking constantly. Add the soaked gelatin and stir until dissolved. Allow to cool. When mixture begins to set, whip cream until moderately stiff and fold in. Add chopped walnuts and fold in gently with cream. Put in individual dishes and chill until set. Decorate with whipped cream and a piece of walnut. Eve notes that the mousse freezes and keeps well if covered with plastic wrap. Needs very little defrosting before serving. *Makes 6-8 luxurious servings.*

Chocolate Cream

🐝🐝

RUTH AND HAL PEETS, *Innkeepers*
THE UNION HOTEL,
Normandale, Ontario

Serve this velvety, chocolate dessert topped with lightly sweetened whipped cream and orange zest (rind).

1 cup	granulated sugar	250 mL
½ cup	water	125 mL
8 squares	unsweetened chocolate	8 squares
1 Tbsp.	Cointreau	15 mL
2 cups	heavy cream (35%)	500 mL

Put the sugar and water in the top of a double boiler. Heat over simmering water until the sugar is dissolved. Add the chocolate. Melt carefully until blended. Remove from the heat. Allow to cool to room temperature. Add the Cointreau. Whip the cream until soft peaks form. Gently fold in the chocolate mixture and place the bowl into another larger one filled with crushed ice or ice cubes. Continue beating until stiff. Spoon into sherbet dishes and refrigerate. *Makes 6-8 servings.*

Chocolate Cheese Mocha Torte

🌸🌸🌸🌸🌸🌸🌸🌸🌸🌸🌸🌸🌸🌸🌸🌸🌸🌸🌸🌸🌸🌸🌸🌸🌸🌸🌸🌸🌸🌸🌸🌸🌸🌸

SUE AND ROBBIE SHAW, *Innkeepers*
SHAW'S HOTEL,
Brackley Beach, P.E.I.

Like most cheesecakes, this one is at its best when it is made and refrigerated at least one day prior to serving.

Crust

1¼ cups	graham wafer cracker crumbs	300 mL
3 Tbsps.	granulated sugar	45 mL
3 Tbsps.	unsweetened cocoa powder	45 mL
⅓ cup	butter, melted	75 mL

Cheesecake

4 8-oz. pkgs.	plain cream cheese, softened	4 250-g pkgs.
¾ cup	granulated sugar (second amount)	175 mL
2	eggs	2
1 Tbsp.	coffee liqueur	15 mL
1 tsp.	vanilla	5 mL

First Topping

1 8-oz.	carton sour cream	1 225-g
1 square	semi-sweet chocolate, grated	1 square
¼ cup	roasted hazelnuts	50 mL

Final Topping

1½ tsp.	instant coffee	7 mL
2 Tbsps.	boiling water	25 mL
4 squares	semi-sweet chocolate (second amount)	4 squares
4	eggs, separated	4
⅓ cup	granulated sugar (third amount)	75 mL
1 Tbsp.	coffee liqueur (second amount)	15 mL
½ tsp.	vanilla (second amount)	2 mL
½ cup	heavy cream (35%)	125 mL

Garnish

chocolate curls

Preheat the oven to 350°F. (180°C). Blend the crumbs, 3 Tbsps. (45 mL) sugar, cocoa and butter together until well mixed. Press firmly into the bottom and sides of a 9 in. (22 cm) spring-form pan. Bake for 10 minutes. Cool while preparing the remainder of the torte.

Beat the cream cheese until light and fluffy. Add the sugar. Add the 2 eggs, one at a time, beating well after each addition. Add the liqueur and vanilla. Pour mixture into the cooled shell. Bake for 30 minutes at 350°F. (180°C). Turn the oven off, open the door several inches and allow the cheesecake to cool completely.

Gently spread the sour cream over the baked layer. Sprinkle with the grated chocolate and roasted hazelnuts. Dissolve the coffee in the boiling water in a double boiler over hot, but not boiling, water. Add the 4 squares of chocolate. Stir until melted and blended. In a bowl, beat the 4 yolks until thick. Gradually beat in the sugar and a small amount of the chocolate mixture. Beat well. Continue adding small amounts of the chocolate mixture to the egg mixture until all has been used. Add the liqueur and vanilla. In a bowl, beat the egg whites until fluffy. Gently fold into the chocolate mixture. Spread over the cooled, baked layer. Refrigerate until ready to serve (preferably 24 hours). Remove from the spring-form pan. Decorate with whipped cream and chocolate curls.

Makes 10 servings.

Wild Raspberry Ice Cream

DEREK HILL AND BETTY JOHNSTON, *Innkeepers*
OLD NOTCH FARM INN,
Sutton, Québec

Wild raspberries grow everywhere in the southern mountains of Québec. Combine them with maple syrup and you have a truly French-Canadian dessert.

4 cups	fresh raspberries	1 L
2	eggs	2
$\frac{1}{2}$ cup	granulated sugar	125 mL
$\frac{1}{2}$ cup	maple syrup (medium grade is fine)	125 mL
1 cup	heavy cream (35%)	250 mL
$1\frac{1}{2}$ cups	half-and-half cream (10%)	375 mL
1 Tbsp.	lemon juice	15 mL

Gently wash the raspberries. Pat dry. Purée them in a food mill or mash them thoroughly. Strain if desired. In a medium bowl, beat the eggs and sugar together until thick and lemon coloured, 4-5 minutes. Stir in the raspberry purée, maple syrup, heavy cream, half-and-half cream and the lemon juice. Freeze in an ice-cream maker by following the manufacturer's directions, or as follows: Pour the ice-cream mixture into a metal 9 in. x 13 in. (3.5 L) pan. Cover with foil and plastic wrap. Freeze until firm, 3-6 hours. Stir 2 or 3 times during that period. For a smoother texture, freeze until almost firm. Scoop it into a large, chilled bowl or into a large, chilled food processor container. Beat with an electric mixer or process the ice cream to break up any lumps. Return to the freezing pan. Cover tightly again and refreeze until solid.

Makes 1 quart (1 L).

Hazelnut Ice Parfait with Rhubarb
Compote and Apple Crème Fraîche

🐝🐝🐝🐝🐝🐝🐝🐝🐝🐝🐝🐝🐝🐝🐝🐝🐝🐝🐝🐝🐝🐝🐝🐝🐝🐝🐝🐝🐝🐝🐝🐝🐝🐝🐝🐝🐝

SINCLAIR AND FREDRICA PHILIP, *Innkeepers*
PIA CARROLL, *Chef*
MICHAEL STADTLANDER, *Chef*
SOOKE HARBOUR HOUSE,
Whiffen Spit Beach, Vancouver Island, B.C.

Michael Stadtlander came to Sooke Harbour House with a mother lode of creativity. He is without question one of the top chefs in Canada. Now, living in a veritable Eden of fresh ingredients, he'll be able to expand his horizons even further — all the while revelling in the gentle climate of Vancouver Island. This is one of the first recipes he created for the Philips.

Hazelnut Ice Parfait

3	egg yolks	3
$\frac{1}{2}$ cup	granulated sugar	125 mL
$\frac{1}{2}$ tsp.	vanilla	2 mL
$\frac{1}{2}$ cup	milk	125 mL
1 cup	heavy cream (35%), whipped	250 mL
$\frac{1}{2}$ cup	Frangelico (hazelnut liqueur)	125 mL
1 cup	hazelnuts, roasted and crushed	250 mL
$\frac{1}{3}$ cup	shaved, semi-sweet chocolate	75 mL

Combine the egg yolks, sugar, vanilla and milk in a bowl over a pot of simmering water and whisk until thickened. Then remove and whip until cool. Fold in the whipped cream, Frangelico, roasted nuts and shaved chocolate. Place in a bowl, covered with plastic wrap, in the freezer overnight.

Rhubarb Compote

3 stalks	rhubarb	3 stalks
$\frac{2}{3}$ cup	granulated sugar	150 mL
1 cup	red wine	250 mL

Peel rhubarb. Cut 1 stalk into two in. (5 cm) pieces. Chop up other two stalks into approximately $\frac{1}{2}$ in. (1 cm) pieces. Place all rhubarb and peelings in a saucepan; add sugar and red wine and bring to a boil until the 2 in. (5 cm) pieces are soft. Remove the 2 in. (5 cm) pieces and keep to one side. In a blender, purée the remaining ingredients to make the rhubarb sauce. When sauce is ready, add the 2 in. (5 cm) sticks to it. Set aside.

Apple Crème Fraîche

2	apples	2
2 Tbsps.	dry, hard, apple cider	25 mL
3 Tbsps.	Crème Fraîche (p. 112)	45 mL
1 Tbsp.	honey	15 mL

Peel apples, remove cores and cut into small pieces. Place in a saucepan; add the cider, bring to a boil and cook until soft. Place in blender with the Crème Fraîche; then sweeten with the honey.

Final Presentation

1	B.C. red delicious apple, unpeeled and julienned powdered cinnamon mint sprigs	1

On a large, white plate, place the rhubarb sticks artistically and spoon the rhubarb sauce over the sticks. Spoon Apple Crème Fraîche into the middle of the plate. Unmold the Hazelnut Ice Parfait and cut into slices. Place on 4 plates over the Apple Crème Fraîche. Arrange the julienned apple over the rhubarb. Sprinkle with powdered cinnamon and place a sprig of mint decoratively. *Makes 4 servings.*

Frozen Cappuccino

LESLIE LANGILLE, *Innkeeper*
BOSCAWEN INN,
Lunenburg, Nova Scotia

1 cup	granulated sugar	250 mL
1 cup	water	250 mL
2 Tbsps.	instant coffee	25 mL
2 cups	semi-sweet chocolate chips	500 mL
2	eggs	2
1 tsp.	cinnamon	5 mL
3 cups	heavy cream (35%), whipped in a large bowl	750 mL

In a saucepan, combine the sugar, water and instant coffee. Bring to a boil and simmer 3 minutes. Put the chocolate chips, eggs and cinnamon into a blender or food processor. Add the boiling coffee syrup and whirl until smooth. Add to the whipped cream and fold together thoroughly but gently. Pour into individual dishes and freeze overnight. To serve, top with a dollop of whipped cream and a sprinkle of cinnamon. *Makes 10-12 servings.*

Le Sabayon Froid aux Perles Bleues de Charlevoix
(Chilled Charlevoix Blueberry Sabayon)

🐾🐾🐾

JEAN AND JANINE AUTHIER, *Innkeepers*
L'AUBERGE LA PINSONNIÈRE,
Cap-à-L'Aigle, Québec

1 cup	heavy cream (35%)	250 mL
2 cups	fresh or frozen blueberries	500 mL
10	egg yolks	10
$\frac{2}{3}$ cup	Dubleuet liqueur	150 mL
$\frac{1}{4}$ cup	dry white wine	50 mL
1 cup	fruit sugar	250 mL

In a small bowl, beat the heavy cream until stiff. Refrigerate until needed. In a blender or food processor, reduce the blueberries to a purée. Set aside. In the upper part of a double boiler over a gentle heat, beat together the egg yolks, the Dubleuet, the white wine, fruit sugar and blueberry purée. Cook, stirring, over simmering water until thickened. Remove from the heat and chill quickly by setting the saucepan in a bowl of ice. Beat until cooled. Gently fold in the whipped cream. Pour the sabayon into 8 dessert dishes. Refrigerate at least 1 hour or until firm. Decorate with some whole blueberries or a small, edible flower. Serve with Almond Shortbread cookies from the Union Hotel. *Makes 8 servings.*

Winds and Brass

🐾🐾🐾

DONNA AND JIM LACEBY, *Innkeepers*
THE AMHERST SHORE COUNTRY INN,
Amherst, Nova Scotia

Donna developed this world-class recipe herself. It has won prizes and has been the delight of many a diner.

6	individual meringues	6
2 cups	sliced, fresh fruit	500 g
	(Donna suggests strawberries, honeydew melon, green grapes and cantaloupe)	

Chocolate Orange Mousse

4 oz.	cream cheese, softened	115 g
$\frac{3}{4}$ cup	sour cream	175 mL
2 Tbsps.	icing sugar	25 mL

2 oz.	semi-sweet chocolate, melted	56 g
1 Tbsp.	Grand Marnier	15 mL
1½ Tbsps.	Cointreau	20 mL

Whip the cream cheese until smooth. Add the sour cream and continue to whip until light and full. Blend in the icing sugar, melted chocolate and liqueurs. Continue to whip until all the ingredients are well blended and the mousse is light and fluffy. Place in a well-sealed bowl and refrigerate. (Donna says that this is best made at least a day ahead and keeps well for a week.)

To assemble: Just before serving, fold the fresh fruit into the mousse. Divide among the meringues. Top with a little dollop of whipped cream. Garnish with grated orange rind and chocolate curls. Serve immediately. *Makes 6 servings.*

Meringue Shells

4	egg whites	4
¼ tsp.	cream of tartar	1 mL
1 cup	fruit *or* extra-fine sugar	250 mL
½ tsp.	vanilla	2 mL

Preheat the oven to 250°F. (125°C). In a large bowl, beat the egg whites and cream of tartar until soft peaks form. Gradually beat in the sugar, continuing to whip until all the sugar has dissolved and the whites are stiff and glossy. Do not underbeat. Fold in the vanilla. Line baking sheets with brown paper. For each shell, drop about ⅓ cup (75 mL) meringue onto paper. With the back of a spoon, shape into shells. Bake for 1 hour. Turn the heat off and leave the meringue in the oven until cooled to room temperature. *Makes 12 meringues.*

Pear Sorbet

LINDA L'AVENTURE AND CECILIA BOWDEN, *Innkeepers*
THE COMPASS ROSE,
North Head, Grand Manan, N.B.

This is a super dessert after one of The Compass Rose's filling Maritime meals. It could also be used as a refresher between courses.

½ cup	dry white wine	125 mL
1 Tbsp.	lemon juice	15 mL
⅓ cup	granulated sugar	75 mL
2	large, firm, ripe pears	2

In a small saucepan, combine wine, lemon juice and sugar. Peel, core and slice pears, then add pears to saucepan mixture. Mix well to prevent discoloring. Boil over high heat for 2 minutes. Cover and simmer until tender. Whirl in blender until smooth, then pour into shallow metal pan and freeze until solid. Let stand at room temperature for a few minutes. Break into pieces and whirl in blender to make a smooth slush. Refreeze in an air-tight container. Will keep for 2 months. *Makes 3-4 servings.*

BAYBERRY HOUSE,
Granville Ferry, Nova Scotia

Anne's Fruit Cream Sauce

🐾🐾🐾🐾🐾🐾🐾🐾🐾🐾🐾🐾🐾🐾🐾🐾🐾🐾🐾🐾🐾🐾🐾🐾🐾🐾🐾🐾🐾🐾🐾🐾🐾🐾🐾🐾🐾🐾🐾

ANNE WANSTALL AND AILEEN ADAMS, *Innkeepers*
BAYBERRY HOUSE,
Granville Ferry, Nova Scotia

Arrange fresh fruits in season on top of the cream that you have spooned onto individual dessert plates. Aileen created a picturesque dessert for us with cantaloupe slices, fresh blueberries, halved green grapes, sliced peaches and a few perfect raspberries. Garnishes could be mint leaves, lemon balm or edible flowers.

1 cup	granulated sugar	250 mL
1 cup	heavy cream (35%)	250 mL
2 cups	sour cream	500 mL

Stir the ingredients together to dissolve the sugar. Refrigerate for at least 2 hours before serving. The sauce will last 2-3 weeks in the refrigerator.
Makes $3\frac{1}{2}$ cups (875 mL).

Fresh Strawberry Ice

🐾🐾🐾🐾🐾🐾🐾🐾🐾🐾🐾🐾🐾🐾🐾🐾🐾🐾🐾🐾🐾🐾🐾🐾🐾🐾🐾🐾🐾🐾🐾🐾🐾🐾🐾🐾🐾🐾🐾

RON AND DOREEN COOK, *Innkeepers*
VICTORIA'S HISTORIC INN,
Wolfville, Nova Scotia

Ron has a selection of refreshing ices to savor between more filling courses. There are few inns that take the time to do this. Garnish with a whole berry, a sprig of mint or lemon balm.

1 qt.	fresh strawberries	1 L
$\frac{3}{4}$ cup	granulated sugar	175 mL
1 Tbsp.	fresh lemon juice	15 mL
1	egg white	1

Hull and slice the strawberries into a medium-sized bowl. Cover with the sugar and let stand 2-3 hours at room temperature or overnight in the refrigerator. In a food processor or blender, whirl together the berries, lemon juice and egg white. Process until very smooth. Pour into a flat pan and spread evenly to a depth of no more than 1 in. (2.5 cm). Cover tightly and freeze for 24 hours. Scoop out into serving dishes and garnish. *Makes 6-8 servings.*

Rhubarb Sherbet

Doris Hall and George Evans, *Innkeepers*
MacNeill Manor,
Chester, Nova Scotia

This sherbet is superb!

1 cup	water	250 mL
1¼ cups	granulated sugar	300 mL
¾ cup	light corn syrup	175 mL
4 cups	chopped rhubarb	1 L
1 cup	heavy cream (35%)	250 mL

Heat the water, sugar and corn syrup until the sugar is completely dissolved. Add the rhubarb and cook until tender. Purée this mixture in a blender. Add the cream, mix well and chill. When cool, turn into a freezer tray or a 9 in. x 13 in. (3.5 L) pan and freeze until firm. Turn frozen mixture out into a large bowl, break up any lumps and beat until smooth. Return to the freezer. Serve in a champagne glass, topped with fresh whipped cream and rhubarb purée. Or better still, serve on top of a large slice of homemade rhubarb pie. *Makes 10-12 servings.*

Raspberry Dubonnet Sauce

Gary and Jean Vedova, *Innkeepers*
Kettle Creek Inn,
Port Stanley, Ontario

This is wonderful over French vanilla ice cream or over wild Raspberry Ice Cream (p. 187).

1 cup	raspberry jam	250 mL
½ cup	apricot jam	125 mL
½ cup	water	125 mL
¼ cup	lemon juice	50 mL
6 Tbsps.	Dubonnet	90 mL

Heat the first 4 ingredients slowly until jam has thinned out. Stir often to prevent burning. Pour through a fine mesh strainer to remove seeds. Stir in Dubonnet. Heat to serve. *Makes 2½ cups (625 mL).*

Oriental Oranges

꧁꧁

EVE AND MICHAEL CONCANNON, *Innkeepers*
MARQUIS OF DUFFERIN LODGE,
Port Dufferin, Halifax County, N.S.

What a way to get your Vitamin C!

12	oranges, peeled, pitted and seeded (Navel oranges are suitable)	12
1 tsp.	orange zest (rind), no pith	5 mL
3-4 Tbsps.	honey	45-60 mL
1	cinnamon stick, in 1 in. (2.5 cm) pieces*	1
4-5	star anise	4-5
5-6	whole cloves	5-6
5-6	cardamon seeds	5-6
	white wine to cover the oranges, as needed	
2-3 Tbsps.	appropriate liqueur; e.g., Grand Mariner, Curaçao	25-45 mL

Section or slice all the oranges. Combine all the ingredients in a deep container (Eve uses a plastic ice-cream container). Leave to marinate in the refrigerator for 2-3 days. Serve over orange sherbet in glass dishes. More oranges can be added as you use the first batch. It will keep for several weeks without deteriorating, but the marinade does become stronger with age.

Makes about 10-12 servings.

The spices may be adjusted to taste. If they are too strong, remove some and add more wine.

"Be not forgetful to entertain strangers; for thereby some have entertained angels unawares" (Heb. 13:2). Found on a needlepoint sampler in the dining room of The Compass Rose, North Head, Grand Manan, New Brunswick.

Directory Index of Recipes by Inn

Please refer to the accompanying map. Each inn has a corresponding number on the map. Happy travelling!

8. **Manana,**
   4760 Brenton-Page Road,
   R.R.#1,
   Ladysmith V0R 2E0
   604-245-2312

   Wild Rice Soup

9. **Hastings House,**
   Box 1110, Ganges,
   Saltspring Island V0S 1E0
   604-537-2362

   Oysters Provençale Blanche

10. **Denman Island Guest House,**
    Box 9,
    Denman Island V0R 1T0
    604-335-2688

    Ling Cod Fillet with Shrimp
    Sauce
    Red Snapper with Clams in
    Wine Sauce

11. **Delphine Lodge and Country,**
    Inn
    Wilmer, Box 21,
    Invermere V0A 1K0
    604-342-9563

    Baby Beef Liver in Tomatoes
    and Onions
    Mincemeat Cake
    Pork Cutlets in Sour Cream Sauce

12. **Deborah's,**
    Sooke Harbour V0S 1N0
    604-642-6548

    Hot Apple Chutney
    Seville Orange Marmalade

13. **Aguilar House,**
    Bamfield V0R 1B0
    604-728-3323

    Orange Oven-poached Spring
    Salmon

ALBERTA

14. **Post Hotel,**
    Box 69,
    Lake Louise T0L 1E0
    403-522-3989
    403-522-3877

    Leg of Lamb with Spinach, Ham and
    Ricotta Stuffing
    Veal with Morels

15. **Mesa Creek Ranch,**
    R.R.#1,
    Millarville T0L 1K0
    403-931-3573 or 931-3618

    Beef Jerky
    Mesa Creek Barbecue Sauce

16. **Black Cat Guest Ranch,**
    Hinton T0E 1B0
    403-866-2107

    Crustless Breakfast Quiche
    Ogre Canyon Saskatoon Pie
    Ranch-Style Onions for
    Hot Dogs, Hamburgers and
    Steak Sandwiches
    Summer Breakfast Pancakes
    Wild Shaggy Mane Mushroom Soup

SASKATCHEWAN

17. **Hearn's Manor House,**
    Box 1177,
    Indian Head S0G 2K0
    306-695-3837

    Shishlikee

18. High Brass Hunting Lodge,
Box 26,
Winnepegosis R0L 2G0
204-656-4954

Creamy Dill Dressing
Wild Duck and Rice

ONTARIO

19. The Windsor Arms,
22 St. Thomas Street,
Toronto M5S 2B9
416-979-2341

Chicken-in-the-pot Windsor Arms

20. The Union Hotel,
Normandale, R.R.# 1,
Victoria, N0E 1W0
519-426-5568

Almond Shortbread
Chocolate Cream
Lentil Soup

21. Sir Sam's Inn,
Eagle Lake,
Haliburton K0M 1M0
705-754-2188

Chicken Dijonnaise

22. The Sherwood Inn,
Glen Orchard, Box 400,
Port Carling P0B 1J0
705-765-3131

Lamb Stew with Sherry

23. The Pillar and Post,
Niagara-on-the-Lake L0S 1J0
416-468-2123
Toronto Line: 361-1931

Apple Frangipane Tart
Breast of Chicken with Cumin and
Peach Sauce
Flaky Pastry
Orchard Onion Soup

24. Old Bridge Inn,
Young's Point K0L 3G0
705-652-8507

Apple-Stuffed Pork Loin
Thee Inn Pâté

25. The Oban Inn
160 Front Street,
Niagara-on-the-Lake L0S 1J0
416-468-2165

Butter Tarts
Caramel Cuts
Chocolate Bars
Crème Fraîche
Hot Mustard
Mary's Scones
Oban's Shortbread
Potatoes and Leeks

26. The Millcroft Inn,
Alton L0N 1A0
519-941-8111

Grilled Rabbit Tenderloin Pommery
Honey Yogurt Dressing
Marinated Salmon with Ginger and
Lime

27. **The Little Inn,**
    Box 100,
    Bayfield N0M 1G0
    519-565-2611

    Pickerel Pâté

28. **Kettle Creek Inn,**
    Main Street, Port Stanley,
    N0L 2A0
    519-782-3388

    Herbed Shrimp Diablo
    Raspberry Dubonnet Sauce

29. **The Horseshoe Inn,**
    Cataract, R.R.#2,
    Alton L0N 1A0
    519-927-5779

    Fresh Rainbow Trout in Puff Pastry
    May's Cauliflower Soup
    May's Sesame Cookies

30. **The Elora Mill Inn,**
    Mill Street,
    Elora N0B 1S0
    519-846-5356

    Calves' Sweetbreads Crozier

31. **The Desert Rose Inn and Café,**
    Mill Street,
    Elora N0B 1S0
    519-846-0433

    Broccoli and Cheese Soup
    Desert Rose Carrot Cake
    Tofu or Tempeh Stroganoff

32. **Breadalbane Inn,**
    487 St. Andrews St. West,
    Fergus N1M 1P2
    519-843-4770

    Strip Loin Cardinal

33. **Benmiller Inn,**
    R.R.#4,
    Goderich N7A 3Y1
    519-524-2191

    Red Onion Marmalade
    Smoked Salmon Cheesecake

34. **Arowhon Pines,**
    Algonquin Provincial Park,
    Huntsville P0A 1K0
    705-633-5661
    or 297 Balliol Street,
    Toronto M4S 1C7 (Winter)
    416-483-4393

    Grouper Singapore-style
    Maple-Glazed Ham

35. **Amaryllis,**
    Rockport K0E 1V0
    613-659-3513

    Campfire Coffee
    Cinnamon-Honeyed Carrots
    Marjorie's Rosemary Chicken
    Pieto's French Toast
    St. Lawrence Fried Fish

36. **Parker's Lodge**
    1340 Lac Pacquin Road,
    Val David J0T 2N0
    819-322-2026

    Tarte Sucre
    Tourtière

    Old Notch Farm Inn,
    Unfortunately Old Notch has
    closed for the 3 R's—Renovation,
    Rest and Recipe Development.

    Derek's Shishkebab Marinade
    Wild Raspberry Ice Cream

37. **Manoir des Erables,**
    220 du Manoir,
    Montmagny G5V 1G5
    418-248-0100

    Magret d'Oie à l'Estragon

38. **Manoir St-André,**
    St-André G0L 2H0
    418-493-2082

    Barbecued Sturgeon
    Champignons Farcis
    Pâté d'Anguille Froid
    Tranches d'Esturgeon au Four

39. **L'Haut Vent**
    Chemin Mt. Echo,
    R.R.#1,
    Sutton J0E 2K0
    514-243-0451

    Cachette Framboise
    Les Fruits de Mer Gratinée

40. **L'Auberge Le Rucher,**
    2368 L'Eglise,
    Val David J0T 2N0

    819-322-2507

    Les Escargots à la Crème et à
    *   l'Estragon*
    Le Lapin en Civet au Luc

41. **L'Auberge La Pinsonnière,**
    124 Rue St-Raphael,
    Cap-à-l'Aigle
    G0T 1B0
    418-665-4431

    Basic Chicken Stock
    Grenadins de Porc aux Bleuets
    Le Flan d'Huitres et Son Coulis de
    Bettraves
    Mignon de Goret aux Perles Bleues de
    *   Charlevoix*
    Salade de Saison

42. **L'Auberge Handfield,**
    St-Marc sur le Richelieu
    J0L 2E0
    514-584-2226

    La Truite du Québec à la Mode de
    *   l'Auberge*

43. **Château Beauvallon,**
    Montée Ryan,
    Mont Tremblant J0T 1Z0
    819-425-7275

    Maple Chicken

44. **Auberge Historique 1867,**
    Chemin Draper Road,
    R.R.#4,
    Sutton J0E 2K0
    514-538-3120

    Dreamy Chocolate Sponge Cake

NEW BRUNSWICK

45. Shorecrest Lodge,
   North Head,
   Grand Manan E0G 2M0
   506-662-3216

Haddock Poached in Sherry
Halibut in Blue Cheese Sauce

46. The Steamers Stop Inn,
   Gagetown E0G 1V0
   506-488-2903

Almond and Broccoli Salad
Chicken (or Turkey) and Dumplings

47. Northern Wilderness Lodge,
   Plaster Rock E0J 1W0
   506-356-8327

Breakfast Muffins
Gerald's Biscuits
Tobique Pancakes

48. Grand Harbour Inn,
   Grand Harbour,
   Grand Manan E0G 1X0
   506-662-8681

Deviled Fish
Fundy Scallops Parmesan
Grand Harbour Rolls

49. Eveleigh Hotel,
   R.R.#2,
   Hampstead E0G 1Y0
   506-425-9993

Old-Fashioned Gingerbread

50. The Different Drummer,
   146 West Main,
   Sackville E0A 3C0
   506-536-1291

Different Drummer Granola

51. The Compass Rose,
   North Head, Grand Manan
   E0G 2M0
   506-662-8570

Brandy Cream Pie
Caesar Salad Dressing
Chocolate Macaroons
Lamb's-Quarters Vichyssoise
Lobster Rolls
Maritime Brown Bread

NOVA SCOTIA

52. The Whitman Inn,
   R.R.#2,
   Caledonia, Queen's County
   B0T 1B0
   902-242-2226

Banana Bread
Ginger Sugar Cookies
Whitman Inn Baking Mix
  • *Berry Muffins*
  • *Pancakes*
Whitman Inn Creamy Tarragon
   Dressing

53. Westway Inn,
   Plympton, Digby County
   B0W 2R0
   902-837-4097

Basic Quick Bread Mix
Fruit-Filled Coffeecake
Oatmeal Muffins

54. Victoria's Historic Inn,
   416 Main Street,
   Wolfville B0P 1X0
   902-542-5744

Cornwallis Vegetable Bisque
Fresh Strawberry Ice
Sausage and Sage Stuffing

55. **Sea Haven,**
    R.R. #2,
    Annapolis Royal B0S 1A0
    902-638-8881

    Elizabethan Sole

56. **Milford House,**
    South Milford,
    R.R.#4,
    Annapolis Royal B0S 1A0
    902-532-2617

    Chocolate Sundae Pudding
    Grape Nuts Puff Pudding

57. **McNeill Manor,**
    Chester B0J 1J0
    902-275-4638

    Armadillo Potatoes
    Seafood Chowder

58. **Marquis of Dufferin Lodge,**
    R.R.#1,
    Port Dufferin B0J 2R0
    902-654-2696

    Brian's Hebridean Poached
      Salmon
    Chicken in Curry Sauce
    Clara's Cream of Carrot Soup
    Maple Walnut Mousse

59. **Liscomb Lodge,**
    Liscomb Mills B0J 2A0
    902-424-5000

    Blueberry Cake

60. **Inverary Inn**
    Shore Road,
    Baddeck B0E 1B0
    902-295-2674

    Bread-and-Butter Pickles
    Scottish Oatcakes

61. **Gramma's House**
    R.R.#3,
    Shelburne B0T 1W0
    902-637-2058

    Baked Stuffed Pork Chops
    Buttermilk Pie
    Gramma's House Herb Bread
    Maple Butter

62. **The Garrison House Inn,**
    350 St. George Street,
    Annapolis Royal B0S 1A0
    902-532-5750

    Acadian Jambalaya
    Poppy Seed Dressing
    Salade Niçoise

63. **Camelot,**
    Musquodoboit Harbour B0J 2L0
    902-889-2198

    Crab Salad Supreme
    Dill Bread
    Camelot Inn Dressing Piquant
    Nova Scotia Blueberry Pie
    Refrigerator Bran Muffins
    Rich Cream of Spinach Soup

64. **Bread and Roses,**
    82 Victoria Street,
    Annapolis Royal B0S 1A0
    902-532-5727

    Maple Granola

65. **Boscawen Inn,**
    150 Cumberland Street,
    Lunenburg B0J 2C0
    902-634-3325

Cold Cucumber Soup
Frozen Cappuccino
Orange, Radish and Scallion Salad
    with Cream Cheese Dressing
Rhubarb Relish

66. **Blomidon Inn,**
    127 Main Street,
    Wolfville B0P 1X0
    902-542-9326

Chicken Elizabeth

67. **Bayberry House,**
    Granville Ferry B0S 1K0
    902-532-2272

Anne's Fruit Cream Sauce
Cucumber with Dill Weed
    or Mint Flakes
Green Beans with Savory

68. **The Amherst Shore Country Inn,**
    R.R.#2, Amherst B4H 3X9
    902-667-4800

Fillet of Sole with
    Crabmeat Stuffing
Fish Chowder
Sliced Cucumber Salad with
    Whipped Cream Dressing
Winds and Brass

PRINCE EDWARD ISLAND

69. **Victoria Village Inn,**
    Victoria-by-the-Sea C0A 2G0
    902-658-2288

Blueberry Buckle
P.E.I Potatoes Romanoff

70. **The Silver Fox Inn,**
    61 Granville Street
    Summerside C1N 2Z3
    902-436-4033

Pumpkin Marmalade
Spiced Grape Jelly

71. **Shaw's Hotel and Cottages,**
    Brackley Beach C0A 2H0
    902-672-2022

Chocolate Cheese Mocha Torte
Dill Sauce

72. **The Dundee Arms Inn,**
    200 Pownal Street,
    Charlottetown C1A 3W8
    902-892-2496

Charlottetown Rye Bread
Chocolate Amaretto Cheesecake
Dundee Bran Muffins
Escargots Dundee
Lobster Pie
Raspberry Bisque

NEWFOUNDLAND

73. **The Village Inn,**
    Trinity A0C 2S0
    709-464-3269

Figgy Duff with Molasses Coady
Newfoundland Pea Soup
Partridgeberry Pie
Patridgeberry Spice Cake

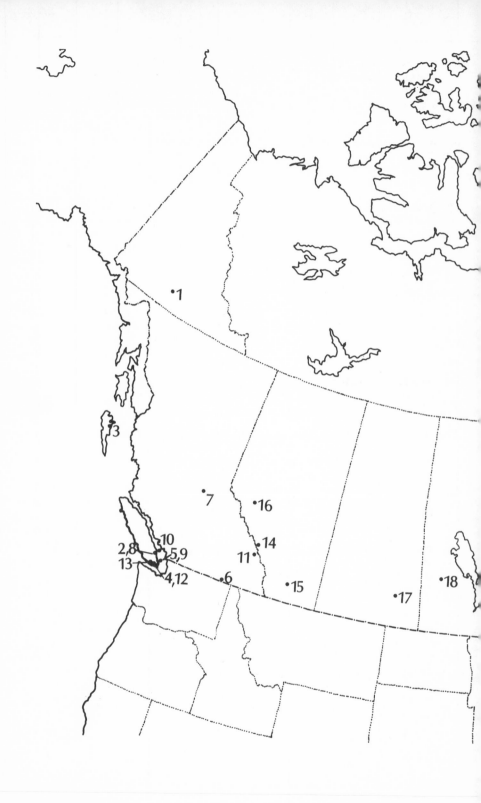

General Index